SO-ASN-906

FLORIDA STATE
UNIVERSITY LIBRARIES

JUN 0 1 2001

TALLAHASSEE, FLORIDA

INTERNATIONAL POLITICAL ECONOMY SERIES

General Editor: Timothy M. Shaw, Professor of Political Science and International Development Studies, and Director of the Centre for Foreign Policy Studies, Dalhousie University, Halifax, Nova Scotia

Recent titles include:

Pradeep Agrawal, Subir V. Gokarn, Veena Mishra, Kirit S. Parikh and Kunal Sen
ECONOMIC RESTRUCTURING IN EAST ASIA AND INDIA: Perspectives on Policy Reform

Deborah Bräutigam
CHINESE AID AND AFRICAN DEVELOPMENT: Exporting Green Revolution

Steve Chan, Cal Clark and Danny Lam (*editors*)
BEYOND THE DEVELOPMENTAL STATE: East Asia's Political Economies Reconsidered

Jennifer Clapp
ADJUSTMENT AND AGRICULTURE IN AFRICA: Farmers, the State and the World Bank in Guinea

Robert W. Cox (*editor*)
THE NEW REALISM: Perspectives on Multilateralism and World Order

Ann Denholm Crosby
DILEMMAS IN DEFENCE DECISION-MAKING: Constructing Canada's Role in NORAD, 1958–96

Diane Ethier
ECONOMIC ADJUSTMENT IN NEW DEMOCRACIES: Lessons from Southern Europe

Stephen Gill (*editor*)
GLOBALIZATION, DEMOCRATIZATION AND MULTILATERALISM

Jeffrey Henderson (*editor*), assisted by Karoly Balaton and Gyorgy Lengyel
INDUSTRIAL TRANSFORMATION IN EASTERN EUROPE IN THE LIGHT OF THE EAST ASIAN EXPERIENCE

Jacques Hersh and Johannes Dragsbaek Schmidt (*editors*)
THE AFTERMATH OF 'REAL EXISTING SOCIALISM' IN EASTERN EUROPE, Volume 1: Between Western Europe and East Asia

David Hulme and Michael Edwards (*editors*)
NGOs, STATES AND DONORS: Too Close for Comfort?

Staffan Lindberg and Árni Sverrisson (*editors*)
SOCIAL MOVEMENTS IN DEVELOPMENT: The Challenge of Globalization and Democratization

Anne Lorentzen and Marianne Rostgaard (*editors*)
THE AFTERMATH OF 'REAL EXISTING SOCIALISM' IN EASTERN
EUROPE, Volume 2: People and Technology in the Process of Transition

Stephen D. McDowell
GLOBALIZATION, LIBERALIZATION AND POLICY CHANGE: A Political
Economy of India's Communications Sector

Juan Antonio Morales and Gary McMahon (*editors*)
ECONOMIC POLICY AND THE TRANSITION TO DEMOCRACY: The Latin
American Experience

Ted Schrecker (*editor*)
SURVIVING GLOBALISM: The Social and Environmental Challenges

Ann Seidman, Robert B. Seidman and Janice Payne (*editors*)
LEGISLATIVE DRAFTING FOR MARKET REFORM: Some Lessons from
China

Caroline Thomas and Peter Wilkin (*editors*)
GLOBALIZATION AND THE SOUTH

Kenneth P. Thomas
CAPITAL BEYOND BORDERS: States and Firms in the Auto Industry,
1960–94

Geoffrey R. D. Underhill (*editor*)
THE NEW WORLD ORDER IN INTERNATIONAL FINANCE

Henry Veltmeyer, James Petras and Steve Vieux
NEOLIBERALISM AND CLASS CONFLICT IN LATIN AMERICA: A
Comparative Perspective on the Political Economy of Structural Adjustment

Robert Wolfe
FARM WARS: The Political Economy of Agriculture and the International Trade
Regime

International Political Economy Series
Series Standing Order ISBN 0–333–71708–2 hardcover
Series Standing Order ISBN 0–333–71110–6 paperback
(*outside North America only*)

You can receive future titles in this series as they are published by placing a standing order.
Please contact your bookseller or, in case of difficulty, write to us at the address below with
your name and address, the title of the series and one or both of the ISBNs quoted above.

Customer Services Department, Macmillan Distribution Ltd
Houndmills, Basingstoke, Hampshire RG21 6XS, England

Canadian–Caribbean Relations in Transition

Trade, Sustainable Development and Security

Edited by

Jerry Haar
Senior Research Associate and
Director, Inter-American Business and Labor Program
Dante B. Fascell North–South Center
University of Miami, Florida

and

Anthony T. Bryan
Professor of International Relations and
Director, Caribbean Program
Dante B. Fascell North–South Center
University of Miami, Florida

First published in Great Britain 1999 by
MACMILLAN PRESS LTD
Houndmills, Basingstoke, Hampshire RG21 6XS and London
Companies and representatives throughout the world

A catalogue record for this book is available from the British Library.

ISBN 0–333–73091–7

First published in the United States of America 1999 by
ST. MARTIN'S PRESS, INC.,
Scholarly and Reference Division,
175 Fifth Avenue, New York, N.Y. 10010

ISBN 0–312–22254–8

Library of Congress Cataloging-in-Publication Data
Canadian–Caribbean relations in transition : trade, sustainable
development and security / edited by Jerry Haar and Anthony T.
Bryan.
p. cm. — (International political economy series)
Includes bibliographical references and index.
ISBN 0–312–22254–8 (cloth)
1. West Indies, British—Relations—Canada. 2. Canada—Relations–
–West Indies, British. 3. National security—West Indies, British.
I. Haar, Jerry. II. Bryan, Anthony T. III. Series.
F2131.C27 1999
303.48'2710729—dc21   99–21784
                                                CIP

Selection, editorial matter and Conclusion © Jerry Haar and Anthony T. Bryan 1999
Chapters 1–10 © Macmillan Press Ltd 1999

All rights reserved. No reproduction, copy or transmission of this publication may be made
without written permission.

No paragraph of this publication may be reproduced, copied or transmitted save with
written permission or in accordance with the provisions of the Copyright, Designs and
Patents Act 1988, or under the terms of any licence permitting limited copying issued by
the Copyright Licensing Agency, 90 Tottenham Court Road, London W1P 0LP.

Any person who does any unauthorised act in relation to this publication may be liable to
criminal prosecution and civil claims for damages.

The authors have asserted their rights to be identified as the authors of this work in
accordance with the Copyright, Designs and Patents Act 1988.

This book is printed on paper suitable for recycling and made from fully managed and
sustained forest sources.

10   9   8   7   6   5   4   3   2   1
08   07   06   05   04   03   02   01   00   99

Printed and bound in Great Britain by
Antony Rowe Ltd, Chippenham, Wiltshire

For Barbara and Eric –
Jerry

For Avril, Roget and Anique –
Tony

Contents

List of Tables   ix

Preface and Acknowledgements   x

Notes on the Contributors   xvi

List of Abbreviations   xx

PART I   OVERVIEW

1   Canadian–Caribbean Relations: A Canadian Perspective
    Jennifer Hosten-Craig   3

2   Canada and the Caribbean: Power without
    Paternalism in the Age of Interdependence
    Ivelaw L. Griffith   22

3   Canada and the Caribbean: Political Commonalities
    and Convergences
    Gregory S. Mahler   36

PART II   CANADIAN VIEWS

4   Canadian and Caribbean Perspectives on
    Security in the Region
    Hal J. Klepak   55

5   A Regional Approach to Sustainable
    Development in the Caribbean: Applying
    the Test of Common Sense (TOCS)
    Patricia A. Lane   79

6   Emerging Linkages: New Brunswick, Nova Scotia
    and the Caribbean
    M.C. Ircha   106

PART III   CARIBBEAN VIEWS

7   Canada–CARICOM Relations since the 1980s:
    An Overview
    Harold Robertson   131

8   Problems and Prospects of CARIBCAN:
    The Early Years
    Sahadeo Basdeo   153

9   Canadian Economic Assistance to CARICOM
    Countries: Assessment and Future Prospects
    Richard L. Bernal and Winsome J. Leslie   190

10 The New Regionalism: The Caribbean–
    Canada Trade Agenda
    Winston Dookeran and Miriam L. Campanella   210

Conclusion
Jerry Haar and Anthony T. Bryan   231

Index   237

List of Tables

6.1   Composition of Canadian imports and
      exports (percentages)   108
6.2   Canada–US trade by rail (tons)   112
6.3   Canada–Caribbean trade (dollars)   114
6.4   Canada–Caribbean trade (tons)   114
6.5   New Brunswick and Nova Scotia trade
      with the Caribbean 1987   116
6.6   Caribbean market size   120
8.1   Caribbean beneficiaries: comparative statistics   163
8.2   Individual country breakdown of official debt
      written off by Canada   170
8.3   Summary of CARIBCAN tariff treatment   174
8.4   Canada's trade with CARIBCAN countries/territories
      and the world   176
8.5   Canada's trade balance with CARIBCAN countries   177
8.6   Value of Caribbean common market exports to
      Canada and the world   178
8.7   Value of Caribbean common market imports
      from Canada and the world   179
8.8   Balance of CARICOM's trade with Canada   180
8.9   Value of CARICOM's imports, Canada   181
9.1   Distribution of CARICOM trade   192
9.2   Canadian Official Development Assistance (ODA)
      to CARICOM countries   197
9.3   Canadian ODA grants for reconstruction in Haiti   203

Preface and Acknowledgements

Since 1884, when local legislatures in Barbados, Jamaica and the Leeward Islands sought to associate their territories formally with Canada, there has been a special relationship between the Commonwealth Caribbean and Canada.

Association with the Commonwealth Caribbean traditionally has allowed Canada to engage in the process of hemispheric development, to serve as a stabilising influence on regional politics and security concerns, and to provide development assistance to foster change and growth among small economies in the region. Having concluded during the 1980s that its role in the region was becoming increasingly important, Canada joined the Organization of American States (OAS) in 1989.

Within the economic sphere – trade/investment, tourism, and economic development assistance – Canadian–Caribbean relations have been especially important. Canada has been supportive of trade development in general as well as of specific organisations such as the Caribbean Association of Industry and Commerce and the Caribbean Community and Common Market (CARICOM). Canada remains an important trading partner for the region and an even more significant partner in banking, offshore financial services, transportation and mining.

In the wake of the Caribbean Basin Initiative (CBI), the nations of the Commonwealth Caribbean sought similar treatment from Canada; thus was born CARIBCAN in 1986. Similar in most ways to the CBI, CARIBCAN provided for the doubling of Canadian aid between 1982 and 1987 (from US$28.5 million to $57 million). Since Canada's regional presence is smaller and perceived as more 'passive' than the US presence (not one mountie was involved in the invasion of Grenada), CARIBCAN was popular from its inception.

Tourism is another area where Canada represents an extremely important market for the Caribbean, even as the US share of the market dominates. The French Antilles, Jamaica, Cuba and several of the smaller islands of the English-speaking Caribbean are important tourist destinations for both Anglophone and Francophone Canadians.

In the area of economic development assistance, Canada has contributed a large proportion of its foreign aid budget to the Commonwealth Caribbean. The Canadian International Development Agency (CIDA) has provided assistance for infrastructure, social needs, health, education and economic development. Initially involved since the early 1960s when the United Kingdom began to shy away from such commitments to development in the West Indies, Canada's attention to the region remains even though governmental resources allocated to the Commonwealth Caribbean are contracting.

In the realm of political and security issues, Canada is perceived in the Caribbean as a 'more benign' neighbour than the United State, and its constructive roles in supporting democratic governance and effective governmental administration have been laudatory. Canada has also played an effective part in training and equipping the military and police forces in the region.

During the last decade, domestic, regional and international forces and factors – economic and political – have ushered in changes in both Canada and the Caribbean and, in turn, have directly impacted the form and dynamics of this particular North–South relationship. Domestically, the consolidation of neoliberal reforms in the Caribbean and the implementation of severe budgetary cuts and other austerity measures in Canada have most definitely affected the relationship. Regionally and internationally, the forces of trade and investment liberalisation, competitiveness, the environment, technological change and immigration have also impacted Canadian–Caribbean relations.

The purpose of this volume is to discuss, evaluate and project the impacts of political, economic and social change on a special relationship in transition – Canada and the Commonwealth Caribbean – during the last decade of the twentieth century. Although there have been contemporary contributions to the literature on Canada and Latin America during the last two years and broader works that focus on politics, democratisation and trade in the region, only one work – Tennyson (1990) – examines Canadian–Caribbean relations. But the work fails to address the major policy issues facing Canada's relations with the Commonwealth Caribbean.

This volume is intended to fill a void in the academic literature by tackling issues of central importance to Canadian–Caribbean relations. At the same time, it is hoped that the book will be useful to policy analysts, non-governmental organisation representatives, and public and private sector decision-makers.

Although there are many areas, topics and themes that traverse Canadian–Caribbean relations, this book focuses on three timely and increasingly important policy issues: trade and commerce, political relations, and security. The globalisation of business and the resurgence of regionalism are two of the most significant trends in the world economy. Will the new regionalism lead to protectionism or deeper trade integration? Will new trading blocs undermine the multilateral system? These are the questions that Winston Dookeran and Miriam Campanella address in their chapter on the Caribbean–Canadian trade agenda. The authors discuss the evolution of Caribbean trade, the promise of export-led growth in non-traditional product areas, and advocate intra-regional corporate and financial integration to promote economic development and enhance the bargaining power of the Caribbean in global accords.

An assessment of CARIBCAN is the subject of Sahadeo Basdeo's chapter, in which he describes the origins, evolution and future perspective of the CARIBCAN agreement between Canada and CARICOM countries. Basdeo argues that since the 1960s, Canada's relationship with the region has expanded beyond its traditional ties to include a host of other issues, such as immigration, security, development assistance, police training, technical and scientific cooperation, investment and environmental concerns. While trade has emerged as the centrepiece, Basdeo concludes that CARIBCAN has not brought about the expected improvements in Caribbean–Canadian trade relations. Not only have the trade flows remained small and somewhat insignificant, but trade has declined relative to that of the European Economic Community and Japan over the same period. Basdeo concludes, nevertheless, that CARIBCAN will continue to be the centrepiece of the relationship; revisions must be made in the value-added content for CARIBCAN produce coverage, and Canadian investment in the region should be promoted. He asserts that the negative impact of the North American Free Trade Agreement (NAFTA) on the region will make these changes all the more urgent.

NAFTA's negative impact is examined in-depth by Harold Robertson, who begins with an historical review of Canada's relationship with the Commonwealth Caribbean, before moving on to a detailed analysis with case examples of the damage that NAFTA will wreak on the Caribbean. He holds that NAFTA will provide Mexico with the huge advantage of duty-free access for precisely those CARICOM products excluded under CARIBCAN.

Regardless of the bilateral, subregional, regional and multilateral evolution of trade relationships, commercial transactions will proceed unimpeded by private sector entities and entrepreneurs who share a common purpose and anticipated financial benefit in conducting business. M.C. Ircha reviews the trade relationship between the Caribbean provinces of New Brunswick and Nova Scotia *vis-à-vis* the Caribbean. He argues that great potential exists for strategic, niche development in commercial relations between Canadian provinces and the Caribbean. Ircha proposes the idea of a 'consolidation centre,' which would spur increased trade between the two zones, with Saint John, New Brunswick, serving as the nexus. His chapter, much like a pre-feasibility study/draft business plan, offers an intriguing and promising – not to mention creative and imaginative – approach to Canadian–Caribbean relations.

In the realm of political relations, Gregory Mahler presents and discusses the uncertainties of the Canadian–Caribbean relationship after NAFTA. He asserts that even though Canada's relative economic influence in the Caribbean has declined over the years, there is a set of factors that can be referred to as political commonalities and convergences that contribute to tie these nations together. However, new realities are changing Canada's relationship with the Caribbean. The reasons are: Canada's budgetary problems, domestic agenda, and greater interests and increasing links with both the United States and other parts of the world.

Perspectives on security in the region are the theme of Hal Klepak's chapter, which examines the historical relationship between Canada and the Commonwealth Caribbean and determines that, since the 1980s, Canada has continued its very limited security assistance to the region but has found itself in a greatly changed context. The changes are the result of the end of the Cold War, the expanded role and activity of the United Nations, membership in the Organization of American States, NAFTA, the growth of the Haitian dimension of Canadian–Caribbean policy, the arrival of the drug trade as a security issue, and the continuing crisis of Cuba. Klepak concludes, however, that in a world where Asia is not interested in a community with Canada, and Europe is looking elsewhere, there must be few options for the future of Canadian international relations that do not take the Americas as the main focus or at least one of them.

A common thread that runs throughout all of the chapter is that the Caribbean remains the only developing area in which Canada, through an integrated set of policies, is capable of exerting significant influence, while Canada remains the most benevolent and reliable developed nation with whom the commonwealth Caribbean interacts and continues to enjoy a special relationship. This unique nexus, in and of itself, merits the attention of researchers, writers, thinkers and policy-makers.

The contributors to this volume represent a diverse mix of scholars, all from Canada and the Commonwealth Caribbean and one from the United States. Rather than seeking to forge a consensus, we have left it to the readers to glean, analyze and evaluate the various contributions presented here. What is irrefutable, however, is the continuing dynamic and evolutionary processes that are shaping Canadian–Caribbean relations within the region and beyond.

The genesis of this volume began with a conference jointly sponsored by the Dante B. Fascell North–South Center of the University of Miami and the Institute of Business at the University of the West Indies, held in Port of Spain, Trinidad, in June 1994. Both the conference and this volume were supported by the generous financial contribution of the North–South Center. Our genuine thanks and appreciation to Ambassador Ambler H. Moss, Jr, Director of the Dante B. Fascell North–South Center; Robin L. Rosenberg, Deputy Director; and Jeffrey Stark, Director of Research and Studies. We also express our gratitude to Dr Bhoendradatt Tewarie, Director of the Institute of Business, University of the West Indies; and above all to Professor Timothy M. Shaw, Director of the Centre for Foreign Policy Studies, Dalhousie University, and editor of Macmillan's International Political Economy Series, and Ms Aruna Vasudevan, editor, Macmillan Press Limited.

JERRY HAAR
ANTHONY T. BRYAN

References

Berry, G.R. (1988) 'The West Indies in Canadian External Relations: Present Trends and Future Prospects', in B.D. Tennyson (ed.), *Canada and the Commonwealth Caribbean* (London: University Press of America).

Braveboy–Wagner, J.A. (1989) *The Caribbean in World Affairs: The Foreign Policies of the English-Speaking States* (Boulder, CO: Westview Press).

Bryan, A. (ed.) (1995) *The Caribbean: New Dynamics in Trade and Political Economy* (New Brunswick, NJ: Transaction Books).

Domínguez, J., R.A. Pastor and R.D. Worrell (eds) (1993) *Democracy in the Caribbean: Political, Economic, and Social Perspectives* (Baltimore: The Johns Hopkins University Press).

Haar, J. and E.J. Dosman (eds) (1993) *A Dynamic Partnership: Canada's Changing Role in the Americas* (New Brunswick, NJ: Transaction Books).

Kempe, R.H. (1986) *Economic Development in the Caribbean* (New York: Praeger).

Klepak. H.P. (ed.) (1993) *Canada and Latin American Security* (Quebec: Meridien).

Levitt, K. (1988) 'Canada and the Caribbean: An Assessment' in J. Heine and L. Manigat (eds), *The Caribbean and World Politics: Cross Currents and Cleavages* (New York: Holmes & Meier).

Mahler, G. (1993) 'Foreign Policy and Canada's Evolving Relations with the Caribbean Commonwealth Countries: Political and Economic Considerations', in *A Dynamic Partnership: Canada's Changing Role in the Americas* (New Brunswick: NJ: Transaction Books).

Momsen, J.H. (1992) 'Canada–Caribbean Relations: Wherein the Special Relationship?' *Political Geography*, vol. 2, no. 5, pp. 501–13.

Rochlin, J. (1994) *Discovering the Americas* (Vancouver: University of British Columbia Press).

Tennyson, B.D. (ed.) (1990) *Canadian–Caribbean Relations* (Sydney, Nova Scotia: University College of Cape Breton).

Thomas, C. (1988) *The Poor and the Powerless* (New York: Monthly Review Press).

Notes on the Contributors

Sahadeo Basdeo is Professor of History and International Relations at Okanagan University College, Kelowna, British Columbia, Canada. Previously, he was on the faculty of the University of the West Indies, St Augustine, Trinidad, in both the Department of History and the Institute of International Relations. He served as a Member of the Senate in Trinidad and Tobago for ten years, and was Minister of External Affairs and International Trade for four years (1987–91). He is the author of *Labour Organization and Labour Reform in Trinidad, 1919–1939*, and has published over forty articles in the fields of history and international relations in several scholarly journals.

Richard L. Bernal has been Jamaica's Ambassador to the United States of America and Permanent Representative to the Organization of American States since 6 May 1991. He is the Chair of the Consultative Committee on Smaller Economies in the Free Trade Area of the Americas process and Jamaica's representative on the Special Trade Committee of the OAS and the Committee for Hemispheric Financial Issues. Ambassador Bernal has been a leading participant in several negotiations on Jamaica's behalf, including debt-reduction agreements and loans from multilateral financial institutions. He has published nearly 100 articles in scholarly journals, books and monographs, as well as opinion editorials in the *Washington Post* and *Wall Street Journal*.

Anthony T. Bryan is Director of the Caribbean Studies Program at the Dante B. Fascell North–South Center and a Senior Associate at the Center for Strategic and International Studies in Washington, DC. Previously, he was Senior Associate at the Carnegie Endowment for International Peace and a Fellow of the Woodrow Wilson Center for Scholars. He served for a decade as the Professor/Director of the Institute of International Relations at the University of the West Indies, St Augustine, Trinidad and Tobago. He is the author of more than seventy articles and the author/editor of several books and monographs on Caribbean and Latin American affairs.

Miriam L. Campanella researches and teaches in the Faculty of Political Science at the University of Turin (Italy). Formerly a visiting scholar at the Center for International Studies, Massachusetts Institute of Technology (MIT), her principal research interest is international economic relations, particularly globalisation and the formation of regional blocs. She has authored chapters in *Transition to a Global Society*, edited by S. Bushrui, I. Ayman and E. Lazlo (1993) and *Cognitive Maps in Biology and Culture*, edited by E. Lazlo (1993).

Winston Dookeran was appointed Governor of the Central Bank of Trinidad and Tobago in July 1997. Previously he served as a Lecturer in Economics at the University of the West Indies and Senior Economist at the United Nations Economic Commission for Latin America and the Caribbean, and as Minister of Planning in the Government of Trinidad and Tobago from 1986 to 1991. During his tenure as a Fellow at the Center for International Affairs at Harvard University he edited *Choices and Change: Reflections of the Caribbean* (1996).

Ivelaw L. Griffith is a Political Science Professor and Associate Dean of the College of Arts and Sciences at Florida International University in Miami, Florida. A specialist in Caribbean and Inter-American security, he has written, edited and co-edited a number of books, most recently *Drugs and Security in the Caribbean: Sovereignty under Seige*, and has published articles in many scholarly journals. He is a consultant with several security agencies, book review editor of *Hemisphere*, a member of the Advisory Board of Caribbean Studies, the Peace and Security in the Americas Network of the Woodrow Wilson International Center for Scholars and of its Working Group on Urbanization, Environment and International Security.

Jerry Haar is Senior Research Associate and Director of the Inter-American Business and Labor Program at the Dante B. Fascell North–South Center and Research Affiliate at Harvard University's David Rockefeller Center for Latin American Studies. He is an international business researcher and consultant specialising in global management and marketing, country risk assessment, and trade and investment strategy. A former Director of Washington Programs for the Council of the Americas, Dr Haar has received research grants from both the Canadian Government and the Government of Quebec. He has authored or co-authored a number of books, including *A Dynamic Partnership: Canada's Changing Role in the Americas* (1993).

Jennifer Hosten-Craig is Senior Program Officer, Canadian International Development Agency (CIDA), where she manages twenty-five sustainable development projects and programmes in Latin America and the Caribbean, Africa and Asia. During 1998, she served as Technical Advisor to the Regional Negotiating Machinery of CARICOM and the Organization of Eastern Caribbean States (OECS). She is the author of *The Effects of the North American Free Trade Agreement on the Commonwealth* (1992) and contributed to *Free Trade in the Americas* (1992). She received the Award of Excellence from the Information Services Institute of the Public Service Commission of Canada in 1993.

M.C. Ircha is Assistant Vice-President for Academic Affairs and Professor of Civil Engineering at the University of New Brunswick. Formerly an urban planner and city engineer, his research interests focus on the evaluation of maritime port reform, urban public works systems and local government administration. He is a consultant in marine transport and ports and has authored nearly a dozen works on maritime policy, transportation, commercialisation and the privatisation of seaports.

Hal J. Klepak is Professor of Latin American Military and Diplomatic History at the Royal Military College of Canada and on sabbatical as Director of the Governance and Security Program at the Canadian Foundation for the Americas (FOCAL). Formerly a strategic analyst with the Department of National Defence and a professor at the Collège Militaire Royal de Saint-Jean, he is the editor of *Natural Allies? Canadian and Mexican Perspectives on International Security* (1996).

Patricia A. Lane is President of Lane Environment Limited, a firm that specialises in environmental assessments and sustainable development planning throughout the world. She is also a Professor of Biology at Dalhousie University and has served as Visiting Professor and Lecturer in human ecology at Harvard University's School of Public Health. Dr Lane has carried out consulting assignments and conducted research in the Caribbean in environmental risk assessment and sustainable development policy. She currently serves as a Senior Advisor to the Cuban Environmental Agency on policy, planning and training.

Winsome J. Leslie is the Economic Attaché to the Embassy of Jamaica in Washington, DC. Prior to her current assignment, she was Assistant Professor of Political Economy at the American University and

Adjunct Professor at the Johns Hopkins School of Advanced International Studies. She is also a former Marketing Officer in Institutional Investment with Chemical Bank in New York, and has served as a consultant on debt, structural adjustment and political economy to various organisations both in New York and Washington, DC. She has published two books on structural adjustment and development in Africa and is the author of several articles on development in Africa and the Caribbean.

Gregory S. Mahler is Provost and Professor of Political Science at Kalamazoo College. Formerly chair of the Department of Political Science at the University of Mississippi, he has authored or edited twenty-odd books and numerous articles dealing with comparative politics, with a focus on legislatures and constitutionalism. An authority on the Canadian political system, his forthcoming books include *Politics in North America: Canada, the United States and Mexico* and *Comparative Politics: An Institutional and Cross-National Approach*.

Harold Robertson, a senior career diplomat in the Ministry of Foreign Affairs of Trinidad and Tobago, is currently his country's High Commissioner to Lagos, Nigeria. A historian by training, he has taught at the University of the West Indies, St Augustine Campus, Trinidad and Tobago. He has published in several international journals and presented scholarly papers and presentations at numerous international conferences.

List of Abbreviations

ACCC	Association of Canadian Community Colleges
ACS	Association of Caribbean States
BPT	British Preferential Tariff
CANEXPORT	Canadian export promotion organisation
CARIBCAN	Canada–CARICOM Trade and Economic Cooperation Agreement
CARICOM	Caribbean Community and Common Market
CBI	Caribbean Basin Initiative
CCBCO	Canada–Caribbean Business Cooperation Office
CDB	Caribbean Development Bank
CEA	Canadian Exporters Association
CEMPOL	Control and Evaluation of Marine Pollution
CEP	Programme on the Environment of the Caribbean
CEPNET	Information Systems for Management of Coastal and Marine Resources
CESO	Canadian Executive Services Organisation
CF	Canadian Forces
CIDA	Canadian International Development Agency
CMTAP	Caribbean Maritime Assistance Programme
CN	Canadian National Railways
CP	Canadian Pacific Railways
CRISP	Caribbean Regional Institutional Strengthening Project
CTAP	Canadian Training Awards Programme
CTCF	Canadian Technical Cooperation Fund
CUSFTA	Canada-US Free Trade Agreement
CUSO	Canadian University Service Overseas
CXC	Caribbean Examinations Council
EC	European Community
ECLAC	Economic Commission for Latin America and the Caribbean
EEC	European Economic Community
ENACT	Environmental Action Programme, Jamaica
ETA	Education, Training and Awareness
EU	European Union
FAO	Food and Agriculture Organization
FCL	full container load

FEMA	Foreign Extraterritorial Measures Act
FTA	Free Trade Agreement
FTAA	Free Trade Area of the Americas (proposed)
FTL	full truck load
GATT	General Agreement on Tariffs and Trade
GPT	General Preferential Tariff
IDB	Inter-American Development Bank
IDRC	International Development Research Centre
IMF	International Monetary Fund
IPID	Integrated Planning for Industrial Development
JAMPRO	Jamaica Promotions
JTEC	Joint Trade and Economic Committee
LCL	less than container load
LDC	least developed country
LTL	less than truck load
MERCOSUR	Southern Cone Common Market
MFA	Multi-Fibre Agreement
MFN	most favoured nation
NAFTA	North American Free Trade Agreement
NATO	North Atlantic Treaty Organization
NGOs	non-governmental organizations
NORAD	North American Air Defense
NRCA	National Resources Conservation Authority
OAS	Organization of American States
ODA	Official Development Assistance
OECS	Organisation of Eastern Caribbean States
ONUCA	UN observer group in Central America
ONUSAL	UN observer mission in El Salvador
PAHO	Pan American Health Organisation
PIOJ	Planning Institute of Jamaica
PURE	Plan d'Urgence de Reconstruction Economique (Haiti)
RCMP	Royal Canadian Mounted Police
SAFTA	South American Free Trade Area
SELA	Latin American Economic System
SMEs	small and medium-sized enterprises
SNAP	Soil Nutrients for Agricultural Productivity
SPAW	Specially Protected Areas and Wildlife in the Wider Caribbean
TOCS	test of common sense

UNCED	United Nations Commission on Environment and Development (Brundtland Commission)
UNDP	United Nations Development Programme
UNEP	United Nations Environmental Programme
UNHCR	United Nations Higher Commission for Relief
UNICEF	United Nations International Children's Fund
VRAs	Voluntary Restraint Agreements
WCED	World Commission on Environment and Development
WTO	World Trade Organization

Part I
Overview

1 Canadian–Caribbean Relations: A Canadian Perspective

Jennifer Hosten-Craig

INTRODUCTION

The 'special relationship' that has existed between Canada and the Commonwealth or English-speaking Caribbean embodies trade and aid, sustainable development, civil society, security, and relations with Cuba in light of the Helms–Burton law. It is a special relationship that is one of the oldest in the area, going back to the early eighteenth century. Canada is as much a part of the Caribbean region as the Caribbean is a part of Canada.

Nevertheless, to many, the Commonwealth Caribbean has suffered a severe downgrading in Canadian foreign policy and aid in the past five years, and many openly question the direction of the relationship. A number of factors appear to be responsible. Among them are the declining role of the Commonwealth in Canada's foreign policy, perhaps more fundamentally the Canadian government's decision to make choices concerning where it should focus its resources in the face of fiscal and economic problems and the ongoing constitutional challenges posed by the possible separation of the province of Quebec.

Added to these factors is the growth of a new and fairly strong Canadian relationship with Latin America and particularly with Mexico through the North American Free Trade Agreement (NAFTA). More than anything else, NAFTA, since coming into force in 1994, has served to focus Canadian attention – in a sense for the first time – on Latin America as a legitimate area for Canadian interest.

Since the mid-1980s, successive Canadian governments have been preoccupied with reducing the budget deficit, high interest rates, minimising the disparity between provinces, and the on-going issue of the separatist threat in Quebec. Because Canada is essentially a trading nation, the perceived solution has been to maximise trading opportunities for Canadian business as well as to increase Canada's competitive advantage in the new global economy. The Canada–US Free Trade Agreement (CUSFTA) and NAFTA have been part of an aggressive Canadian strategy to improve its competitive advantage in the new global economy. Reasons for the changing Caribbean Community and Common Market (CARICOM) relations include the current importance Canada is placing on trade relations and the growing perception that, because of its relatively small market, the Caribbean is not as important as the countries of Central and South America.

TRADE

Traditionally, trade has been the basis of the Canada–Caribbean relationship. However, over time that relationship has come to include a number of related services, such as banking, insurance and shipping. Trade is no longer as significant. In 1964, for example, Canada exported more to the Commonwealth Caribbean (US$70 million) than to India ($64 million) or to any other Commonwealth country in the developing world. In turn, Canada was ranked third, after Great Britain and the United States, as a destination for Caribbean exports. Between 1980 and 1990, two-way trade with the region had declined to around $6 billion. Indeed, despite the implementation of CARIBCAN, the non-reciprocal agreement allowing duty-free entry of a large number of Commonwealth Caribbean exports to Canada, the decline has not been reversed.

CARIBCAN

Writing about CARIBCAN in 1993, Sahadeo Basdeo described the agreement as one manifestation of the special relationship between Canada and the Caribbean (pp. 55–79). The agreement, which was signed in 1986, was the result of the disappointment of Caribbean leaders with the Caribbean Basin Initiative (CBI), a preferential trading agreement promoted by the US administration as a mechanism for reversing negative trade imbalances with the region. The CBI was not fulfilling those expectations, but instead was being used as a political tool by the administration of US President Ronald Reagan to divide the region along ideological lines at the height of the Cold War.

Although many regard the CARIBCAN agreement as patterned after the CBI, typically the agreement is not considered to have been politically motivated. The programme, like the CBI, has excluded certain items for which the region is considered to have a comparative advantage – textiles, clothing, leather garments, footwear, lubricating oils and methanol products, competing with import-sensitive production in Canada – but, in recent years, the programme has led to an increase in trade in non-traditional items produced in CARIBCAN beneficiary countries. The era when Canadian cod, lumber and other staples were exchanged for West Indian rum, sugar, molasses and spices has now given way to a new quality of trade, characterised by a more sophisticated, diversified grouping of products. In recent years, products have included goods and services such as machinery, technical and consulting services, telecommunications equipment, agricultural technology, consumer goods, food products and resource commodities, in exchange for such imports as petroleum and petroleum products, steel, textiles, sugar, bauxite, alumina, ores, rum and other alcoholic beverages, molasses, fish and food products.

The main point made by Basdeo is that trade has always served to foster other relationships with the region. In the early eighteenth century, as a result of trade between eastern Canada and the Commonwealth Caribbean, other services, including banking, insurance, investment, aid and tourism developed. Similarly in the 1980s and 1990s, CARIBCAN, whose purpose was to improve trade with the region, has also achieved other goals. Although CARIBCAN's success is regarded at best as marginal, it has succeeded in expanding the goods and services traded between the region and Canada. The agreement has helped to maintain a level of communication between Canada and the region through such mechanisms as the Joint Trade and Economic Committee (JTEC), which enables officials on both sides to discuss related issues. Over time, the CARICOM agreement has undergone a series of revisions, offering more opportunities for Caribbean producers to trade in items for which they enjoy certain comparative advantages. These include the allowance of in-bond bottling of Caribbean rum, leather luggage, and certain vegetable fibre products, items previously excluded from the agreement. Another offshoot is the Canada Caribbean Business Cooperation Office, which was set up to improve investment flows between Canada and the region.

One is impressed by the fact that, although its success has been moderate, CARIBCAN could have as much influence as it has had, which supports the view that a relatively small amount of Canadian aid can go a long way in an area such as the Caribbean. Furthermore, it is an indication of the significant level of influence enjoyed by Canada in the region.

Basdeo (1993) makes several interesting suggestions in his essay. The first is that official CARIBCAN discussions may be used as a barometer to judge official Canadian thinking. Another is that CARIBCAN could serve to enhance mutilateral relations in the future, including accession of CARICOM countries to NAFTA. These points are being discussed in more detail in light of recent recommendations made by the Senate Foreign Affairs Committee on relations with the region and in discussions of the results of the JTEC meeting in Ottawa.

NAFTA

Perhaps the greatest challenge to the current trading regime between Canada and the countries of the Caribbean is the North American Free Trade Agreement. It is now openly admitted that the signing of NAFTA by Canada, the United States and Mexico has heralded a significant change in relations with the region. Several studies (see, for example, Hosten-Craig, 1992) have concluded that NAFTA poses a threat to CARICOM countries, stemming from North America's important share in CARICOM exports, similarities between patterns of CARICOM and Mexican exports, and the size of the tariff preferences conceded to Mexico. The most direct effect of NAFTA on CARICOM countries is in apparel, particularly for Jamaica. Multi-Fibre Agreement (MFA) quotas on Mexican exports to North America will be eliminated within five years, but quotas for CARICOM countries will be phased out over a ten-year period. The result will be trade diversion, which will be compounded by the availability of cheaper goods from low-income Asian countries.

A Senate of Canada Report on Free Trade in the Americas (Senate of Canada, August 1995) made recommendations designed to lessen the impact of NAFTA and other globalizing trends on the current trading regime between Canada and the Caribbean. Five principal recommendations emanated from those hearings:

- First, the Canadian government should consider expanding the coverage of items formerly excluded under CARIBCAN, inasmuch as these items will now be subject to greater international competition as a result of NAFTA. This, the Committee argued, would be a useful interim measure to offset some of the trade and investment diversion arising from NAFTA, while providing CARICOM countries with tangible evidence that the Canadian government remains committed to maintaining a special relationship with the region.

- Second, support plans should be provided for regional integration at the CARICOM level.
- Third, there should be support for differential treatment for Caribbean countries that want to join NAFTA. That support would be provided either on an individual basis (as desired by Trinidad and Tobago) or in the form of advice on the economic reforms necessary for eligibility in NAFTA. Support would be provided through the JTEC, the current forum for on-going monitoring of Canadian–CARICOM trade relations. Alternatively, it was suggested that Canada could lend its support to Caribbean countries by sponsoring their accession to NAFTA or by supporting those that would like to join the FTAA as a regional group.
- Fourth, there should be assurance that Canadian development assistance to the Caribbean will focus to some extent on encouraging those sectors likely to be competitive in regional and hemispheric free-trade arrangements. The World Bank and the Inter-American Development Bank (IDB) should also be encouraged to consider the manner in which their lending might support key sectors.
- Fifth, a conference should be convened between the Prime Minister of Canada and leaders of Commonwealth Caribbean countries to discuss mutual trade relations. The primary purpose of the conference would be to evaluate ways of improving Canada–Caribbean cooperation in the areas of trade, investment, taxation, financial services, technology transfer, training, licensing and franchising. The meeting would also address ways in which Caribbean countries can help themselves adjust economically to the formation of regional trading blocs and prepare themselves for possible accession to NAFTA or an FTAA.

In conclusion, the Committee felt that Canada needed to take into account the interests of the Commonwealth Caribbean in formulating its trade policy. It was felt that currently attention was placed more heavily on negotiating trading agreements with larger partners. However, many of the reasons that had helped to forge the special relationship between Canada and the region, such as geography, linguistic and cultural proximity, historic and current trade connections, extensive two-way movements of individuals, long-standing investment and other non-official involvement still apply. The Canadian government should make a clear determination to adopt a policy, with special attention to the region and its development.

It has been noted that while the report by the Senate Committee on Foreign Affairs struck an optimistic note concerning the future of Canada–CARICOM relations, the Committee only has the power to recommend. Nonetheless, a review of Canadian government actions since the report's release provides good insight into the true nature of the relationship, with some hints for future developments.

At a JTEC meeting held in Ottawa in November 1996, several decisions were made in relation to the Senate recommendations. One was to extend the life of the CARIBCAN agreement for ten more years. It was also decided that the Canadian government would hold meetings with the business community to discuss items currently excluded from the agreement. (Textiles and apparel are still regarded as somewhat sensitive.) The Canadian side reported on the results of those meetings and presented recommendations in 1997.

The JTEC meeting also agreed to provide technical and financial assistance to aid the regional integration process at the CARICOM level, and the countries of the region subsequently identified areas of importance for them. This list, provided to Prime Minister Jean Chrétien during the Commonwealth Heads of Government meeting in Edinburg, Scotland, in October 1997, is currently being assessed. Technical assistance most likely would include continued preparation for NAFTA/FTAA accession by countries in the region, and, in the future, it would probably replace direct aid more and more often. In addition, assistance was provided to coordinate the approach and logistics of the World Trade Organization (WTO) meeting in 1997, Canada thereby supporting the region's efforts to act as one body. Additional on-going support for the University of the West Indies is another part of the strategy to support a coordinated approach in a region that risks being increasingly marginalized as a result of its size and regional insularity.

In 1997, Prime Minister Chrétien met with Caribbean leaders in Grenada. The meeting, recommended by the Senate Committee in its Interim Report, demonstrated significant progress in carrying out the recommendations of the Committee. The Canadian government clearly decided to follow the Committee's recommendations and remains committed to assisting the region, despite indications of declining interest in the subregion.

Aid

Canada's 'special relationship' with the Commonwealth Caribbean is best reflected in its aid programme. The Commonwealth Caribbean has received one of the highest proportions of Canadian development assistance given to any region of comparable size. The Canadian International Development Agency (CIDA) is responsible for managing and distributing Canadian development assistance.

Ten years ago, the aid programme for the eastern Caribbean was in the vicinity of $80 million. Today, it is only about $30 million. While this amount may appear reasonable, given the region's relatively small population, it is a great deal for a 'special relationship'. The objective of CIDA's programme in the eastern Caribbean is to enable the people of the region to strategically plan and manage their own development process, in the face of changing economic circumstances, for the purpose of achieving fiscally and environmentally sustainable development.

Caribbean Development Assistance studies (CIDA, 1993, 1995) indicate that the major challenge facing the eastern Caribbean is sustained economic growth. CIDA has accordingly replaced the composition of its eastern Caribbean programme with one placing greater emphasis on sustainablity, human resources development, institutional strengthening and economic management. Governments in the region have expressed their satisfaction with multi-island program mechanisms addressing issues on a flexible basis in response to the specific needs of each country. This trend is likely to continue, with new projects or programmes being conducted on a multi-island basis.

Cuts in a number of CIDA programmes have increased competition for aid from other regions. More aid has been designated for Haiti, in keeping with the government's focus on human rights, democracy and good governance. In addition, Cuba is now eligible for some forms of Canadian development assistance. Increased competition has encouraged certain critics to argue that the Commonwealth Caribbean receives too large a proportion of Canadian aid, given the region's size and level of development, and that aid to the region has not been effective. These challenges might, it is believed, encourage CARICOM countries to consider more strategic approaches toward obtaining Canadian development assistance.

CIVIL SOCIETY

Contemporary Canada–Caribbean relations must take into consideration the growing influence of the 140 000-strong Caribbean community in Canada (Basdeo, 1993, pp. 55–79). This growing population has increased the political relevance of the area in the corridors of power and influence in Ottawa. Canadians with Caribbean backgrounds currently occupy positions in the Canadian Senate, Parliament and many government departments and agencies.

The influence of the Caribbean community is also evident in civil society. Civil society includes non-governmental organizations (NGOs), such as sports and professional associations, church groups, trade unions and other organizations. The growth of internationally active civil society actors is an important component of the evolving democratization of both the international system and individual nations. Civil society has been defined as 'the sum of all social institutions and associations (excluding family) which are autonomous, independent of the state, and capable of significantly influencing public policy'.

A major concern for regional observers, particularly those with a special interest in the Caribbean, is the slow pace of the regional integration process. Frustration has increased since implementation of NAFTA and the apparently concomitant decline in priority given the region over the past five years. There has also been a noticeable absence of concrete measures to address what many see as the only viable option for the region. The rationale for regional integration stems from the region's small size relative to markets, its small population base, and the vulnerability of small independent states in an increasingly global economy. Added to this is the perception that the territories are competing against one another and making little effort to work together (Senate of Canada, 1994).

Although it was believed for some time that progressive regional leaders would promote regional integration, evidence has proven the contrary. There has been little follow-up on the findings of the West Indian Commission conducted in the early 1990s to explore the regional integration option. Hope now appears to rest on the ability of civil society to recognise the benefits of the regional option and to demand that political leaders further this cause. Civil society in Canada has come to play a proactive role in influencing government policy. This is evident in the direction taken by Canadian policy in past years, one that clearly favours consultation with Canadian NGOs. The government of Canada currently holds extensive consultations with NGOs, which enjoy more efficacy than ever before, and NGOs are playing a key role in shaping and promoting Canadian values at home and abroad. This is believed to be less the case in the Commonwealth Caribbean, with the notable exception of the Caribbean Conference of Churches. Like most other sectors of society, however, many NGOs are currently feeling the effects of budget cuts and added pressures in rationalising their operations to stay in business.

The pressures faced by NGOs, such as Canadian University Service Overseas (CUSO), are important in understanding the current challenges faced by Canadian and other NGOs due to fiscal and budgetary cuts. CUSO has had one of the longest-standing relationships of any NGO in the Caribbean. It was in the Caribbean where many CUSO representatives cut their teeth, so to speak, before venturing into development work in the more distant lands of Asia and Africa (Smillie, 1985).

In the 1960s and 1970s, CUSO had more than 160 volunteers in the Caribbean working in 15 different islands and territories. They were stationed throughout – from Barbados to Belize in the southeast, to Jamaica in the northern part of the region. This is no longer the case today, however. Instead of a separate Caribbean section, CUSO's Caribbean operation has been merged with Latin America. Because of this decision, which is currently being implemented by numerous organisations including the Canadian government, CUSO has only one small office in Jamaica to serve all of the Commonwealth Caribbean. Furthermore, the Caribbean section in Ottawa currently consists of only one support officer.

The experiences of CUSO and other NGOs over the years in the Caribbean are important. Early workers found that real social change posed a major threat to conservative governments in the region (Smillie, 1985). Other factors include a long-standing Canadian paternalism and exploitation of the area based on general misunderstandings concerning the diversity of the culture, politics and terrain. These attitudes took their toll on volunteers working directly with the people in the region (*ibid.*). Experience suggests that more homework needs to be done on the area and its people if Canadian assistance is to be regarded as meaningful and equitable. Canadians tend to believe that they are familiar with the area because of its geographic proximity, but too often this approach has backfired. Similar findings have been reported by NGOs working in Latin America.

Are the Caribbean and Latin America sufficiently similar to warrant an assimilation of the region in Canadian NGO and other programming? Some like Klepak argue that this measure may ensure the survival of regional programmes (1994). Others, however, realizing that the majority of the programmes are currently focused on Latin America, believe that the Caribbean will suffer further loss of profile and a concurrent loss of interest in Canada. Despite these losses, Canada provides support for Caribbean NGOs in such areas as agriculture, rural development, health, education and community development (Basdeo, 1993). Assistance has been facilitated through the Canada Fund for local initiatives, accessible through accredited regional Canadian diplomatic missions. The fund enables missions to provide timely assistance to grass-roots organisations, while complementing other CIDA bilateral or multilateral aid.

Canadian aid has also facilitated educational links between institutions in Canada and their counterparts in the region. Organisations such as the Association of Canadian Community Colleges (ACCC) have forged strategic partnerships in Barbados and are currently involved in sharing knowledge and resources with their regional counterparts. Indications are that this type of partnership is the way of the future, as organisations and institutions seek to maximise resources in the face of budget cuts.

Another area of Canada–Caribbean cooperation involves farm workers from the Caribbean. Under an agreement between Canada and several Caribbean countries, seasonal workers from the region provide manual labour for farmers on tobacco and fruit farms in Quebec and southern Ontario. Canadian farmers have experienced difficulty employing Canadians to do similar jobs. Seasonal workers spend a limited period of time in Canada, under strict conditions, and remit foreign currency to their families in the Caribbean. Despite some difficulties concerning living and working conditions on the farms over the years, the programme appears to have worked well. It is valued by Canadian farmers and contributes to the economies in labourers' home countries. It is interesting to note that in the past five years, the number of workers from the Caribbean has declined in favour of a growing number from Mexico. While some see this trend as having evolved over time, others believe it is another manifestation of the NAFTA effect favouring Mexican over Caribbean workers.

PERCEPTIONS OF THE CARIBBEAN COMMUNITY IN CANADA

Immigrants arriving in the 1960s from the Caribbean faced heavily restrictive rules of entry, which required a high educational level and professional or skill potential. These rules also applied to those entering the country as domestics. In 1965, for example, 24 per cent of West Indians admitted were professionals, compared to just 2 per cent of

Italians (Smillie, 1985). Many of the earlier immigrants made a very positive impression in their new homes. Some of these include the Honourable Jean Augustine, MP, Rosemary Brown, a former member of the British Columbia legislature and a prominent advocate of women's and minority rights, Chief Justice Julius Isaacs, as well as others representing a broad section of Canadian society. The efforts of these individuals have been instrumental in fostering Canada–Caribbean relations.

Some observers of Canadian immigration trends view relaxation of Canadian immigration ground rules in the mid- and late 1970s as having had a negative impact on the way Canadians view the Caribbean community. They say that the less-restrictive rules have enabled a significant number of the less-desirable elements of Caribbean society to enter Canada. Settling in urban centres such as Toronto and Montreal, without the skills and social support of earlier immigrants and under tough economic circumstances, these more recent arrivals have found adjusting to their new homes difficult.

Statistics reporting a very high level of criminal activity by Jamaican gangs in Toronto have contributed especially to a negative perception of West Indians in Canada, and involvement of some Toronto-based Jamaican gangs in drug trafficking has received considerable press coverage in the country (Klepak, 1994). As a result, a certain mythology has developed about Jamaicans in Canada; anyone who participates in antisocial activities is believed to be Jamaican. This negative image has unfortunately spread and coloured the perception of the region in the eyes of many Canadians. Fortunately, though, there has also been a long tradition of success in international competitions by Canadian athletes with Caribbean connections. The recent spectacular performances of the Canadian men's sprint team in the Olympic track and field events at least partially offsets the negative media images of Caribbean Canadians.

Although Canadians still think of the Caribbean as a sun and holiday destination, the feeling is less reciprocal in terms of the welcome Caribbean visitors receive in Canada. This attitude is now reflected in current immigration laws requiring Caribbean visitors to Canada to have visas, a practice that has encouraged accusations of racism. Charges of racism are not new in Canadian–Caribbean relations, however, and incidents attributed to racism have been levied against Canadian policies and some institutions (Smillie, 1985). However, efforts are being taken to improve communication with the Caribbean community, particularly in large urban centres, and progress has already been reported.

SECURITY

Security is another area in which Canada has been involved in the Caribbean, although almost always as a reluctant partner. Initially, it was the Commonwealth tie that pulled the strings. There evolved though a need to help fill the void left by Great Britain's withdrawal from the region and following the independence of small, defenseless countries in Canada's front yard. Later on, Canada became involved because of its tourism link and also as a counterweight to the United States, acting as a partner in whom confidence was great.

Following the Second World War, Canada's reluctance to commit its defense resources has been attributed to two main factors. The formation of the North Atlantic Treaty Organization (NATO) and the participation of Canadian forces in peacekeeping operations in sensitive areas around the world left Canadian military resources stretched. Other reasons have included the desire to lessen Canada's dependence on the United States and the possibility of getting drawn into military maneuvers in the region, which have had the potential to expand into Central and South America (Klepak, 1994). This fear was at the heart of Canada's reluctance to join the Organization of American States (OAS) for many years.

Nonetheless, the Commonwealth tie resulted in defense links with the Caribbean. Assistance was provided in the form of a Canadian presence (ships) on the occasion of independence celebrations, officer and cadet training for Jamaica, Guyana, Belize and the Eastern Caribbean, as well as technical assistance. By 1982, under Canadian Prime Minister Pierre Trudeau, technical assistance was expanded to include the coastguard, although Canada had expressed its reluctance to become involved in a military option prior to the invasion of Grenada in 1993. Indeed, it is this distinction in Canadian and US security policy that highlights the differences between the two nations' approaches to the region.

Since 1980, Canada has continued its limited security assistance in the Caribbean (Klepak, 1994), although its form has changed. Contributing international factors have been the end of the Cold War, membership of the OAS, the expansion of the role of the UN in international security, and the establishment of NAFTA. Other regional factors have included the increased attention given to problems facing Haiti, the prominence of the drug trade (which has become a major security issue for many countries, including the United States), and the longevity of the Castro government in Cuba, regarded as somewhat of an anomaly, particularly by the US administration in light of the decline of Communism and the end of the Cold War.

Expansion of the UN's role has required a much greater security contribution from countries such as Canada. This involvement saw Canadian forces active in Central America between 1989 and 1992, and in El Salvador up to the present time. Canadian navy ships were also sent to Haiti in the late 1980s to support that country's democratic efforts, and the Royal Canadian Mounted Police (RCMP) have provided training for Haitian police. Canada's policy has enabled it to demonstrate commitment to La Francophonie, the French counterpart of the Commonwealth, of which it is a member.

One aspect of the contemporary security scene is the characterisation of the drug trade by the US as a major security threat. Typically, Canadians view the issue as having a social dimension and involving issues of health and education, rather than as a national security question focused on the elimination of the international drug trade (Klepak, 1994). This perception has at times put Canada out of step with the United States on the security issue. Nonetheless, Canada has played a more active role in the fight against drugs and drug trafficking by the United States and other countries.

Canada's accession to the OAS and NAFTA are also factors that have influenced its greater activity in regional security. When Canada joined the OAS in 1989, it sought to exclude Chapter V of the agreement, which dealt with defense. However, time soon changed this resolve, and, as Canada's involvement and focus on the Americas south of the US border grew, it found itself promoting, along with Argentina, a commission to advance outstanding security issues in that part of the world. Similarly, with the NAFTA agreement came the decision that a security element was necessary to ensure that free trade mechanisms would not be exploited by those involved in the drug trade.

Another aspect of the current security issue is immigration, which has taken on new importance with the changing face of regional security concerns in the 1990s. The two hot spots in the Caribbean are Haiti and Cuba, with considerable resources being diverted from the Commonwealth Caribbean to this end. Concurrent with reallocation of resources to Haiti in particular has been a steady increase in interest in Mexico as well as Latin America itself. This interest has grown at the same time as the observed worldwide decline in the Commonwealth relationship.

Notwithstanding, security assistance to the Commonwealth Caribbean has continued. Canada recognises that for the Caribbean, the drug trade poses a serious threat to democracy and regional stability. One risk governments face is that of officials being subverted by the lure of financial reward, as has already occurred in some parts of the region. Other challenges are concerned with crime and social instability as a result of dependency on drugs. Recognising these threats, the government of Canada has provided support in the form of an RCMP liaison officer stationed in Kingston, Jamaica, with responsibility for coordinating the efforts of other Caribbean states, as well as in Bogota and Mexico City (Klepak, 1994). Cooperation has been given for coastguard operations, which combine security and anti-drug training in the region. Canadian authorities, at the same time, are careful to point out that the more effective solution to the issue is one that focuses attention on demand for drugs, one that still comes largely from North America.

Given the historical relationship between Canada and the Caribbean on security matters, the Caribbean is more likely to prefer Canadian to US assistance in this area, as there may be fewer strings attached. On the other hand, Canada probably will not be willing to devote significant resources to this form of assistance, although the issue is important to the Caribbean and Canada. Furthermore, as the Grenada invasion demonstrated, Canada is unlikely to be drawn into missions that involve military invasions (Haar and Dosman, 1993), and, consequently, the Caribbean probably will depend both on the United States and Canada in the sensitive area of defense. Canadian assistance becomes more likely if coordinated with multinational organisations such as the UN and the Commonwealth. For historical and practical considerations, the latter scenario would be more probable.

CANADA–CUBA RELATIONS

Although the United States has maintained a trade and investment embargo against Cuba for more than 30 years, Canada has pursued an independent foreign policy stance. In fact, Canada and Mexico were the only countries in the Americas that did not sever relations with Cuba after the Cuban revolution. Canada's independent policy mainly reflected the view that foreign governments enjoying popular support should be recognised diplomatically (Kirk *et al.*, 1995).

A number of initiatives have been undertaken over the years to cement the relationship between Canada and Cuba. For instance, Prime Minister Trudeau visited Havana in 1976, thus becoming the first leader of a NATO country to visit the island, and the Cuban government still remembers. As a result of the exchange, two-way trade between the countries increased from $50 million to $649 million between 1968 and 1981. Cuba has become a favourite winter destination for Canadian tourists, and in 1998 215 000 Canadians visited Cuba, pulling ahead of Italy as the number one source of incoming tourists.

At a conference held in Havana in June 1994, Secretary of State for Latin America and Africa, Christine Stewart, announced a number of adjustments in Canada's policy towards Cuba. These changes allowed for more consultations with Cuban ministers and officials by parliamentarians; support for full Cuban membership in the OAS; funding for Canadian NGOs involved in development work in Cuba and access by Cuba to Canadian government development assistance; provision of further humanitarian relief; and trade promotion support and assistance for Canadian firms doing business in Cuba (Saint-Amand, 1995).

Canadian trade with Cuba is becoming more and more important. In 1994, Canada exported about Canadian $108 million in merchandise to Cuba, making the island the seventh largest market for Canadian goods in Latin America and the Caribbean. These figures were noticeably boosted during the last 10 months of 1996, when Canadian exports to Cuba jumped to $200 million, making Cuba second only to Mexico, which was just under $10 million. Similarly, in 1994 Cuba shipped about $194 million worth of goods to Canada, and during the last 10 months of 1996 Cuban exports to Canada averaged about $360 million. The leading imports from Cuba were nickel, sugar, rock lobsters and shrimps, precious metal scrap, clothing and cigars (Statistics Canada, 1996).

The Cuban economy is struggling at this time. Since the collapse of Communism in 1989 and the withdrawal of financial support by the Soviet Union, the Cuban economy has shrunk by nearly one-half, while exports and imports represent less than one-third of their value in 1989. Shortages of food, medicine, consumer goods and electric power are common (*ibid.*). Another source of the struggle for survival of the Cuban economy is the long-standing US embargo against the island. For over 35 years the United States has banned its citizens from any commercial relations with Cuba. Investments by firms from other countries in Cuba are vulnerable to compensation claims from US companies and Cuban-Americans whose properties were confiscated when Communists seized power (Saint-Amand, 1995).

More recently, the threat of even greater restrictions against companies doing business with Cuba has been introduced by the US administration in the form of the Helms–Burton Act. Under this act, US nationals may launch lawsuits in US courts against Canadian and other foreign firms and individuals allegedly 'trafficking' in property expropriated from those US citizens. US President Clinton announced on 16 July 1996 that this right to sue would be suspended for a six-month period.

Canada has expressed strong opposition to the act, along with Mexico, the Caribbean and a number of other countries, and in December 1996, the government of Canada introduced legislation to counter the Helms–Burton Act. The Canadian legislation amends the Foreign Extraterritorial Measures Act (FEMA) to protect Canadian companies from unacceptable foreign laws such as Helms–Burton. In doing so, the Foreign Affairs Minister, Lloyd Axworthy, said, 'These amendments send an important signal that Canada continues its vigorous opposition to Helms–Burton' (Department of Foreign Affairs and International Trade, 1996). At the same time, Mr Axworthy restated Canada's belief that the best way to encourage democratic development in Cuba is through engagement and dialogue.

When in force, the amended FEMA would provide protection for Canadian firms in three ways. By ensuring that judgments handed down under Helms–Burton would not be enforced or recognised in Canada; by permitting Canadians to recover in Canadian courts any amounts awarded under Helms–Burton, along with their court costs and consequent damages – a measure known as 'clawback'; and by giving the Attorney General of Canada the authority to amend a schedule listing objectionable foreign legislation that violates international law. Prior to implementing the FEMA, Canada had announced that it would participate as a third party in the European Union's (EU) challenge to the Helms–Burton legislation at the World Trade Organization (WTO). In addition, Canadian officials have held consultations with the US under NAFTA and pursued the issue in international organisations, such as the Organisation for Economic Cooperation and Development (OECD) and the OAS.

Canada's position *vis-à-vis* Helms–Burton has received strong support from Mexico, Canada's other NAFTA partner, and other Caribbean countries, all of which have objected to the US attempt to extend its law to other jurisdictions. The Helms–Burton Act puts the otherwise excellent relations of Canada and the United State to the test. The bill has provided yet another example of why Caribbean countries turn to

Canada to play its middle power role in the region. Cuba is currently a full charter member of the Association of Caribbean States (ACS), and its membership will ensure the solidarity of that grouping of Caribbean countries. Both Canada and Mexico, with the support of the Caribbean countries and other nations, have advised the United States that any new measures taken by the United States to isolate Cuba will not affect their relations with Cuba.

THE AMERICAS

Canada's involvement in the Americas is a complex challenge. Economies of the Americas are liberalising their trade regimes and improving their economic management. However, poverty, income inequalities, weak institutions and environmental degradation threaten to undermine the Americas' promising economic prospects and the still fragile democratisation process. With the ratification of NAFTA and the commitment expressed at the December 1994 Summit of the Americas to set up a 'free trading system' by the year 2005, Canada has vested economic and security interests in the Americas. As these interests expand, the priorities of Canadian Official Development Assistance become even more important.

The 1996–97 budget for the Americas was estimated at US$145 million. These resources were primarily divided among country-specific and regional programmes regrouped under three subregions: Caribbean with 39 per cent of the resources (Commonwealth Caribbean, Haiti and Cuba); Central America 22 per cent (Honduras, Nicaragua, Costa Rica, El Salvador and Guatemala); and South America 39 per cent (Peru, Bolivia, Brazil, Colombia and Ecuador). Canadian assistance is delivered also through small Canada Funds in Panama, Mexico, Venezuela, Paraguay, Argentina, Chile and Uruguay (Canadian International Development Agency 1996–97).

Consistent with CIDA's programme priorities, the developmental challenge in the Americas will be to pursue programme activities that support political stability, economic liberalisation, social equity and sound environmental management. Consideration of women as full partners in development will also continue to be fully integrated in programming activities as critical cross-cutting issues.

ENVIRONMENT

In 1996–97, programme activities focused on improving the management of natural resources and increasing the environment and natural resources management capacity of key institutions. Over the following eight years from 1997 to 2005, $12 million has been allocated to the Environmental Action Programme in Jamaica. This initiative will assist in the development of environmental education programmes and awareness-building, and strengthen institutional capacity in environmental management.

CONCLUSION

Historically, Canada has enjoyed a great deal of influence in the Caribbean, and recently this influence has resulted in the early support of those countries in opposing the Helms–Burton bill. This support has provided momentum for additional regional and international support for Canada's opposition to the US plan to further isolate Cuba. In turn, the future support of partners such as Canada and Mexico can enable the region to withstand pressure to take actions against regional interests.

If Caribbean countries do not always seek Canada's help in security matters, it is because Canada is often recognized to be a reluctant partner in such activities. Canada's membership in the OAS and in NAFTA can, however, enable it to play a stronger role as a middle power in conflict-mediation and as a trusted mentor in the region. It will also be up to the region to ensure that the Caribbean is not forgotten in Canada. A more proactive people-to-people approach at a variety of levels would go a long way towards strengthening ties, while forging strategic partnerships for the future. These partnerships could work to promote positive images and success stories.

Recent decisions to extend the CARICOM agreement and to discuss measures that would, if implemented, help the countries of the region to strengthen their fragile economies in preparation for eventual integration into the world economy are concrete indications of continued goodwill towards the region. Despite signs to the contrary, the special relationship between Canada and the Caribbean is not dead. Actions speak louder than words. The resilience of this relationship over time, and despite geographic and cultural barriers, is remarkable, particularly in light of current challenges.

References

Basdeo, S. (1993) 'Caribcan: A Continuum in Canada–Commonwealth Caribbean Economic Relations', *Canadian Foreign Policy*, vol. 1, no. 2 (Spring), pp. 55–79.

Campbell, F.A. (1992) *Refueling a Special Friendship, Canada and the Caribbean States* (Ottawa: North–South Institute).

Canadian International Development Agency (CIDA) (1993) *Canadian Development Assistance in Latin America and the Caribbean* (Ottawa–Hull: Americas Branch, CIDA).

Canada International Development Agency (CIDA) (1996–97) *Estimates Part III. Expenditure Plan* (Ottawa: Canada Communication Group).

Department of Foreign Affairs and International Trade (DFAIT) (1996) 'Legislation to Counter Helms–Burton Act to come into force January 1'. News Release, Ottawa: DFAIT, 30 December.

Haar, J. and E.J. Dosman (eds) (1993) *A Dynamic Partnership: Canada's Changing Role in the Americas* (Coral Gables, FL: North–South Center Press).

Hosten-Craig, J. (1992) *The Effect of a Free Trade Agreement on the Commonwealth Caribbean* (Lewiston, NY: The Edwin Mellen Press).

Issues of the Day (1993) *Canadian Speeches: A National Forum of Diverse Views* (Toronto: Southam Electronic Publishing), February.

Kirk, J. *et al.* (1995) *Back in Business: Canada–Cuba Relations after 50 Years*, Canadian Foundation for the Americas.

Klepak, H.P. (ed). (1993) *Canada and Latin America Security* (Quebec: Meridien).

Klepak, H.P. (1994) 'Canadian and Caribbean Perspectives on Security in the Region', unpublished paper presented to the Conference on Canadian Caribbean Relations: The Search for New Directions.

Mahler, G. (1993) *Canada and the Caribbean: Political Commonalities and Convergences*, Department of Political Science, University of Mississippi.

National Journal (1994) 'The Cuban Conundrum', 17 September.

Saint-Amand, A. (1995) 'U.S. Firm Challenges Sheritt Cuban Project', *The Financial Post* (11 March).

Senate of Canada (1994) *Foreign Affairs: Proceedings of the Standing Senate Committee*. Issue no. 6 (29 November).

Senate of Canada (1995) *Free Trade in the Americas Interim Report* (August).

Smillie, I. (1985) *The Land of Lost Content: A History of CUSO* (Toronto: Deneau Publishing).

Statistics Canada (1993) *Touriscope: International Travel*. Catalogue no. 66–201.

Statistics Canada (1996) *Imports by Country*. Catalogue 65-006. Ottawa: Statistics Canada.

2 Canada and the Caribbean: Power without Paternalism in the Age of Interdependence

Ivelaw L. Griffith

It can be asserted, without fear of contradiction, that, although scholars of international politics disagree about many things, there are two denominators of the international system about which they agree unanimously. The first is that the system is an anarchical one. There is, of course, disagreement over the extent to which life in this anarchical society is nasty, brutish and short, for whom it is so, and why it is so. The other denominator is that the international community is living in an age of interdependence. Again, there is dispute over the nature, scope and manifestation of this interdependence.

Two trailblazers of the interdependence school have argued that:

> From the foreign policy standpoint, the problem facing individual governments is how to benefit from international exchange while maintaining as much autonomy as possible. From the perspective of the international system, the problem is how to generate and maintain a mutually beneficial pattern of cooperation in the face of competing efforts by governments (and nongovernmental actors) to manipulate the system for their own benefit. (Keohane and Nye, 1989, p. 249)

This is essentially a two-dimensional strategy question. From a Caribbean perspective, a response to both of its aspects – the individual government and the international system – would feature Canada. For almost every Caribbean government, exchanges with Canada bring benefits without any covert or overt design to diminish or undermine the position of the government in question. And in terms of the international system, Canada is willingly invited to be a power broker, especially because its policies and pursuits are shorn of crass self-interest and tactics of manipulation.[1]

Our anarchical international society has always been characterised by hierarchical gradations of power, although the power distribution and definitions of the hierarchy have been altered by the end of the Cold War (see, for example, Hoffman, 1990, pp. 115–22; Nye, 1992; Kegley, 1993, pp. 131–46). However, post-Cold War alterations have not essentially changed Canada's place in the international system as a middle power. Indeed, as Foreign Minister Lloyd Axworthy told the 13 December 1996 meeting of the National Forum on Foreign Policy in Manitoba, 'Canadians remain committed to an active, internationalist foreign policy. The issues and the setting may have changed, but Canadian support for an activist middle-power approach is as strong as it was 40 years ago' ('Notes for an Address', 1996). Post-Cold War alterations have also not transformed the basic character of Caribbean countries as small, subordinate states. Space limitations do not permit a full examination of the nature, scope and meaning of all of the interdependence dynamics between middle-power Canadian and small, subordinate states of the Caribbean. Nevertheless, any attempt to come to terms with the essence of those dynamics necessitates an appreciation of the exchanges in at least two areas: commerce and trade, and security and governance.

COMMERCE AND TRADE

A few general observations on the nature and scope of Canadian–Caribbean relations are in order before turning to the first interdependence arena. The first and very obvious one is that Canada's contacts in the region are not uniform. There is variation in the nature and extent of political, economic, security, cultural, educational and diplomatic dealings. For example, although Canada maintains diplomatic relations with all of the independent nations in the region, diplomatic missions are only maintained in Barbados, Cuba, the Dominican Republic, Guyana, Haiti and Jamaica. The variation notwithstanding, Canada–Caribbean relations are multilateral and multifaceted; they exist both bilaterally and multilaterally, and involve government-to-government as well as non-governmental organisational contacts. Canada–Caribbean contacts have also been long-standing, predating the birth of independent nations in the Caribbean and even of the Canadian federation itself. In 1865, for example, two years before the federation came into being, the MacDonald/Cartier government sent its first Canadian commercial mission to the region. The contacts extend so far back that one vice president of the Canadian International Development Agency (CIDA) remarked, 'After Columbus, we came' (Hyett, 1993, p. 59).

The commercial and trading contacts between Canada and the Caribbean were consolidated in the aftermath of the American Revolution, as British Caribbean colonies began to depend increasingly on northern Canadian provinces for supplies to keep their plantation economies afloat. A former Trinidad and Tobago foreign minister explained, 'It was this maritime commercial connection that established the foundation of early Canadian–Caribbean relations and which subsequently became the vehicle through which Canadian missionaries, bankers, businessmen and tourists entered the British Caribbean' (Basdeo, 1993, p. 49).

As might be expected, the commercial and trading contacts have varied over time. Basdeo has noted:

> The most striking feature of recent Canadian–Caribbean trade relations is the extent to which the trade has broadened from its historically narrow base. The era when Canadian cod, lumber, and other staples were exchanged for West Indian rum, sugar, molasses, and spices has now given way to a new quality of trade – one characterized by a more sophisticated and diversified group of products. (Basdeo, 1993, p. 55)

During the 1990s, Canadian products sold in the Caribbean have included goods and services such as machinery, technical and consulting services, telecommunications equipment, agricultural technology, consumer goods and food products. From Caribbean countries have come petroleum and petroleum products, nickel, steel, textiles, sugar, rum, bauxite, alumina, gold, diamonds, fish, food products and tropical fruits and animals.

Finance and mining are among the areas with the largest and longest Canadian investment in the region. The operations of the Royal Bank of Canada (then known as the Merchant's Bank of Halifax) in Trinidad and Tobago and Bermuda date back to the 1880s. By the 1930s, the Royal Bank of Canada, the Bank of Nova Scotia, the Canadian Imperial Bank of Commerce and the Bank of Montreal were all fully operational in the region. Canadian banks still tower over the region's banking and financial landscape. Three of the four dominant private banks in the Caribbean are Canadian: the Royal Bank of Canada, the Canadian Imperial Bank of Commerce, and the Bank of Nova Scotia (Basdeo, 1993, pp. 49–50; Hyett, 1993, p. 59). The other is Barclays of the United Kingdom.

In the area of mining, Alcan continues to feature prominently in the bauxite industries of Guyana and Jamaica. Canadian companies are also major players in nickel and oil operations in Cuba and in gold and diamond operations in Guyana. In the case of Guyana, the phenomenal boost in the quantity and efficiency of gold production over the last decade is attributable to the investment and production initiatives of several Canadian companies, including Gold Star Resources, Cambior, and Omai Gold Mines, Ltd. In November 1996, Omai, which had suspended production for four months following a cyanide chemical spill in May 1995, announced a US$53 million investment expansion. The expansion brings the company's investment in Guyana to $253 million and will boost gold production from 13 000 to 20 000 ounces daily (Griffith, 1993, p. 56; *New York Carib News*, 1996).

Canadian trade with the English-speaking Caribbean has actually declined over the past two decades. But the decline has not affected the strong bonds of friendship between Canada and the Commonwealth Caribbean because their interdependence is not predicated primarily on trade and commerce. As Kari Levitt remarked, 'Canadian relations with the countries of the Commonwealth Caribbean serve Canadian political, as distinct from economic or commercial, objectives' (1988, p. 230). The Canada–Commonwealth Caribbean relationship is considered a special one, influenced by common colonial history, political culture and Commonwealth ties. What K. Levitt wrote in 1988 is still accurate a decade later:

> For Canada, the Commonwealth Caribbean constitutes perhaps the only place in the world where Canada enjoys a 'presence' in the international relations sense of the term. The priority accorded to the Commonwealth Caribbean, 'in the overall external policy of Canada' ... bears testimony to the fact that Canada places an importance on its relations with countries of the English-speaking Caribbean that is altogether disproportionate to their small size, and their rapidly diminishing importance in terms of trade and investment. (p. 230)

It is essentially this special relationship that explains the launching of CARIBCAN, which was announced in February 1986 and passed into law four months later as a tangible expression of that relationship. With a close resemblance to the US-sponsored Caribbean Basin Initiative (CBI), CARIBCAN aims at strengthening the exporting capacities of Commonwealth Caribbean countries and promoting Canadian investment in the region. Its most important feature is the preferential duty-free entry to the Canadian market for all categories of Commonwealth Caribbean exports. CARIBCAN has a programme to strengthen the export potential of beneficiary countries and seminars for their diplomats and businesspeople to learn how to develop markets for Caribbean products in Canada, among others.

One University of the West Indies economist indicated that it is difficult to assess the full impact of CARIBCAN on Commonwealth Caribbean–Canadian commercial and trade relations, mainly because Canada also has a generalised system of preferences (Ramsaran, 1996, p. 39). Many assessments of CARIBCAN, however, have concluded that, so far, it has been a qualified failure in its main objective. A 1991 CARICOM Secretariat study of Canadian–CARICOM trade indicated that there was an adverse balance in CARICOM merchandise trade with Canada for each year between 1984 and 1990, CARIBCAN's introduction in 1986 notwithstanding. Canada's export performance to the region has improved, however, increasing 5 per cent annually between 1987 and 1990 (Basdeo, 1993, p. 64). A look at Ramsaran's terms of trade comparison for 1986 and 1994 also does little to instill confidence in the value of CARIBCAN for Caribbean trade. In 1986, trade balances – in millions of US dollars – were as follows: Bahamas, 0; Barbados, 10; Belize, 2; Guyana, −16; Jamaica, −51; and Trinidad and Tobago, 27. In 1994, they were: Bahamas, −24; Barbados, 11; Belize, −11; Guyana, −159; Jamaica, −114; and Trinidad and Tobago, 33 (Ramsaran, 1996, p. 39).

If there is a single place in the region outside the Commonwealth Caribbean with which Canada can be said to have a 'special relationship' in commercial and trading terms it is Cuba. One noted Canadian specialist on Cuban observed, 'The Canadian presence in Cuba is unmistakable. From the moment that one arrives there (either at the new Varadero air terminal or the revamped one in Havana – both built by Canadian companies) it is impossible not to be aware of Canada's role' (Kirk, 1995, p. 145). Canada did not follow the US lead in breaking diplomatic relations with Cuba in 1960, following Fidel Castro's arrival on the scene the previous year, and it has long sought 'normalcy' in its dealings with the island's leaders. The Canada–Cuba special relationship itself dates back to the Pierre Trudeau era of the 1970s, a highpoint of which was the 1976 visit by Trudeau and his family to Havana. Trudeau's remarks at a February 1983 Commonwealth–Western

Hemisphere conference in St Lucia offer an explanation of Canada's approach to Cuba, 'In our view, states have the right to follow whatever ideological path their peoples decide. When a country chooses a socialist, or even a Marxist, path it does not necessarily buy a "package" which automatically injects it into the Soviet Orbit' (cited in Mahler, 1993, p. 86). Commercial and trading contacts between Canada and Cuba are quite significant. For instance, 1994 merchandise trade between both was valued at $237 million, which increased by 66 per cent in 1995 to $393 million. Cuba sells nickel, cobalt, sugar, seafood, rum and cigars to Canada. Canada, in turn, exports machinery, cars and car parts, electrical equipment, grains, lumber, pulp and paper, foodstuffs and manufactured goods to Cuba. As far as investment is concerned, Canadians invest mainly in mining, tourism and manufacturing. Canada is now among Cuba's top five trading partners – along with Spain, Mexico, Russia and China – with over 300 Canadian companies operating on the island (Freudmann, 1996).

Cuba–Canada business dealings involve both individual investments and joint ventures. In January 1996, records at the Canadian embassy in Havana listed 17 joint ventures, with 20 more under negotiation. One successful example of such a venture involves Sherritt Inc. of Alberta, which has interests in the production of oil, gas, fertilizers and industrial materials. A Sherritt subsidiary, Sherritt International of Toronto, owns cobalt and nickel mining and refining operations, agricultural lands and tourism businesses in Cuba. Sherritt is reputedly Cuba's single largest foreign investor, with some $650 million in assets and cash. Sherritt took its Cuba dealings a step further in December 1994 by entering into a joint venture with the Cuban government. Metals Enterprise was the result of this arrangement, with each party having a 50 per cent interest in the new company (Freudmann, 1996; Wells, 1996, pp. 22–4). Tourism is also a key aspect of the Cuban–Canadian connection. Canada provides tourism investment, tourism management and tourists. The largest single group of tourists to Cuba are Canadians – some 30 per cent of all tourists visiting the island. An estimated 200 000 Canadians visited Cuba in 1996, with 54 planes leaving from various parts of Canada every week. The tourism sector is not just huge, it also is growing. Wilton Properties Ltd, for example, has signed joint-venture agreements with Cuban hotel developer Grand Caribe to develop 11 hotels, all of which will carry five-star amenities, such as golf courses, equestrian facilities, tennis clubs and health spas (Wells, 1996, pp. 22–4; Morris, 1996, p. 17).

Given this economic and trade interdependence, it is fully understandable that Canada would be high on the Helms–Burton rage list. Christine Stewart, Canada's Secretary of State for Latin America and Africa, stated in May 1996 that:

> It is no surprise that Canada is opposed to the Helms–Burton legislation. For one thing, it represents an approach to Cuba that diverges significantly from Canada's. Second, in our view, it magnifies the problems of US–Cuba relations: it is like throwing oil instead of water on an unwanted fire. Third, we believe it is the wrong instrument as it not only targets Cuba, but threatens trading partners and friends and disrupts international trade and investment. (Griffith in *Helms–Burton and International Business*, 1996, p. 3)

Canada has implemented a range of domestic and international measures to thwart the aims and impact of the US legislation, including the pursuit of arbitration under the North American Free Trade Agreement (NAFTA), action before the World Trade Organization (WTO), and its own legislative action (see DePalma, 1996, p. A8; Swardson, 1996; and Myers, 1996, pp. 1A, 14A). Action on the legislative front took the form of amendments to the Foreign Extraterritorial Measures Act, passed in 1984. These amendments took effect from 1 January 1997 (*The Miami Herald*, 1997).

SECURITY AND GOVERNANCE

Canada features prominently in the security and governance affairs of the Caribbean, and it is especially in international political terms where Canada's power without paternalism is most manifest, which allows it to stand on certain international high moral ground. For Canada, not only is there linkage between security and governance, but the linkage is multifaceted. As one high-ranking foreign ministry official explained, 'In Canada's view, security really begins with the consolidation of democracy; the firm establishment of constitutionally-based legal systems and irrevocable rule of law. Security can be guaranteed only where there is respect for human rights and dignity; where there is sustainable economic development and social justice for all member of society. These are the real elements of security. They go far beyond armies and arsenals' (Sinclair, 1995, p. 134).

It is precisely this thinking that has motivated a variety of security and governance interchanges with the Caribbean. Hal Klepak, Canada's leading hemispheric security expert, has explained:

> In a number of areas, Caribbean security issues have been of concern to the Canadian government. If the Caribbean is writ large, then these are many, including the evolution of the situation in our new North American Free Trade Agreement (NAFTA) partner Mexico, the peace process in Guatemala and other parts of Central America, the insurgency in Colombia, civil–military relations in a number of Caribbean Basin states, the Panama Canal, and the like. However, even if the Caribbean is writ small, there are still some. These are: (1) the Haitian dilemma, (2) the international drug trade, (3) the stability of the small states in the Commonwealth Caribbean, and (4) ensuring peaceful change in Cuba. (1996, p. 89)

Attention is paid to some of these 'writ small' area issues below, but it is important first to offer a preliminary comment on Canada's security and governance contacts with the region.

There have been three schools of security policy-thinking concerning the Caribbean as mentioned: the defense and security school, the peace and development school, and the national interest school. The first stresses the linkages between Western strategic interests and the region. The second is suspicious of military security assistance and regards economic cooperation as the best security guarantee. The third pushes for economic and diplomatic cooperation and non-entanglement in disputes that could damage the country's reputation and positive image internationally. Each school has weighed heavily in Canada's security and governance dealings with the Caribbean, sometimes acting in combination. The 1990s have seen a marked influence of the peace and development school and the national interest school. Canada's security interchanges with the region have, therefore, not been significant in terms of military hardware, but in terms of police and coast-guard training, airport and seaport security measures, intelligence sharing and intelligence training, and communications equipment and training. Interchanges have been mainly with the Commonwealth Caribbean and Haiti (Griffith, 1993, p. 206).

As regards Haiti, Canada's security and governance role is well known. While US leadership has been critical in restoring security and governance, Canada's leadership has been central in sustaining them.

In assessing the Haitian situation in the Summer of 1996, two US officials noted, 'The last US soldier serving as part of the UNMIH [United Nations Mission in Haiti] departed Port au Prince April 17, 1996. The remaining force of 1,900 Canadian, Pakistani, and Bangladeshi troops is led by a Canadian general' (Oakley and Dziedzic, 1996, p. 1). In a December 1996 policy statement, the Canadian government took justifiable pride in stating, 'Canada has been leading efforts to restore democracy in Haiti since the September 30, 1991 coup d'état . . . We consider that UNMIH has been a success to date, and that our contribution of 500 military and 100 police officers, including the commander of the UN Civilian Police, has been a large factor in this success . . . Canada's participation in UNMIH is one of the most important contributions to global security which we are making at this time' (Canadian Policy toward Haiti, 1996).

In the context of the multidimensional approach to security and governance shared by both Canada and the Caribbean, the issue of drugs has recently been the subject of increasing interchange. As both Canadian and Caribbean statesmen and scholars have acknowledged, the drug issue constitutes a multidimensional dilemma, part of which is security-related. The dilemma is not a security matter simply because of the multidimensionality of drug operations – drug production, consumption-abuse, trafficking and money laundering. It is so primarily for four reasons: (1) drug-related operations have multiple consequences and implications, including marked increases in crime, systemic and institutional corruption, and arms trafficking; (2) the operations and their consequences have increased in scope and severity over the past decade; (3) they have had dramatic impact on agents and agencies of national security and good governance, in military, political and economic ways; and (4) the sovereignty of many countries is severely tested and subject to infringement by both state and non-state actors because of drugs.[2]

Canada's drug relationship with the Caribbean has two basic forms: (1) the provision of equipment and training by Canada to combat drug trafficking and money laundering and to strengthen criminal justice; and (2) the sharing between Canada and Caribbean countries of intelligence pertaining to trafficking and organised crime. The relationship, on the other hand, is not motivated only by Canada's interest in the security and good governance of the Caribbean. It is also driven by (1) Canada's increasing problems of drug trafficking and abuse, money laundering and related crimes; and (2) the fact that some of the trafficking and other problems have direct and indirect Caribbean connections.

Some of those connections are facilitated by Caribbean posses operating in Canada.

Posses are organised gangs of Jamaican origin and comprised primarily of Jamaicans or people of Jamaican descent. Although known mostly for their trafficking in drugs and weapons, they have also been implicated in money laundering, fraud, kidnapping, robbery, burglary, prostitution, forgery and murder. They initially trafficked in marijuana that came mainly from Jamaica, but gained a foothold in the wider illegal drug business as their leaders recognized the potential for expanding the range of drugs and related 'services'. As their networks became over-extended and there was need for manpower, the posses began to recruit from outside the Jamaican national group, using 'outsiders' primarily as mules and street-level dealers to minimise their vulnerability to law-enforcement countermeasures. African-Americans, Guyanese, Panamanians, Trinidadians and Nigerians are now increasingly brought into posse operations. Cooperation with Colombians and Dominicans is also said to be on the rise. More than this, though, white females are reportedly now being used as couriers and arms purchasers. Chinese, whites, and Indians of Jamaican descent are also said to be recruited.

The Shower, Sprangler, Dunkirk and Jungle posses are regarded as among the largest and most well-known groups. The Shower posse's distribution network, based in New York and Miami, reputedly extends to Atlanta, Boston, Buffalo, Chicago, Cleveland, Dallas, Denver, Detroit, Hartford, Los Angeles, Pittsburgh, Toronto, Quebec and elsewhere. In Europe, this posse is known to have operated in Great Britain, the Netherlands and Germany. According to the US National Drug Intelligence Center, the Shower posse has its own airplanes and pilots for smuggling, as well as a variety of legitimate businesses, such as car rental and travel agencies, to assist with its money-laundering operations. Over the years, economic incentives and law-enforcement countermeasures have created shifts in posse operations, away from traditional centres in New York and Miami to areas of upstate New York and to Connecticut, Massachusetts and several cities in the US Midwest and Southwest. Expansion in Canada has included Montreal, Toronto, Oshawa, Kitchener, London, Windsor and Hamilton.[3]

In recent years, security and governance relations between Canada and the Caribbean have extended to the area of security confidence-building. Canada has been an important broker of confidence-building initiatives with the OAS, and protector of Commonwealth Caribbean interests in the subject within the organization. Among other things, it has facilitated Caribbean participation in forums where security confidence-building has been either the sole or a main agenda item. For example, it underwrote the participation of Commonwealth Caribbean government and academic specialists at the OAS meeting on the subject held in Buenos Aires, Argentina, in March 1994. Moreover, the Commonwealth Caribbean delegates to the meeting of hemispheric defense and security ministers in San Carlos de Bariloche, Argentina, in October 1996 were transported to Argentina with the Canadian delegation in a Canadian military aircraft.

Pursuit of the subject of confidence building by the OAS assumed an appreciably different thrust and character with the formation of a permanent Commission on Hemispheric Security by the OAS in 1992. For the Caribbean, the most significant among the Commission's several initiatives was the holding of a special conference on the security concerns of Caribbean island states in October 1996 in Washington. Combining its national interest pursuits in the work on hemispheric security confidence-building with its special interest in security challenges facing the Caribbean, Canada not only facilitated the participation of Commonwealth Caribbean governmental and academic experts at the Washington meeting, but also commissioned a special study on Caribbean security confidence-building, which it presented to the Washington meeting.[4]

CONCLUSION

The networks of interdependence between Canada and the Caribbean discussed above are part of the contemporary reality of Caribbean international relations. A significant part of this reality is the fact that although post-Cold War global power alterations have not changed the basic character of Caribbean states as small and subordinate, they have already begun to reveal changes in the wider global networks of interdependence. Many of the changes already severely constrain the political and economic autonomy of Caribbean states, and many stand to impose even further limitations on Caribbean autonomy and sovereignty.[5] Under these conditions, Caribbean leaders look to sources of power within the international community, placing hope, if not confidence, on the willingness of big and middle powers to help them maintain their capacity for state action. Canada is one of the powers to which small Caribbean states look primarily because Canada is a power that acts without paternalism. Absence of paternalism is generally not a characteristic of relationships between states with such power asymmetries as those between Canada and the countries of the Caribbean. It is precisely this feature in Canadian–Caribbean relations that offers the for hope small Caribbean states that life in this anarchical, interdependent global society is not necessarily destined to be nasty, brutish and short.

Notes

1. This is not to suggest that Canadian foreign policy is totally devoid of self-interest. One leading Canadian political scientist has asserted the following, for instance: 'Canada's development assistance is designed primarily to benefit the interests of Canada's foreign policy makers; other beneficiaries, whether in Canada or in underdeveloped countries, are of distinctly secondary importance'. See Kim Richard Nossal, 'Mixed Motives Revisited: Canada's Interest in Development Assistance', *Canadian Journal of Political Science*, vol. 21 (March 1988), p. 38.

2. For more on the security and governance implications of drugs for Canada and the Caribbean, by Canadian and Caribbean scholars, see, Hal P. Klepak, 'Canadian Security Interests in Latin America', in Hal P. Klepak (ed.), *Canada and Latin American Security* (Quebec: Méridien, 1993), esp. pp. 120–32; Hal P. Klepak, 'The Impact of the International Narcotics Trade on Canada's Foreign and Security Policy', *International Journal*, vol. 49 (Winter 1993–94), pp. 66–92; Ivelaw L. Griffith, 'Drugs and Security in the Commonwealth Caribbean', *Journal of Commonwealth and Comparative Politics*, vol. 31 (July 1993), pp. 70–102; Ivelaw L. Griffith and Trevor Munroe, 'Drugs and Democratic Governance in the Caribbean', in Ivelaw L. Griffith and Betty N. Sedoc-Dahlberg (eds), *Democracy and Human Rights in the Caribbean* (Boulder: Westview, 1997), pp. 74–94; and Ivelaw L. Griffith, *Drugs and Security in the Caribbean: Sovereignty under Siege* (Philadelphia: Pennsylvania State Press, 1997).

3. For more on posse operations, see Laurie Gunst, *Born Fi' Dead* (New York: Holt, 1995); and Griffith, *Drugs and Security in the Caribbean*, Chapter 5.

4. The study, *Confidence Building: Managing Caribbean Security Concerns* (Ottawa: Ministry of Foreign Affairs and International Trade, 1996), was undertaken by James Macintosh of Canadian Security Research, a private security consulting firm, and Ivelaw Griffith of Florida International University.

5. For a discussion of some of the implications of Post-Cold War global changes for the Caribbean, see J.I. Domínguez, 'The Caribbean in a New International Context: Are Freedom and Peace a New Threat to its Prosperity?' in A.T. Bryan (ed.), *The Caribbean: New Dynamics in Trade and Political Economy* (Miami: North–South Center, 1995), pp. 1–23; Ivelaw L. Griffith, *Caribbean Security on the Eve of the 21st Century* (Washington,

DC: National Defense University Press, 1996), pp. 19–27; and J. Rodríguez
Beruff and H. García Muñiz (1996), 'Introduction: Challenges to Peace
and Security in the Post-Cold War Caribbean', in J. Rodríguez Beruff and
H. García Muñiz, *Security Problems and Policies in the Post-Cold War
Caribbean* (New York: St Martin's Press), pp. 1–12.

References

Basdeo, S. (1993) 'Caribcan: A Continuum in Canada–Caricom Economic
Relations', *Caribbean Affairs*, vol. 6 (April–June).
'Canadian Foreign Policy' (1996) December. Posted at www.dfiat-maeci.gc.ca/
english/geo/lac/haiti.htm.
DePalma, A. (1996) 'Canada and Mexico Join to Oppose U.S. Law on Cuba',
New York Times (13 June).
Domínguez, J.I. (1995) 'The Caribbean in a New International Context: Are
Freedom and Peace a New Threat to Its Prosperity?' in A.T. Bryan (ed.), *The
Caribbean: New Dynamics in Trade and Political Economy* (Coral Gables, FL:
North–South Center Press).
Freudmann, A. (1996) 'Canada's Trade with Cuba Skyrockets Embargo or No
Embargo', *Journal of Commerce* (7 February).
Griffith, I.L. (1993) *The Quest for Security in the Caribbean* (Armonk, NY: M.E.
Sharpe). *Helms–Burton and International Business: Legal and Commercial
Implications*, 'Keynote Address', Proceedings of a conference sponsored by
the Canadian Foundation for the Americas and the Center for International
Policy, 16–17 May 1996.
Griffith, I.L. (1993) 'Drugs and Security in the Commonwealth Caribbean',
Journal of Commonwealth and Comparative Politics, vol. 31 (July).
Griffith, I.L. (1996) *Caribbean Security on the Eve of the 21st Century* (Washington, DC: National Defense University Press).
Griffith, I.L. (1997) *Drugs and Security in the Caribbean: Sovereignty Under Siege*
(Philadelphia: Pennsylvania State Press).
Griffith, I.L., and T. Munroe. (1997) Drugs and Democratic Governance in the
Caribbean', in I.L. Griffith and B.N. Sedoc-Dahlberg (eds), *Democracy and
Human Rights in the Caribbean* (Boulder, Colo.: Westview).
Gunst, L. (1995) *Born Fi' Dead* (New York: Holt).
Hoffman, S. (1990) 'A New World Order and Its Troubles', *Foreign Affairs*, vol.
69 (Fall).
Hyett, C. (1993) 'Caribcan: Canada's Response to the Caribbean Basin Initiative', in A.B. Bakan, D. Cox, and C. Leys (eds), *Imperial Power and Regional
Trade* (Waterloo: Wilfrid Laurier University Press).
Kegley, C.W. (1993) 'The Neoidealist Moment in International Studies? Realist Myths and the New International Realities', *International Studies Quarterly*, vol. 37 (June).
Keohane, R.O. and J.S. Nye, Jr. (1989) *Power and Interdependence*, 2nd edn
(Glenview: Scott, Foresman & Co.).
Kirk, J.M. (1995) 'Unraveling the Paradox: The Canadian Position on Cuba', in
A.R.M. Ritter and J.M. Kirk (eds), *Cuba in the International System* (London: Macmillan).

Klepak, H.P. (1993) 'Canadian Security Interests in Latin America', *Canada and Latin American Security* (ed.) H.P. Klepak (Quebec. Méridien).

Klepak, H.P. (1993–94) 'The Impact of the International Narcotics Trade on Canada's Foreign and Security Policy', *International Journal*, vol. 49 (Winter).

Klepak, H.P. (1996) 'Canada and Caribbean Security', in J.R. Beruff and H.G. Muñiz (eds), *Security Problems and Policies in the Post-Cold War Caribbean* (London: Macmillan).

Levitt, K. (1988) 'Canada and the Caribbean: An Assessment', in J. Heine and L. Manigat (eds), *The Caribbean and World Politics* (New York: Holmes & Meier).

Macintosh, J. and I. Griffith (1996) *Confidence Building: Managing Caribbean Security Concerns* (Ottawa: Ministry of Foreign Affairs and International Trade).

Mahler, G.S. (1993) 'Foreign Policy and Canada's Evolving Relations with the Caribbean Commonwealth Countries: Political and Economic Considerations', in J. Haar and E.J. Dosman (eds), *A Dynamic Partnership: Canada's Changing Role in the Hemisphere* (Coral Gables, FL: North–South Center Press).

Miami Herald (1997) 'Anti-Helms–Burton Act Takes Effect in Canada' (1 January).

Morris, N. (1996) 'Can Cuba Change?' *Maclean's* (15 January).

Myers, S.L. (1996) 'Clinton Troubleshooter Discovers Big Trouble from Allies on Cuba, *New York Times* (23 October).

New York Carib News (1996) 'Omai Boosts Investment' (26 November).

Nossal, K.R. (1988) 'Mixed Motives Revisited: Canada's Interest in Development Assistance', *Canadian Journal of Political Science*, vol. 21 (March).

'Notes for an Address by the Hon. Lloyd Axworthy, Minister of Foreign Affairs, to a Meeting of the National Forum on Foreign Policy "Canadian Foreign Policy in a Changing World"', Winnipeg, 13 December 1996, posted on www.dfait-maeci.gc.ca.

Nye, J.S. Jr. (1992) 'What New World Order?', *Foreign Affairs*, vol. 71 (Spring).

Oakley, R. and M. Dziedzic (1996) 'Sustaining Success in Haiti', *Strategic Forum*, vol. 77 (June).

Ramsaran, R.F. (1996) 'Small Economies, Trade Preferences, and Relations with Latin America: Challenges Facing the Anglophone Caribbean in a Changing World', paper presented to a conference on Caribbean–Mercosur Relations, Buenos Aires, Argentina, 5–6 September.

Rodríguez Beruff, J. and H. García Muñiz (1996) 'Introduction: Challenges to Peace and Security in the Post-Cold War Caribbean', in J. Rodríguez Beruff and H. García (eds), *Security Problems and Policies in the Post-Cold War* (New York: St Martin's Press).

Sinclair, J. (1995) 'The OAS and Hemispheric Security: A Canadian Approach', in L.E. Kjonnerod (ed.), *Hemispheric Security in Transition: Adjusting to the Post-1995 Environment* (Washington, DC: National Defense University Press).

Swardson, A. (1996) 'Canada Vows Sanctions against U.S. for Enforcement of Anti-Cuba Trade Law', *Washington Post* (18 June).

Wells, J. (1996) 'Business Moves In', *Maclean's* (15 January).

3 Canada and the Caribbean: Political Commonalities and Convergences

Gregory S. Mahler

INTRODUCTION

As many scholars have indicated, the relationship between Canada and the Caribbean is a well-established one. Through the Commonwealth, the Francophonie, and more recently through such associations and programmes as the Organization of American States (OAS) and CARIBCAN, Canada has continued to have an active interest and presence in the Caribbean. In recent years, a substantial degree of uncertainty has been injected into this situation as a result of the North American Free Trade Agreement (NAFTA). With Canada expanding its formal ties with other hemispheric partners – the United States, and in many respects more importantly Mexico – the question is: what will happen with Canada's ties with the Caribbean?

This chapter addresses two different and fundamental concerns. First, some of the more concrete relationships that have existed in recent history between Canada and a number of the Commonwealth Caribbean nations will be briefly examined. Although these relationships have been more fully developed elsewhere, it is important to reestablish their centrality in order to appreciate the second point to be raised here: the non-trade-based commonalities between and among Canada and the Caribbean Commonwealth nations.

These non-trade-based commonalities are considerably more abstract and, correspondingly, more difficult to analyse than straightforward trade or business figures. If, as will be suggested here, Canada's relative economic influence in the Caribbean has declined over the years, what accounts for Canada's continued interest in the region and the region's continued interest in Canada? This interest, it will be argued, does exist, but it exists for reasons other than 'obvious' financial ones.

More important, if NAFTA causes Canada to have even less trade interaction with the Commonwealth Caribbean in the future, what can be seen as a justification for a continued healthy relationship between these countries? It will be suggested here that in addition to the more 'traditional' trade and economic factors, there is a set of factors that can be referred to as *political commonalities and convergences* that continue to tie these nations together when economic and security considerations no longer are, strictly speaking, strong enough to do so.

THE HISTORICAL PERSPECTIVE

Canada has had a presence in the Caribbean for a very long time. Ties between Canada and several of the Leeward Islands were discussed as long ago as 1884, and 'as recently as 1974 the State Council of the Turks and Caicos Islands asked that their territory be annexed by Canada' (Thomas, 1988, p. 338). Indeed, in a 1988 article dealing with relations between Canada and the Turks and Caicos Islands, it was noted that:

> The new Government, under Mr. Skippings, stated that one of its first priorities will be a close examination of the relationship between Canada and the Turks and Caicos Islands, and, provided Britain agrees, within the next few months, major steps towards forming some type of Association between the two countries is a very real possibility. (Stuart, 1988, p. 18)

Another scholar in the field has observed that the Caribbean Commonwealth 'is the area of the Third World with which Canada has the longest and closest ties' (Levitt, 1988, p. 229).

Canada's relations with the Commonwealth Caribbean can be viewed in two different spheres: economic and political. Economic relations include, among other dimensions, trade, tourism and development assistance; while political relations include, among others, Canada's role in Caribbean security considerations. For many years, Canada has been a supporting member of the Caribbean Commonwealth. For example, the Canadian International Development Agency (CIDA) was a major supporter of the Caribbean Association of Industry and Commerce (see Thomas, 1988, p. 333). Over the years, between 1981 and 1987, Canada's Ministry of External Affairs significantly increased aid programmes, directly affecting Caribbean development (Levitt, 1988, p. 236).

The 1986 culmination of Canada's Caribbean initiative – CARIBCAN – was seen as a very attractive alternative to the earlier US-sponsored

Caribbean Basin Initiative (CBI) in 1982. Concern about the US 'strings' attached to the CBI made the Reagan administration's initiative a mixed blessing, since duty-free entries to the US market, tax credits to businesses investing in the Caribbean, and direct aid from the United States were attractive, while other aspects were not. 'The most disturbing aspect of the CBI, however, is its link with the US government's military and security interests and the fact that, like the Alliance for Progress in Latin America in the 1960s, it was prompted by cold-war considerations' (Thomas, 1988, p. 337). On the contrary, CARIBCAN was popular with many of the Caribbean nations because 'Canada has a lower profile in the region and, therefore, arouses fewer fears in government circles about its big-power ambitions' (Thomas, 1988, p. 338).

Tourism, as noted, was another major link between Canada and the Caribbean (Kempe, 1986, p. 49). Although Canada's control of much of the Caribbean tourist trade has been taken over by the United States, Canada still provides a major proportion of tourists to the Commonwealth Caribbean each year (Thomas, 1988, pp. 147–51; Kempe, 1986, p. 49). A recent study indicated that, 'Some 474,000 Canadians annually go to the Caribbean and spend about 30 million dollars in the process' (Stuart, 1988, p. 20).

Trade figures show that Canada no longer plays as significant a role in the Caribbean economy as it once did (see Braveboy-Wagner, 1989, pp. 230–1; Ahmad, 1990, pp. 30–65). The Caribbean has traditionally been an attractive market for Canada despite its small size, primarily because of its 'relative stability as a market, proximity, and acceptance of North American standards and technology' (Donley, 1986, p. 110). As well, Canadian banking has traditionally been very interested in the Caribbean and has had a significant impact on the region. According to one study, 'The monetary regulating systems of Jamaica, Trinidad and Tobago, Guyana, Barbados and the Bahamas were established on the Canadian model' (Guy, 1987, pp. 304–436).

Through the mid-1980s, Canadian exports to the region were not significant: including Mexico, Venezuela and Cuba, trade was 'about three per cent of total Canadian trade, or about 15 per cent of Canada's total trade outside of that which we have with the United States' (Donley, 1986, p. 109). One study showed that while Canada's trade with the Commonwealth Caribbean made up 13 per cent of its trade with developing areas in 1970, by 1987 that figure had fallen to 8 per cent (Guy, 1987, p. 438). Nonetheless, the Caribbean Commonwealth nations continue to have a visibility in Canada far beyond that which might be justified by direct economic factors:

For Canada the Commonwealth Caribbean constitutes perhaps the only place in the world where Canada enjoys a 'presence,' in the international relations sense of that term . . . Canada places an importance on its relations with the countries of the English-speaking Caribbean that is altogether disproportionate to their small size, and their rapidly diminishing importance in terms of trade and investment. The relationship is primarily a political one, which offers Canada the opportunity for active participation in a North–South dialogue within the culturally familiar setting of the Commonwealth fraternity. (Guy, 1987, p. 438)

This economic situation evolved over a period of many years in the relationship described above. While at an earlier point in history, Canada was a dominant player in the Commonwealth Caribbean nations' economies, the point has been reached today where both Canada and Commonwealth Caribbean nations have higher proportions of trade with the United States than they have with each other.

In recent years, the negotiation and ratification of NAFTA has been the cause of significant concern for many nations of the Commonwealth Caribbean. Prior to the signing of the agreement, these economies were relatively insignificant and had only small shares of the North American (primarily Canadian and US) markets. The situation has deteriorated further since conclusion of the agreement, however, because Commonwealth nations now face the possibility of being 'shut out' of many of their markets and of having relatively inexpensive labour in Mexico assume some of the limited markets (for example, textiles) developed by Commonwealth Caribbean nations over the years.

In the area of economic development assistance, Canada continues to maintain active ties with the Caribbean Commonwealth at the government-to-government level. Bilateral aid has continued to be an important dimension, even if the aid has not increased as fast as the Caribbean nations would like (see Levitt, 1988, pp. 235–6; Braveboy-Wagner, 1989, p. 83).

Canada's political relations with the Commonwealth Caribbean can be briefly traced in two dimensions: the Caribbean's perception of Canada and Canada's participation in Caribbean security arrangements. Briefly, Canada is seen by many of these nations as less 'threatening' than the United States. The United States made no secret of the fact that the Reagan administration's CBI had a 'Cold War' and 'anti-Cuba' dimension. When the United States referred to the Caribbean as one of its borders against Communism, the reaction from the Caribbean was not one of gratitude.

Canada, on the other hand, has traditionally taken a much less restrictive perspective. In Prime Minister Pierre Trudeau's speech in St. Lucia in 1983 – very widely cited by Commonwealth Caribbean political leaders – he explicitly observed that, 'In our view states have a right to follow whatever ideological path their peoples decide. When a country chooses a socialist, or even a Marxist, path it does not necessarily buy a "package" which automatically injects it into the Soviet orbit' (Levitt, 1988, p. 227). Canada has been relatively consistent in following this doctrine, and while the era of Prime Minister Brian Mulroney may have placed more of an emphasis on the 'selling' of Canada in the United States, or, phrased another way, on close international economic ties with the United States, it has not violated the general principles articulated by Trudeau over a decade ago. Canada, therefore, continues to be seen as a non-threatening, attractive benefactor in many Third World nations, including the Caribbean.

As far as security concerns go, Canada continues to be a force in the development of security considerations for the Commonwealth Caribbean nations.[1] It is worth noting that following the US intervention in Grenada, many have suggested that the relative importance of Canadian security activity has decreased while the relative importance of US security activity has increased in the region, a fact becoming increasingly visible in the context of the US war on the drug trade. This is not to say that Canada's contribution has disappeared, however. Canada still provides a security presence, assists in training, and offers other support for Caribbean nations in this regard (see Braveboy-Wagner, 1989, pp. 39–47; Levitt, 1988, p. 241). However, Canada has traditionally hesitated to get involved in any long-term security linkage in the hemisphere, and many observers have suggested that it is 'unlikely to move boldly' in this area in the long run (Harbron, 1986, p. 123).

So, what we see is a pattern of a *historic* close association between Canada and the Commonwealth Caribbean nations, although, by all objective standards, the relationship has decreased over time and has become relatively insignificant in scope (that is, compared to that with the United States). Why have the trade, aid and security relations between Canada and the Commonwealth Caribbean nations declined over the years? Three reasons have been suggested as contributing to the policies leading to this situation.[2]

- First, Canada had been having budgetary problems – like the United States and many other nations – and has not been *able* to provide the level of assistance to these nations that it would like.
- Second, Canada's domestic agenda has been distracting to many Canadian policy-makers. Issues such as constitutional reform, relations between Quebec and the rest of the federal system, and the future of Canadian Confederation have pushed CARIBCAN out of the public's view, to a large extent.
- Third, the political agenda of Brian Mulroney had placed relatively more emphasis on good relations with the United States than did that of Pierre Trudeau, and consequently the government had been more willing under Mr Mulroney than it was under Mr Trudeau to step back and avoid confrontations with the United States, including those related to the Caribbean.

Most indicators would suggest that the *material* dimension, therefore, of relations between Canada and the Commonwealth Caribbean has not been, relatively speaking at least, as big, as healthy, or as dynamic, as many suggested it would be. Thus, it could be argued – and is argued here – that there is what can be called a 'mythology' involved.

This so-called 'mythology' can be described in rather direct terms. A student interested in Canadian–Caribbean relations can find numerous references to the 'special relationship' that exists between Canada and the Commonwealth Caribbean. Many scholars have even discussed this 'special relationship (see, for example, Preston, 1988, pp. 303–17; and Dosman, 1987, p. 823). However, when we search for concrete, material indicators, the relationship does not appear to be all that special, at least if 'special' is interpreted as meaning 'big', 'substantial' or 'important'. Indeed, many scholars in the mid- to late-1980s began questioning the use of the term 'special' for the relationship. J.J. Guy suggested that, in the context of Canadian foreign policy, 'The term "special" has been most frequently applied throughout Canada's ties as an independent country to the island states of the Caribbean. Indeed, Ottawa has treated the Caribbean as a single political entity longer than for any other region or country in the world including the USA' (1987, p. 424).

Scholars have pointed out, however, that 'In spite of declining trade and various kinds of irritation, other contacts between Canada and the West Indies have grown appreciably since 1945 (Preston, 1988, p. 308). If, as this perspective would seem to suggest, 'special' can be interpreted as meaning that 'there isn't a good business or political reason for the association, but we do it anyway', then we can say that there does appear to be a 'special' relationship. How can we explain the ties that appear to exist here? Although one explanation has focused on 'maritime commerce, common membership in both the English and French empires, and independence of the USA' (Guy, 1987, p. 435), other reasons are equally important and merit discussion.

CHANGE

Current concerns are that NAFTA may seriously compromise whatever 'special' relationship has existed by leaving the Caribbean Commonwealth nations *outside* of the customs union arrangement created by NAFTA. Many of the markets so carefully developed by Caribbean nations over the years (for example, hemp, textiles, oil, sugar, fish and bananas) may now simply be taken over by Mexican labour and resources. Even if economic barriers develop, however, the relationship between Canada and the Commonwealth Caribbean can still remain 'special' for *non*-economic/trade/security reasons. In this objective, materialistic world, what could possibly be the basis of a 'special' relationship if it *is not* trade, aid or security?

It can be suggested that 'family ties' are a significant variable in the equation loosely referred to as 'international relations'. There is a parallel between 'family ties' and the title of this chapter: 'political commonalities and convergencies'. When our children grow up and move away from home, we resolve to 'keep in touch', and they still have a special relationship with us. This, of course, is one way to describe the international political relationship that we know as 'The Commonwealth': as the developing nations of the Caribbean matured, they slowly left Great Britain but still kept in touch via the Commonwealth.

As Great Britain pulled back from the hemisphere in the 1950s, 1960s and 1970s, Canada's role as what can only be called 'a substitute Great Britain' increased to some extent, especially in trade, aid and security matters. Although these roles have diminished and have been assumed by the United States (to continue the metaphor a bit, an old 'friend of the family' that is *not* related), the 'family' link remains.

To press the metaphor further, if Britain can be considered the *mother* of parliamentary democracies and the Commonwealth Caribbean nations are grown children, Canada would be the oldest daughter/son of the family who still looks out for her/his younger siblings. And, to some extent, these siblings still look up to Canada. Furthermore,

Canada may still feel protective of these siblings, even if no significant material, economic or security ties remain.

What do these nations have in common? What is 'the family tie?' Although several aspects must be taken into consideration in answering this question, two important ones must be addressed. One involves *people* and the other involves *political structures and institutions*. The first of these will only be briefly developed here; the second will be the focus of the remainder of this chapter.

By *people* is meant the actual individuals who tie nations together. Over the years, there has been substantial Caribbean immigration to Canada and less numerous but still important Canadian migration to the nations of the Commonwealth Caribbean. The issue of Caribbean immigration to Canada has generated a great deal of discussion over the years as a consequence of a 'brain drain' from the Caribbean to Canada. Indeed, this phenomenon has combined with the general selectivity of Canadian immigration policy, and perhaps with recollection of the overtly discriminatory policies of the past, to make immigration the most significant source of friction in Canada–Caribbean relations (Berry, 1986, p. 362).

Large Caribbean populations do exist in Canada. Toronto, for example, has a large Caribbean population. It publishes a Caribbean newspaper, holds Caribbean holidays (Cropover and Carnival, for example), and Caribbean cuisine is readily available there. Similarly, a number of Canadian expatriates live in Commonwealth Caribbean countries and have helped to created important links between the two settings.

By *political structures and institutions* is meant what many have referred to as 'the Westminster model' of government and membership in the Commonwealth. The Queen is Head of the Commonwealth, and in most of the nations (except Trinidad[3]) actually holds a constitutional position as head of state. Other political structures, such as those in the legislatures, are very similar as we move through the region. Heads of government meet regularly, as do delegations of legislators through the Commonwealth Parliamentary Association. In short, this is a family that *has* resolved to 'keep in touch'. And even if Canada's direct material relations with the Commonwealth Caribbean nations are not as strong as they once were – or maybe we can more accurately say, 'are not as dominating as they once were' – a family attachment still exists.

This is what is meant by 'political commonalities and convergences'. Institutional linkages do exist between Canada and the Commonwealth Caribbean nations that are *not* based on trade, aid, tourism or security, such as the Commonwealth Parliamentary Association. The remainder of this chapter will be dedicated to *one* of these 'commonalities and convergences', the Westminster Model of government, how it has adapted to the needs of the small democracies of the Caribbean, and the similarities that exist between Canada and the Commonwealth Caribbean in this regard.

POLITICAL COMMONALITIES AND CONVERGENCES: THE 'WESTMINSTER MODEL'

The Concept of the 'Westminster Family'

The British Parliament is often referred to as the 'mother of parliamentary democracies'. Many parliamentary democracies around the world were at one time governed from Westminster, and as many of them gained independence and established their own governments, they chose to incorporate – sometimes directly and sometimes with some modifications – many of the institutions and practices referred to today as composing the 'Westminster Model' of parliamentary government.

To pursue the 'mother' parallel further, as the 'children' have grown up and 'moved away from home' – and have become independent political actors – at least two very interesting phenomena have ensued. First, we have seen the rise of the Commonwealth, a thoroughly unique type of political association. Second, these parliamentary 'children', the sovereign legislatures of the many Commonwealth nations, have been faced with problems of their own and in many cases have developed *their own* solutions. In some instances, the parliamentary institutions and patterns of behaviour that have evolved have been very similar to those developed by 'mother' at Westminster. In other cases, however, entirely new institutions and patterns of behaviour have evolved in response to present challenges.

Apart from the existence of the basic 'Westminster Model' of parliamentary government,[4] it is not *necessarily* the case that the political institutions, practices and behaviour that have evolved and been adapted at Westminster will be, correspondingly, the best political institutions, practices and behaviour in all other legislative settings in the Commonwealth. This means, of course, that we can reasonably expect substantial differences between and among the nations discussed here when their political institutions are examined.

Political institutions work best when they are *appropriate* for their respective political settings. The United Kingdom has had over 300 years of generally stable political history, time to industrialise and develop economically, in which the 'Westminster' political traditions and practices have developed. It is easy to see that those political practices that might work very well indeed in the United Kingdom might *not* work so well in a newer, non-industrialised political system without the British history of political stability and the ensuing legitimacy of government that it suggests.[5]

The Structures Examined

By 'structures' is meant those institutions and patterns of behaviour thought of as being part of the 'legislative arena'. These structures can be broken down into two groups, those that exist *within* the legislature and those that exist *outside of* the legislature.

Many books have been written on legislative structures and the legislative system in general (see, for example, Kornberg and Musolf, 1970; Kornberg, 1973; Olson, 1980; Hirsch and Hancock, 1971; Eldridge, 1977; Loewenberg and Patterson, 1979), not to mention countless articles in journals. In this literature, authors distinguish between structures that exist *within* the legislature, such as bicameralism, legislative staff and office space, rules governing debate, and the legislative process (for example, who can introduce bills, under what conditions, and how often), and other structures that actually exist *outside* of the legislature, such as electoral laws of the regime (proportional representation elections versus single-member-district elections, for example), the power of the legislature *vis-à-vis* the executive, and so on.

Some of the structures that exist in the legislative arenas of Commonwealth Caribbean nations will be examined to see how these structures have evolved while yet retaining a great deal in common with Canada. To take an example, many of the Caribbean Commonwealth nations have written constitutions that describe in some detail the natures of their political structures, including the position of leader of the opposition, for example, while in the Canadian constitution this is still considered to be unwritten. The question is: is this the best thing for them to do (see White, 1991, pp. 499–523)?

Canada operated with essentially an 'unwritten' constitution from the date of its functional independence in 1867 until 1982, when the Constitution Act was passed. The Caribbean Commonwealth nations all began their existences with relatively structured constitutions. The difference can partly be explained by Canada's relative maturity at the time of its independence compared with the Caribbean nations' relative immaturity at the times of theirs. However, one can still see that the institutions that existed in these nations were essentially similar: the 'Westminster Model' of government existed throughout. These are the types of commonalities and convergences that are referred to as being so important.

Most area legislatures are bicameral, as is the Canadian legislature and the legislature at Westminster, a system developed over a period of several hundred years (see Bailey, 1958, pp. 12–20) for reasons appropriate at the time.[6] However, certain legislatures have special procedures, such as occasionally sitting in joint session, as is the case in St Vincent and the Grenadines. Thus, even though a first-time observer will recognise the commonalities of legislative institutions between Canada and the Caribbean Commonwealth nations, he or she will also recognise that they are not the *same*.

For most the world, the 'Westminster Model' of government is synonymous with the notion of strong party discipline. Indeed, many would say that it is difficult to imagine the existence of a parliament without a highly disciplined party system (see Lemco, 1988, pp. 283–302; Harmel and Hamm, 1986, pp. 79–91; see also Mahler, 1985–86, pp. 19–21). Here again it is clear that many of the Commonwealth nations have decided that what is good for parliament at Westminster and in Canada may *not* be best in their particular settings. Some systems appear to feel that the British level of partisan activity is more than is needed in their systems, while others believe that a more rigorously controlled party structure in the legislature than that existing in Britain or Canada is appropriate for their respective systems (see Hewitt, 1989, p. 157).

Caribbean variations on the Westminster practice appear to be working well, and simply demonstrate once again that the systems once governed from Westminster need not, necessarily, automatically copy the Westminster design down to the last detail. The evolution of institutions to *fit the needs of the particular political culture* has taken place, and although it has resulted in some institutional differences between Canada and the Commonwealth Caribbean, the political actors involved still 'speak the same language' and have a substantial amount in common. Unfortunately, although virtually all Commonwealth legislators may be in agreement that *more* legislative and office staff, travel budgets, research resources, and the like would be both helpful and, ultimately, useful to the citizens (and taxpayers) of their respective countries, it is usually the case that these are not high priority expenditures in the many political systems of the Commonwealth. In some Commonwealth nations, the legislators do have more office space and staff than that afforded individual legislators at Westminster, but it is much more commonly the rule that legislative staff is equally unavailable, and legislative office space equally rare (Hammond, 1984, pp. 271–318).

Although the actual legislative process varies throughout the Commonwealth, most Westminster structures can be found to be well-entrenched, including such well-known parliamentary institutions as Mr Speaker, the Clerk at the Table, Question Time, Private Members' Bills, and the like. Here again, though, there are certain differences in practices and procedures, but there is a very strong similarity overall between provincial and national legislative behaviour in Canada, and corresponding legislative behaviour in the Commonwealth Caribbean.

Canadian provincial and national legislators meet with legislators from Commonwealth Caribbean nations annually at the Commonwealth Parliamentary Association Conference to discuss problems of mutual concern. Canadian observers visit Caribbean legislatures, and Caribbean legislators attend parliamentary seminars in Ottawa. In brief, there is a great deal of commonality in this regard. The actual details of the legislative process vary on a nation-by-nation basis. Some legislative arenas require legislative proposals to lie on the table longer than others. Some permit more debate than others, some limit amendment more than others, and some offer more opportunity for legislative initiatives by private members than others. In all of these respects, however, although the general Westminster Model of parliamentary government exists, Commonwealth legislatures have found it both reasonable and, in some cases, necessary to adapt Westminster structures to their particular needs.

One of the most important structures in the legislative process is the legislative committee. Although the role of committees is not very important in the United Kingdom, that is not always the case as one moves away from Westminster, either in the direction of Canada or the Caribbean. Committee autonomy and power at Westminster would work against the principle of party discipline and government power (see Thomas, 1978, pp. 683–704); away from Westminster, especially in settings in which party discipline is not as strong, the role of committees may be correspondingly larger, permitting a system of legislative *specialisation* (see Zwier, 1979, pp. 31–42) to develop.

Even a very cursory examination of 'Westminster Model' institutions in Canada and Commonwealth Caribbean nations shows that these institutional 'commonalities' that exist between the two regions are really quite impressive. These commonalities offer tremendous support for the 'family' metaphor: the actors are obviously not identical, but there are substantial similarities among political institutions.

CONCLUSION

While one has heard a great deal about bilateral relations between Canada and a number of Commonwealth Caribbean nations and a great deal about trade, aid and security – all very important issues – it can be suggested that there are other, non-material matters that contribute to the 'special' relationship heard so much about over time.

This is not meant to suggest that these 'family' factors can always take the place of security, trade or aid issues in cementing linkages between nations. On the other hand, however, this chapter does seek to suggest that a special relationship can continue to exist between and among these nations, even if the other, more concrete linkages are no longer so clearly significant. There can continue to be a special relationship between Canada and the Caribbean, regardless of how visible the United States becomes in drug and security issues, how much non-Canadian tourists dominate in the tourist realm, or how small – relatively speaking – Canada's trade relations with the Commonwealth Caribbean nations ultimately become.

Notes

1. It should be noted that from the Canadian perspective, there are many reasons why it is in *Canada's* security interests to be active in the Caribbean. See Edgar Dosman (1987), 'Points of Departure: The Security Equation in Canada–Commonwealth Caribbean Relations', *International Journal*, vol. 62, pp. 821–47.
2. These are discussed at some length in my 1993 essay, 'Canada's Evolving Relations with the Caribbean Commonwealth Countries: Political and Economic Considerations', in J. Haar and E. Dosman (eds), *A Dynamic Partnership: Canada's Changing Role in the Americas* (University of Miami, North–South Center), pp. 79–92.

3. Trinidad and Tobago is a republic, with an elected president. There, the Queen retains her status as Head of the Commonwealth but has no legal status in the government.
4. This includes the following four characteristics: (1) the Head of State and the Chief Executive are not the same person; (2) the executive power is vested in the Prime Minister and cabinet, usually not mentioned in law; (3) the government is composed of members of the legislative branch; and (4) the government is ultimately responsible to the legislature. See Gregory Mahler (1992), *Comparative Politics: An Institutional and Cross-National Approach* (Englewood Cliffs, NJ: Prentice Hall), p. 222.
5. The importance of the *context* within which legislatures operate is something that has been widely discussed in the literature. See, among other sources, D. Nelson (1982), 'Communist Legislatures and Communist Politics', in D. Nelson and S. White (eds), *Communist Legislatures in Comparative Perspective* (New York: State University of New York Press); M. Mezey (1983), 'The Functions of Legislatures in the Third World', *Legislative Studies Quarterly*, vol. 8, pp. 511–50; M. Kornblith (1991), 'The Politics of Constitution-Making: Constitution and Democracy in Venezuela', *Journal of Latin American Studies*, vol. 23, no. 1, pp. 61–89; F. Baumgartner (1987), 'Parliament's Capacity to Expand Political Controversy in France', *Legislative Studies Quarterly*, vol. 12, pp. 33–54; and W. St Clair-Daniel (1985), 'Caribbean Concepts of Parliament', *The Parliamentarian*, vol. 66, no. 4, pp. 211–13.
6. A good longitudinal study of British political institutions can be found in L. Robbins (ed.) (1987), *Political Institutions in Britain: Development and Change* (New York: Longman).

References

Ahmad, J. (1990) 'Canada's Trade with Development Countries', in G. Helleiner (ed.), *The Other Side of International Development Policy: The Non-Aid Economic Relations with Developing Countries of Canada, Denmark, the Netherlands, Norway, and Sweden* (Toronto: University of Toronto Press).

Bailey, S. (1958) *British Parliamentary Democracy* (Boston: Houghton Mifflin).

Baumgartner, F. (1987) 'Parliament's Capacity to Expand Political Controversy in France', *Legislative Studies Quarterly*, vol. 12.

Berry, G.R. (1986) 'The West Indies in Canadian External Relations: Present Trends and Future Prospects', in B. Tennyson (ed.), *Canada and the Commonwealth Caribbean* (Lanham, MD: University Press of America).

Braveboy-Wagner, J.A. (1989) *The Caribbean in World Affairs: The Foreign Policies of the English-Speaking States* (Boulder, CO: Westview Press).

Donley, C. (1986) 'Canadian Trade and Investment in the Region', in B. MacDonald (ed.), *Canada, the Caribbean, and Central America* (Toronto: The Canadian Institute of Strategic Studies).

Dosman, E. (1987) 'Points of Departure: The Security Equation in Canada–Commonwealth Caribbean Relations', *International Journal*, vol. 62.

Eldridge, A. (ed.) (1977) *Legislatures in Plural Societies: The Search for Cohesion in National Development* (Durham, NC: Duke University Press).

Guy, J.J. (1987) 'Canada and the Caribbean: How "Special" the Relationship?', *The Round Table*, vol. 304.

Hammond, S. (1984) 'Legislative Staffs', *Legislative Studies Quarterly*, vol. 9.

Harbron, J. (1986) 'Is There a Canadian Role in Regional Security?', in B. MacDonald (ed.), *Canada, the Caribbean, and Central America* (Toronto: The Canadian Institute of Strategic Studies).

Harmel, R. and K. Hamm (1986) 'Development of a Party Role in a No-Party Legislature', *Western Political Quarterly* vol. 39, pp. 79–91.

Hewitt, V. (1989) 'The Congress System is Dead: Long Live the Party System and Democratic India?', *Journal of Commonwealth and Comparative Politics*, vol. 23, no. 2.

Hirsch, H. and M.D. Hancock (eds) (1971) *Comparative Legislative Systems* (New York: The Free Press).

Kempe, R.H. (1986) *Economic Development in the Caribbean* (New York: Praeger).

Kornberg, A. (ed.) (1973) *Legislatures in Comparative Perspective* (New York: David MacKay).

Kornberg, A. and L. Musolf (eds) (1970) *Legislatures in Developmental Perspective* (Durham, NC: Duke University Press).

Kornblith, M. (1991) 'The Politics of Constitution-Making: Constitution and Democracy in Venezuela', *Journal of Latin American Studies*, vol. 23, no. 1.

Lemco, J. (1988) 'The Fusion of Powers, Party Discipline, and the Canadian Parliament', *Presidential Studies Quarterly*, vol. 18, no. 2.

Levitt, K. (1988) 'Canada and the Caribbean: An Assessment', in J. Heine and L. Manigat (eds), *The Caribbean and World Politics: Cross Currents and Cleavages* (New York: Holmes & Meier).

Loewenberg, G. and S. Patterson (1979) *Comparing Legislatures* (Boston: Little, Brown).

Mahler, G. (1985–86) 'Parliament and Congress: Is the Grass Greener on the Other Side?', *Canadian Parliamentary Review*, vol. 8, no. 4.

Mahler, G. (1992) *Comparative Politics: An Institutional and Cross-National Approach* (Englewood Cliffs, NJ: Prentice Hall).

Mahler, G. (1993) 'Canada's Evolving Relations with the Caribbean Commonwealth Countries: Political and Economic Considerations', in J. Haar and E. Dosman (eds), *A Dynamic Partnership: Canada's Changing Role in the Americas* (Coral Gables, FL: North–South Center Press).

Mezey, M. (1983) 'The Functions of Legislatures in the Third World', *Legislative Studies Quarterly*, vol. 8.

Nelson, D. (1982) 'Communist Legislatures and Communist Politics', in D. Nelson and S. White (eds), *Communist Legislatures in Comparative Perspective* (Albany, NY: State University of New York Press).

Olson, D. (1980) *The Legislative Process* (New York: Harper & Row).

Preston, R. (1988) 'Caribbean Defence and Security: A Study of the Implications of Canada's "Special Relationship" with the Commonwealth West Indies', in B. Tennyson (ed.), *Canada and the Commonwealth Caribbean* (New York: University Press of America).

Robins, L. (ed.) (1987) *Political Institutions in Britain: Development and Change* (New York: Longman).

St Clair-Thomas, W. (1985) 'Caribbean Concepts of Parliament', *The Parliamentarian*, vol. 66, no. 4.

Stuart, I.A. (1988) 'Canada and the Turks and Caicos Islands', *Canadian Parliamentary Review* (summer).

Thomas, C. (1988) *The Poor and the Powerless: Economic Policy and Change in the Caribbean* (New York: Monthly Review Press).

Thomas, P. (1978) 'The Influence of Standing Committees of Parliament on Government Legislation', *Legislative Studies Quarterly*, vol. 3.

White, G. (1991) 'Westminster in the Arctic: The Adaptation of British Parliamentarism in the Northwest Territories', *Canadian Journal of Political Science*, vol. 24, no. 3.

Zwier, R. (1979) 'The Search for Information: Specialists and Nonspecialists in the U.S. House of Representatives', *Legislative Studies Quarterly*, vol. 4.

Part II
Canadian Views

4 Canadian and Caribbean Perspectives on Security in the Region

Hal P. Klepak

Only a few short years ago, it would have been curious indeed to have a chapter on comparative views on security in a work on future Canadian–Caribbean relations. This relationship undoubtedly had some security dimensions in the past, particularly the rather distant past, and was one where this aspect of international relations played a small and unexceptional role.

A vast number of recent changes in the relationship, however, as well as in the security context of both Canada and Caribbean countries, has meant that this area of interest is no longer a stranger to discussions of future patterns in the connection. Some of these patterns have developed out of the dramatic events of the end of the Cold War, while others from the evolution of the Commonwealth, Francophonie, the Organization of American States (OAS), and even the United Nations (UN). All have been related to the vast implications of the US victory in the Cold War, growth of great regional economic blocs, and the generalised crisis of much of the Third World.

Most Caribbean countries are now independent, although the majority only so in the last three decades. They are also small and vulnerable in the area of security, a fact of life for most small states in the region as elsewhere.[1] This they have learned through lessons in the fields of civil–military relations, the drug 'war', terrorism, the illegal arms trade, sovereignty, and the general political, economic and social stability of many of their countries. These problems have led them to continue or to develop linkages with other countries in the security field that can help them address difficulties that far exceed their individual offensive capacities.

Canada's links with the region have experienced difficult times of late, and many question marks appear on the horizon in terms of where the relationship is going. This, undoubtedly, reflects the declining role of the Commonwealth in Ottawa's foreign policy, but also the more fundamental choices being faced by the Canadian government, as its fiscal and economic problems burgeon and its ability to be as present as it would like throughout the world becomes a thing of the past. At the same time, the growth of a new and reasonably strong Canadian relationship with Latin America, and especially with Mexico through the North American Free Trade Agreement (NAFTA), has in a real sense for the first time focused Canadian attention on the Americas south of the United States.[2] Increasingly, Canadian diplomats, and the public at large, see Latin America as a legitimate area for Canadian interest and of real importance to the future of the country. The Caribbean in this sense may have a new lease on life where Canadian priorities are concerned, as its importance in the hemisphere as a whole takes shape.

These trends all have security dimensions and have been the topic of some academic and official study as a result. It must be understood, however, that neither in the Caribbean nor in Canada is the security dimension much to the fore except where thorny issues make its presence inevitable. In recent years, this has essentially meant Haiti, although the evolution of events in Cuba, the drug issue in many of its aspects, and good governance have made it impossible to ignore wider security themes present in the area.

This chapter will first take a very brief look at the historical security contexts for both Canada and the Caribbean, then, just as cursorily, the historic security connection between the Caribbean and Canada, followed by an assessment of major issues of the recent past and present in light of security concerns for Ottawa and regional capitals. Finally, the question of where these trends may be leading us will be analysed.

CANADA'S SECURITY CONTEXT

The essential factors of Canada's geostrategic situation have remained remarkably constant since it became part of New France in 1608. It is a country with a very small population spread over a vast, cold and generally inhospitable land, next to a major power that dwarfs it in terms of population, economic strength, political and military clout, and ideological and cultural drawing power. It profits and suffers from its bicultural and bilingual status and its multicultural makeup.

In recent decades, this context has been modified by two major trends. One is the growth of close relations with its large neighbour, following centuries of war and attempts at conquest. The other is the increase in the value of Canadian territory, airspace and sea lanes to the United States as a result of their location along the lines of any potential major attack on the United States from its Soviet rival, thereby making Canada of enormous strategic importance to Washington. Needless to say, this importance has been reduced significantly in very recent years. Prior to this period, however, Canada saw its major threat as coming from the south. Indeed, under the *ancien régime*, the total population of New France was generally less than one-thirtieth of that of the neighbouring English colonies, making the danger a real one. Geography, weather, conscription and French naval and land power staved off conquest for a century and a half, but eventually it came in 1759 (Morton, 1990, pp. 12–23; Eccles, 1972, pp. 178–217). Most of the troops who besieged and took Québec that year were not British regulars, but rather New England militiamen – a clear indication of the force of the threat.

Under the British Empire, immigration increased and, with time, the British colonies, organised in 1867 into the self-governing Dominion of Canada, were outnumbered *only* by about ten to one by the by-then republic to the south. Unfortunately, the new United States proved to be both expansionist and aggressive, and defense remained a constant concern for the Dominion as it had been for the colonies before them. Even before Manifest Destiny took formal root as a plank of US foreign policy – indeed from before the Declaration of Independence itself – Canada was a target for US conquest. Only the power of the Royal Navy and the determination of Canadian and British forces stopped the repeated invasions that took place during both the American Revolutionary War and the War of 1812 (Lanctot, 1965, pp. 13–25; Stanley, 1960, pp. 106–77).

Canada was not, however, to be allowed to forget that it was the only part of the entire British Empire with a *land* border with a great power and thus much more greatly exposed to conquest than any insular territory or, indeed, territories under the Union Jack that only touched on the lands of small powers. Threats of war continued virtually throughout the nineteenth century, and only slowly in the twentieth century did better relations prevail. Even then, as late as the 1930s, Canadian defense planning still considered the United States a significant potential threat (Preston, 1967, pp. 215–26).

After Canada's experience as an ally of the United States during the First World War, and infinitely more so during the Second, Canadian security concerns about the United States declined enormously. In the first case, there seemed little reason for concern when relations were becoming so close. In the second place, there was not much one could do militarily in case of US attack. The asymmetries of power were simply too great and British decline made meaningful help from that quarter virtually unthinkable. Linkages of all kinds with the United States, especially in the economic field, were in any case growing apace and those with the United Kingdom decreasing markedly (see Cuff and Granatstein, 1975, pp. 3–29; Granatstein, 1989, pp. 21–62).

The Second World War brought formal defense cooperation between the two countries both in North America and abroad. This was carried over into peacetime through a joint defense commission and air defense agreements. These were broadened and brought into a multilateral context through the formation of the North Atlantic Treaty Organization (NATO) in 1949, a made-to-measure alliance for Canada, allowing it to be under the same security roof with both mother countries, while also multilateralising its defense relationship with the United States. A shared air defense arrangement was then set up for North America in the mid-1950s, and Canada became a full partner of the United States in the area of continental defense, at least insofar as the northern half of the Americas was concerned. More will follow on this subject.

This comfortable new context for Canadian security allowed a further international role to flourish, that of contributing to UN and other multinational peacekeeping operations. This field of endeavour made considerable sense for a country anxious for superpower rivalry during the Cold War to halt short of a *hot* war, which might well have meant the end of Canada, placed as it now was, in the era of strategic bombers, nuclear weapons and intercontinental missiles, directly on attack routes between the two antagonistic centres of alliance (see Klepak, 1994a, pp. 201–4). Canada's membership in NATO and the North American Air Defense (NORAD) system ensured that Ottawa shared the general Western desire for winning any competition with the Soviet Union for influence in the Third World. On the other hand, Canadian membership in the Commonwealth, and later on in Francophonie, meant that the country understood the problems of less-developed countries and tended to adopt a more favourable stance towards them than did certain other Western states.

THE CARIBBEAN SECURITY CONTEXT

For centuries, the Caribbean has been anything but united. Instead, it has been a patchwork of differing imperial possessions and a vast mix of races, religions and cultures. Its original peoples to all extent exterminated early on by European colonial conquerors, its population became based on the arrival of immigrants from Europe, in relatively small numbers, and in waves from Africa as slaves for the region's sugar industry. Even this was not a constant pattern, with the larger Spanish colonies of Cuba, Santo Domingo and Puerto Rico tending to develop significant white and mixed-blood populations soon after the conquest.

The Spanish were joined by British, French, Dutch, Danish and, later, US competitors, whose actions would develop the region's present great diversity. Colonial wars over gold routes to Europe and the sugar trade made for a bewildering series of changes in the political status of the plantations, ones which marked the development of the islands and some of the continental lands touching the Caribbean Sea. Thus, no single security picture emerged for the region as it did for the colonies to the far north. The Spanish saw their position in the region under siege by English, French and Dutch privateers, as well as the governments of those states. London, the Hague and Versailles saw Madrid as improperly appropriating to itself hegemony in the region, and later on as providing relatively easy pickings for the more successful maritime power that they represented. The links between the colonies and their *métropoles* became essential, while links among the islands were not seen as especially useful, a state of affairs that boded ill for the future. Very differing cultures were established in the various territories, both insular and continental.

The explosion of the United States into the region through Manifest Destiny earlier on but especially through the conquest of Cuba, Santo Domingo and Puerto Rico in the 1898 war with Spain further complicated the region's security context. Following the war, the United States acted to acquire the Panama Canal and a virtual protectorate in Panama. Often using the security argument as justification but just as frequently acting to protect its own economic interests in the area, Washington began to intervene actively, directly and militarily in the affairs of every independent state in the region, but especially in Central America, Haiti and Cuba, while it incorporated Puerto Rico directly into its new imperial arrangements (see Lafeber, 1983; Lemaitre, 1974).

The expulsion of Spain from the area was accompanied by the Hay–Pauncefote Treaty of 1901, an agreement with Great Britain by which London confirmed US hegemony in the area (Queuille, 1969, pp. 158–9). In the next decade, Washington eliminated through purchase the Danish position in the Caribbean. Neither the Netherlands nor France counted significantly in the region by the twentieth century, although they have held onto their respective territories up to the present day. By the 1914 opening of the US-dominated Panama Canal, the Caribbean had become *de facto* a US lake, even though the flags of several powers continued to fly over parts of it.

The Second World War did little but increase US dominance. Latin American states, already members of the US-led Pan American Union, were incorporated into an inter-American security system. That system felt itself legitimately entitled to regulate the future of the French and Dutch West Indies (Garrié Faget, 1968, pp. 4–8). And even the British were obliged to lease a number of bases to the United States in return for naval assistance in the early years of the war when the Commonwealth alone was fighting the Axis, an arrangement that meant effective US presence in much of the British West Indies really became greater than that of the British themselves.

European weakness during the war was followed by a vast decolonization process. Caribbean countries, while rather late to the process due largely to the questions about the viability of small states, were rapidly becoming independent by the 1960s. While French and Dutch colonies tended to form special arrangements with their mother countries, aiming to establish a special associated status, most British possessions simply became independent members of the Commonwealth. The new states found themselves the object of considerable concern in the security area as a result of the presence of Cuba in the region, its policy in the early and mid-1960s of 'exporting revolution', its great interest in expanded relations with the rest of the Caribbean countries, its support for leftist movements throughout the region, and Washington's fear that Havana was acting as a mere surrogate of the Soviet Union, expanding the latter's influence in the Americas in general and in the vital Caribbean area in particular.[3] At times, US interest could be helpful as in obtaining assistance from the regional superpower. At other times, given the obvious fact that a major security threat, real or imagined, to the United States would be a security *problem* at least to Washington's neighbours, this concern could lead to undue pressures or even direct intervention against Caribbean states. The cases of Grenada and Nicaragua are merely the most dramatic of these.

CANADA AND CARIBBEAN SECURITY

The links between Canada and the region where security is concerned have been significant at times, and less so at others, throughout the last three and a half centuries. New France was linked by common security interests to the French West Indies and by trade ties from early on. When French naval power increased, the security of all of the American colonies grew. When it fell, those colonies could expect to share the same fate.

It is little wonder that French colonial troops were used more than once in the defense of the West Indian colonies, so important for French wealth and so vulnerable to British attack. Since Canada could provide considerable numbers of white soldiers, either through conscription for militia service or through the locally-raised but more permanent *troupes de la marine*, such deployments were virtually assured. After all, neither the population base nor the social and racial makeup of the French West Indian colonies made their self-defense possible. New France's most famous military commander, Le Moyne d'Iberville, in fact died on one such West Indian campaign and was buried in Havana.

Under the British Empire, economic links between Canada and the West Indies grew even more. The North Atlantic trade triangle incorporated both. British naval supremacy, however, when combined with the end of conscription in Canada and the reduced level of threat generally in the West Indies, created less need for security links. What cooperation there was came through the mere common membership of that imperial family.

This did not change with Dominion status for Canada, although the Second World War did bring about some changes in the relationship. London was faced immediately with the need to reduce its regular garrisons in the colonies and bring them home to fight in Europe. For the West Indies, this would have meant the end of those garrisons at a time when a real threat actually might present itself either in the form of Axis forces or, more likely, through the pressures of irredentist claims presented by Latin American states, especially Argentina, Venezuela and Guatemala. Westminster asked Ottawa if Canada could find reserve regiments, then being mobilized to take on the job of garrisoning Great Britain's US possessions, and the reply was yes. Thus, Canadian infantry units were used to garrison British possessions from Bermuda to the Falklands, despite the potential diplomatic difficulties this could have created with Buenos Aires, Caracas and Guatemala City. They represented the first direct Canadian military presence in the West Indies since the eighteenth century.

As British power declined during and after the war, Canada's special place in the Commonwealth and the Americas made it a likely partner for the Commonwealth Caribbean, especially as it gained independence.

Indeed, on more than one occasion, incorporation of the Turks and Caicos Islands into the Dominion was touted more or less formally. More realistically, Ottawa was considered a provider of assistance in a number of areas, a source of tourism, a potential counterpoise to the United States, and a general partner in whom confidence was great.

In the security field, this had some, if little, echo. Canada was not particularly interested in commitments outside North America and the North Atlantic, and these commitments were already significant once NATO was given muscle in 1950 and the Korean War broke out that same year. When commitments to UN peacekeeping were seriously undertaken after 1956, Ottawa's resources were stretched reasonably thin, despite the great expansion of the Canadian Forces (CF) after 1950. More importantly, interest in such commitments was slim because of the fear that hemispheric links would draw Canada closer to the inter-American security system and Latin America. Neither of these were appealing to governments that were anxious to avoid both further US domination in the security area, and closer military ties with the then frequently sinister armed forces of Latin American countries (Rochlin, 1994, pp. 33–48; Klepak, 1990, pp. 26–36, 82–98 and 167–73).

The Commonwealth tie did result in defense linkages, however. Canadian ships were very present during various independence celebrations in the Caribbean. First, through the Royal Canadian Mounted Police, then through the armed forces themselves, Canada cooperated closely with Jamaica in setting up the latter's national security organisations. Cadet training schemes were followed by reciprocal high-level military visits and consultations. Aircraft were sold to Jamaica, and pilot training was undertaken. Technical assistance was initiated and expanded to include joint training exercises. Elsewhere, officer training was begun early on for Guyana and was extended over the years to include Barbados, Belize and several of the Eastern Caribbean states. Under Prime Minister Pierre Trudeau, training and technical assistance was expanded, and emphasis by 1982 was placed especially on the coast-guard as part of the Caribbean Maritime Training Assistance Programme (Griffith, 1993, pp. 134–5, 206–8; see also Serbin, 1993, pp. 66–7, 156). Indeed, Mr Trudeau intimated that the future of Belize was of importance to Canada, a point taken by many as meaning Ottawa would be gaining more interest in the security of the colony as it moved toward independence. Department of External Affairs officials were soon to clarify this by assuring all parties that Canada's interest did not extend to the national defense field.

Since the 1980s, Canada has continued its very limited security assistance in the Caribbean. Assistance has found itself in a greatly changed context, due to the end of the Cold War, expansion of the role and activity of the UN in the international security area, membership of the OAS, establishment of the NAFTA, growth of the Haitian dimension of Canadian Caribbean policy, development of the drug trade as a very important security issue for many countries, including the United States, and the crisis of the Cuban revolutionary government.[4] The end of the Cold War has meant a major reduction in Canadian commitment to the defense of Europe, whatever governments in Ottawa have publicly said about the decision to withdraw their army and air force elements deployed there since the early 1950s. In the same measure, it has meant a decline in the importance of Canadian defense cooperation for the United States, as the direct threat of a Soviet (now Russian) attack on North America came close to disappearing (see Sokolsky, 1994, pp. 171–98). Thus, both continental and North Atlantic security have suffered a reduction in priority for Ottawa in recent years. It is also true that the developing Asian dimension of Canadian foreign policy has so far not found an echo in the security field commensurate with its economic importance.

The US victory in the Cold War has heralded what Fidel Castro has termed 'triumphalism' in Washington, where subsequent years saw US President George Bush declare a new world order under US leadership and where US activity is still both global and dramatic. Military interventions in Panama, the Gulf region, Somalia and Haiti have shown that the United States is alone on the world stage in being able to complement its economic power, ideological and cultural punch, and diplomatic and political importance with an exclusive military and strategic *reach* never before known in international affairs and shared with no-one in today's world. The United States is thus the only *world* power, and, whether the current situation is a unipolar *moment* or a unipolar *era*, what is not in doubt is that it is *unipolar* (Nye, 1990; Ornstein, 1992, pp. 1–16; Merle, 1991). While many in the United States are far from interested in the role of world policemen, such a choice may not offer itself to them in any real sense in the current international turbulence that threatens their leadership and the peace of the world from which they gain so much.

The United States is thus free to act almost anywhere it wants and has more options to do so than anyone else – political, economic, cultural, ideological and military.[5] The implications for Canada are very great indeed, as Ottawa is repeatedly called upon to show itself to be

'Ready, Aye, Ready.' And the nature of increasingly close relations with Washington, exemplified by North American free trade and withdrawal of forces from Europe to this continent, means that the comfortable multilateralism of NATO is often not available in this new context. With the traditional counterpoises of Europe affected by that continent's increasing self-absorption, and by Canada's acceptance of its membership in the Americas after turning a blind eye for decades, the country is entering a truly new phase in its history. The asymmetries of North American life, the implications of which have been countered largely and successfully for centuries, will now constitute a huge challenge to Canadian cultural, political and, perhaps, economic survival.

The expansion of the UN's role in the security area has meant vast growth in the scope and number of peacekeeping and related missions around the world, and has called for a huge increase in Canadian deployments to this activity. After decades of representing a small percentage of CF operations, such taskings have come to be the single largest effort of the nation's military. In the Americas, this has meant, in conjunction with or separate from the OAS, the first deployments of Canadian troops to the region south of the United States since the Second World War. Two major missions in Central America have been deployed. The first, the UN observer group in Central America (ONU-CA), was in place from 1989 to 1992, and saw Canada provide the largest national contingent. The second, the UN observer mission in El Salvador (ONUSAL), has been deployed to El Salvador since the same period and is still there. In addition, the Canadian Navy sent ships to the waters off Haiti on at least two occasions since that country began its painful move toward democracy in the late 1980s. Although those units have formed part of international operations under the auspices of both the UN and the OAS, they have reflected as well Ottawa's partnership with Washington and Paris as most interested nations in the Haitian case. Thus, the actual presence of the CF in the greater Caribbean region has known a revolutionary increase in the last half-decade.

In addition to its relationship to these developments, the OAS has also become an important forum for Canadian security objectives in the hemisphere. Canada's reluctance to join the OAS, and its pre-1948 predecessor the Pan American Union, was linked closely to a desire to reduce dependence on the United States and to avoid defense entanglements outside North America, especially those related to military forces that most Canadians considered somehow unsavoury (Soward and MacAulay, 1948, pp. 30–41; Rochlin, 1994, pp. 14–48; Klepak, 1990, pp. 105–43, especially pp. 105–13). Even in 1989, when the decision to join was finally made, Chapter V of the OAS Charter, which deals with defense, was specifically excluded from those commitments that Canada was assuming. As well, Canada declined to sign the Rio Pact, the main basis of the inter-American security system. Thus, for Canada, given its historical experience, the OAS was to be a community with no security connections.

Time would quickly prove this to be impossible, and it was not only the major military deployments in Haiti and Central America that made it so. It soon became clear that membership in the inter-American community meant that one was involved in hemispheric security issues whether one liked it or not. Ottawa wished to strengthen democratic government in the hemisphere through its leadership of, and support for, the OAS's Unit for the Promotion of Democracy, and this meant a role in civil–military relations issues in the hemisphere. Canada wanted to use its experience and prestige to press for progress with disarmament and nuclear proliferation goals in the Americas; this also brought it to the fore in security areas. Indeed, Canada, along with Argentina, was instrumental in obtaining the establishment of a Security Committee in the OAS, charged with examining ways to advance outstanding security issues within the hemisphere, and the making of this committee permanent in 1995.

North American free trade has also had its effects on Canadian security affairs, although so far they have been slight. There is a widespread feeling that one cannot find a community of the NAFTA kind without it having certain security implications, but those have not been overly obvious. Canada has opened its first military attaché's office in Latin America in Mexico City, with responsibility for Cuba and Central America as well. The Department of Foreign Affairs has also held its first workshop with Mexico on common security interests. The US National Defense University has held a trilateral workshop on NAFTA and security. It remains to be seen what security elements will eventually be put into place on the basis of this community. Given the asymmetries faced by both Mexico and Canada in their relations with the United States, there is considerable reluctance to go too far too quickly in this key area.

It cannot be denied, however, that certain security facts of life for Canada and Mexico will become more stark now that there is a NAFTA community. When, for example, the United States considers something a security *problem*, whether it is drugs, immigration or the environment, it will become at least a security *issue* for neighbouring countries. Although this was always the case, it became clearer at

Ogdensburg and after Pearl Harbor, when dramatic changes in US security perceptions automatically impacted both neighbours. And indeed, security matters were discussed openly during President Zedillo of Mexico's visit to Ottawa in the spring of 1996. Ottawa and Mexico City agreed to cooperate much more in the future on security matters of mutual interest, as well as to seek out ways to help with the international security agenda.[6]

The security dimension of Canada's relationship with Haiti has been all too clear. The 1991 coup against the government of President Aristide caused an international outcry because of the curtailment of Haiti's very brief flirtation with democracy. Occasional pressures by the community on the military regime that ousted Aristide saw Canadian warships involved early on in patrolling the sea lanes off the republic, and much later taking a large part in the UN-imposed blockade of the island. When the United States was to land its forces in September 1994 under the President Carter-brokered settlement with Haitian strong-man General Raoul Cedras, the Canadians agreed to provide both a fairly large number of Royal Canadian Mounted Police (RCMP) officers to help train a reformed Haitian police force and troops for the maintenance phase of the UN-sponsored operation. This accord was, of course, never to stick, but the US invasion and occupation of the island later that fall saw the Canadians following up with police training and a major contingent of total UN deployment for the mission. Thus, more uniformed Canadians were deployed to Haiti than had been in either of the Central American missions earlier in the decade. The French-speaking capabilities of both the CF and the RCMP made Canada an ideal source for both trainers and troops, not to mention other forms of supporting the country's move toward sustainable democracy.

A long-term Canadian interest in Haiti thus became more direct and very much linked to security matters. However, this was not easy to carry out, given the international community's unwillingness to risk the lives of its troops in order to *liberate* the country. Canada, which had been very outspoken in its calls for strong action against the Cedras regime, was less than keen on joining an essentially US operation that was almost completely unsupported by other national forces willing to participate in the fighting phase of an invasion. Ottawa was very reluctant to be seen as participating in an essentially unilateral attack mounted by Washington. The Canadian stake in Haiti was to grow steadily, however. After the first extension of the mission and the departure of the bulk of US troops, Canada was asked admirably by Washington and New York to take command and ensure the operation's continued success. Ottawa acquiesced in the full knowledge that the risks were great and that there well could turn out to be a lengthy, even open-ended commitment. The establishment and anchoring of democracy, as well as other wishes on the part of the international community where Haiti was concerned, were long-term objectives difficult to achieve. Canada's security connection with the Caribbean was transformed by one decision in a way unthinkable only months before.

No issue is more fraught with difficult questions, including those concerning security, than how to handle the international drug trade. Under present circumstances, where the problem is seen by the United States so often in security terms and where US goodwill is so vital for almost every Latin American and Caribbean country, it is no surprise that many other states have followed Washington's lead in equating the drug trade with a security threat. First Mexico then a dozen other regional states began to call drugs their 'No. 1 security threat', or at least a serious security threat for which a response would be partly military. Caribbean countries did not in the same token need Washington's lead to understand the security dimensions of the drug trade. Here, Canada was somewhat on the outside. Having considered drug abuse largely a health, education and social dilemma, Canadians were out of step with the growing militarisation of the problem and emphasis on elimination of the drug trade rather than on reduction of demand. While this approach often was appreciated by producer or transit countries because the problem would have to be addressed jointly among suppliers, consumers and middlemen rather than just on suppliers, it was, nonetheless, out of line with the militarisation trend.

Since the late 1980s, Canada had begun to use the CF for anti-drug purposes. If aircraft, ships or personnel, for example, were needed by other agencies with direct responsibilities for combating drug trafficking (such as the Coast Guard, Customs Service and others, but especially the RCMP), they could be provided with minimal administrative assistance and quick response time. CF personnel have been trained to take on naval boarding and search operations, aerial surveillance and interception missions, and related tasks. Several dramatic events have highlighted the now routine nature of such military assistance to civilian authorities.

Cooperation with the United States in this area has been reasonably smooth, despite some vibrant criticisms that Parliament has not been consulted in an area where Canadian and US policy have differed markedly as to what is the best approach.[7] Equally, the use of the effective but enormously expensive apparatus of the NORAD system, originally set up to provide interception capabilities *vis-à-vis* Soviet bombers, has been widely criticised as wasteful and clear 'overkill'.

The Caribbean dimension of the problem is of interest to Ottawa. An RCMP liaison officer is maintained in Kingston, Jamaica, to cooperate with Caribbean states in this area, as well as other such officers in Bogota and Mexico City. The participation of Jamaican gangs in Toronto in drug distribution rings has received considerable press coverage in Canada. Ottawa has provided police support as well as further very limited security assistance in this area. While the assistance provided Colombia has received the most attention in the press, cooperation with the Commonwealth Caribbean has been both more consistent and readily available. As mentioned, the Coast Guard cooperation scheme with several Caribbean states has a strong anti-drug connection, as does most police training.

In the early 1990s, the annual conferences of commanders of the armies, navies and air forces of the hemisphere's nations were held with the largest attendance ever of Commonwealth states of the Americas. At an air force meeting in 1993, the drug issue was discussed and accords were reached, the details of which have not as yet been made public, aiming at further cooperation in the anti-drug area (see Andean Commission of Jurists, 1993, p. 3). There may be fallout from this for Canada and the Commonwealth Caribbean countries represented at these meetings. Certainly, the Army Commanders Conference in 1995 in Bariloche, Argentina, emphasised more than ever the role that armies in the hemisphere would have to assume in this field. Canada will want to continue to prioritise the suppression of demand at home and control of money laundering and precursor chemicals more broadly. Nonetheless, it may prove impossible to ignore calls from other countries, particularly the United States, to establish and maintain further initiatives aimed at supply and transit, some of which will continue to be turned over to military and other security forces (Klepak, 1992, pp. 525–8; and 1994, pp. 66–92).

To this day, the Cuban situation retains some, if few, of the more traditional security dimensions. Gone is the rather far-fetched idea of Cuba being a direct military threat to the United States and NATO. With the demise of the Soviet Union, such an argument fails to hold even the limited appeal it had during the Cold War (Schoultz, 1987; Suárez Salazar, 1990, pp. 79–87). The government is far from tempted to support even leftist insurgency, not to mention terrorism, in the region or elsewhere. Nor would it have the means to do so even if it chose. Furthermore, the end of the Soviet connection has ended any potential Cuban assistance to Moscow in the event of war with the United States.[8] While there are those in Miami who still speak of the presence of a Cuban menace, the reality is that such talk is now patently absurd. Instead, any Cuban threat is the product of the instability that the crisis of the current government and society brings to the island and the Caribbean region as a whole. As was seen in the *balsero* crisis of the summer of 1994, the economic crisis in Cuba could cause the United States a major problem, one that only military means could bring under immediate control and only negotiations with Havana could show any hope of halting. As with Haiti, so with Cuba, the immigration card is a strong one. Immigration's influence in the Caribbean in the context of redefining security in the post-Cold War era, and especially in light of the Cuban and Haitian examples, shows just how much potential there is for destabilising international relations and become a source of security and wider-ranging difficulties.

The extension of the crisis on the island, or the collapse altogether of social peace there, could make the current level of immigration seem a trickle. Widespread fighting could draw US military intervention and even encourage protracted guerrilla warfare, a threat taken seriously by many, including the Pentagon. And for Canada, such a situation would be embarrassing. Ottawa tried to keep Washington from intervening, even though it could not offer itself a solution to such real-life problems. It is little wonder then that Canada sees a peaceful transition as more than merely advisable and efforts like Helms–Burton as little less than madness.

Thus, Canada's international strategic position has changed to a great extent over the last half-decade, and these changes have been reflected in the Caribbean as much as in other parts of the world. The general decline of the Commonwealth relationship has paralleled growth in the level of interest in Haiti and a vastly increased connection with Mexico and Latin America.

CARIBBEAN PERSPECTIVES ON REGIONAL SECURITY

The wide differences among the Caribbean states make it difficult to speak of one regional security context. For a start, many of the actors in Caribbean affairs whose shores touch that sea do not consider themselves primarily Caribbean nations. Major cases in point are the United States (North American, North Atlantic, Pacific, even Arctic), Mexico (North American, Pacific, Latin American), both Colombia and

Venezuela (Andean, South American, Latin American), and all of Costa Rica, Guatemala, Honduras, Nicaragua and Panama (Central American, Pacific, Latin American). These countries necessarily have foreign and security policies that reflect these different pulls, not to mention historical circumstances separating them from, as much as uniting them with, the Caribbean.

The islands themselves are a patchwork of different influences and contexts. Cuba, a country of some 11 million people, has a critical mass, making it the obvious 'Pearl of the Antilles', as it had been at the time of the Spanish Empire. Spanish-speaking but heavily influenced by the slave culture so prominent under Spain, the island is in many ways a mix of Iberia, America and Africa. Under enormous US influence during its first six decades of independence beginning in 1898, which the Soviet Union came to replace between 1961 and the beginning of this decade, Havana is now isolated to a degree unknown before and suffers the multiple problems resulting from a US embargo, the end of Russian and East European assistance, and hopelessly inadequate economic policies at home. The continuing crisis makes US military intervention far from unthinkable, and civil strife a real fear. In addition, the situation has meant that Cuba's major influence in much of the Caribbean following Castro's victory in 1959 has disintegrated. All of this makes for a nearly hopeless security situation at a time when the end of Warsaw Pact assistance has meant an enormous and precipitate decline in national defense capabilities (Klepak, 1991, pp. 666–8).

It is too soon to speak of Haiti's eventual security situation, as it has so recently been placed under the tutelage of the United States and the UN. Suffice it to say that its situation is far from resolved and may yet present further challenges. What is clear is that its connection with Canada will not soon disappear and the prospects for an easy withdrawal from these increased responsibilities for Haiti, if things were to go wrong, are not favourable.

Historically, the Dominican Republic's main security problem has been Haiti. Now, furthermore, with it unlikely for Haiti to present a threat in the next few years, Santo Domingo can concentrate on the usual problems of domestic affairs and drugs.[9]

Against the experiences of these Latin American countries stands the much more recent, and generally happier, history of the Commonwealth Caribbean's larger states of Jamaica and Trinidad and Tobago. Despite problems of all kinds, these countries have been able to retain democratic governments, general political stability, and have founded security forces that, with few exceptions, have been kept under civilian control. Jamaica's crime and drug problems are, of course, great, and there have been moments of serious difficulties where domestic order is concerned. Nonetheless, those moments have been overcome successfully, and domestic outlets such as emigration have helped stabilise the country. It is still true, however, that the country's economic situation is rocky and further internal disorder must remain a constant concern for the government. As for so many countries of the region, the challenges posed by NAFTA and its expansion are neither easily fully perceived nor adequately answered.

Trinidad and Tobago has known both disorder and military unrest, although it has been kept under control up to the present. Economic predictions are not, however, universally good, and there is a danger of further destabilisation. The drug trade is a vastly troubling issue that keeps the armed forces and the police busy. The danger of officers and government civilian officials being bribed is great, given, as usual, drug traffickers' large financial resources.

If these problems appear to be serious for the larger English-speaking islands, they are much more so for the smaller ones. Attempts to pool their resources have known some success, but the challenges are tremendous (Griffith, 1992, pp. 465–75). Only such a degree of unity or cooperation as could truly deal with the threats facing the smaller islands can be expected to bring anything like a real improvement in their security situation. While everyone recognises that the threats posed by terrorism, the drug trade, international crime, shaky civil–military relations, foreign domination and domestic instability can only be faced together, few are willing to make real sacrifices of their sovereignty to achieve unity. Efforts to establish such unity, both before and after independence, have so far failed.

There are still concerns about the security of the two ex-British colonies of Guyana and Belize. Guatemala's return to democracy eventually led in the early 1990s to a *de facto* recognition of Belize and then to the lifting of the claim to its territory going back centuries. And while subsequent governments in Guatemala have been less than fully clear about this, there is much less to worry about than in the past, always assuming Guatemalan stability after the peace process reaches fruition. The background to this is, of course, that the British garrison some 1800 strong stationed in the country until 1993, which alone provided a real deterrent to any eventual aggressive Guatemalan designs, has been withdrawn, leaving the weak Belize Defense Force (with a small British training cadre) to await events on its own. There have recently been border 'encroachments' that could eventually raise these thorny points again. For Guyana, its long-standing territorial dispute with Venezuela is at a very low key at the moment. However, former coup attempts in the neighbouring country made for greater concern. In the future nationalist and military elements could insist on settling the differences.

Lastly, even the remaining European dependencies have security problems of their own. These are generally related to the international drug trade and these countries' importance as transit points on key routes for that trade. While this situation may appear to be serious at times, as in Aruba, the Turks and Caicos, and the Cayman Islands, these governments can at least count at least on significant resources to deal with the threat. These resources mainly come from their respective mother countries in Europe and only very little from the islands. Furthermore, the amount of the aid becomes all the more important as local authorities have more often than not been willing to be bribed by drug traffickers.

The United Kingdom, France and the Netherlands have all deployed naval and air force units in reinforced numbers to these territories in recent years. It is no secret that their missions are essentially anti-drug operations, which became all the more important after 1992 because of the vastly increased penetrability of European frontiers after Maastricht (see Jamieson, 1992). Missions have served to reinforce local deployments already in place and to strengthen the resolve of local governments and security forces.

MEETING GROUND

In the area of security, there is limited potential meeting ground between Caribbean countries and Canada. Ottawa already feels over-extended in terms of commitments abroad, especially where potential military deployments are concerned. The armed forces have arguably never been busier in *peace*time, and the public, while generally still keen on peacekeeping, is not necessarily so about yet further commitments abroad (see Finan and Flemming, 1995, pp. 291–311). Related to this is the extremely difficult fiscal situation that the Canadian government faces, with one of the worst public debt situations in the developed world. Every government department is under heavy pressure to cut, rather than increase, operations. The National Defense Department has perhaps been hardest hit of all by repeated cuts in recent years. As if this were not serious enough, the Department of Foreign Affairs and International Trade has also been hard hit and has been obliged to make major reductions in programmes previously considered absolutely essential. In turn, the amount of official aid available for dispersement abroad has been reduced dramatically.

There is, on the other hand, a clear interest in the Commonwealth Caribbean to expand this connection. Yet, new programmes can expect to face the severest criticism and must show ever clearer links to other major policy objectives, especially job-creation at home and the expansion of trade abroad. Any programme that cannot demonstrate a clear link with these larger objectives is likely to be underfunded or even left out altogether.

The Caribbean, and especially the Commonwealth Caribbean, is not the priority it once was for Ottawa. The area is small and has a less than impressive total population and combined economic product. Canadian links with these countries of the region are strongest in the cultural and immigration areas, although certain areas of economic interest are still strong and total Canadian regional investment is impressive. At the same time, Canada's connection with Haiti has meant that considerable diplomatic, police and military resources have already been deployed in the region; their presence does not necessarily receive the best press, however. Therefore, it is perhaps not surprising to see something of a 'go-slow' signal as far as other Caribbean commitments in the security area are concerned.

There is, however, an important understanding among key circles concerning the extent of the problems facing Caribbean countries in the area of security. Ottawa is concerned about civil–military relations, the drug trade, international crime, regional instability and survival of democracy, and other fields loosely grouped under the security umbrella. The Defense White Paper and statement of foreign policy entitled *Canada and the World*, both results of long parliamentary reviews of foreign as well as defense policy, express this concern. There is also a feeling that Canada has an advantage in this area of the Americas. In a world where Asia is not interested in a 'community' with Canada, and Europe is looking elsewhere, there must be few options for the future of Canadian international relations that do not take the Americas as the main focus, or at least one of them.

Integration with the Americas is fraught with problems for Canada and its traditional preference for multilateralism and position on the same side as *les grands*. The context could not be more different from NATO's, wherein other major powers also were (and still are) at the table and presented opportunities for the exercise of Canadian independence at little risk. In the Americas, only Canada, Brazil and Mexico are to a large extent major players. Canada must recognise that the full asymmetries of inter-American relations are now for the first time ones that it will have to fully accept and with which it will need to take precautions in this new field of its foreign policy.

CONCLUSION

Whatever the reality suggested, the Americas are becoming a major priority for Canada, and the Caribbean may well not loose its priority for Ottawa if it is subsumed into the more compelling inter-American relationship. In the security field, the growth of Canadian links with Latin America has been extraordinary if compared to its limits only a half-decade ago. The Commonwealth Caribbean should have a special place in any such developments, since it shares few of the negative features of previous security affairs among Latin American states or even between them and the United States. Indeed, it offers room for Canadian action in the Americas that specifically reflects Canadian traditions and ideas, as well as its bilingual status, monarchical preferences and parliamentary government.

A pair of oft-mentioned new members for NAFTA, Colombia and Venezuela, believed by many observers to be probably two of the next three nations in the drive for a Western Hemisphere Free Trade Area, are Caribbean states. Mexico, Canada's second NAFTA partner, is a Caribbean state, and even the United States, our closest collaborator in economic affairs, is also. The Commonwealth and Francophonie are well represented in the region, and both of their mother countries have dependent territories in and touching on the Caribbean Sea. It is hardly surprising that linguistic, cultural, historic and economic links of all kinds exist between them.

Limits on the security relationship have been presented in some detail here. But Canada is beginning to forge a much closer security relationship with the whole of the Americas, and the Caribbean surely will be part of this. Given Canada's confidence in the Commonwealth Caribbean's belief in democracy, it will be easier for Canada to cooperate with these governments in the delicate security field than with others. In many ways, both Canada and the Commonwealth Caribbean are feeling their way in closer inter-American security links, and, together, they may be able to face the evolution of these relations better than they might separately. Limitations are not going to disappear readily; the problems that must be overcome are significant and interrelated. Without proposing enormous advances in this field, it does appear that some security cooperation can continue, and even grow, at relatively little cost to the mutual benefit of all. Canada can help in matters that concern it, and the Caribbean can receive much needed assistance and cooperation in areas of great importance to it.

Notes

1. See the excellent recent work by I.L. Griffith (1993), *The Quest for Security in the Caribbean* (Armonk, NY: Sharpe), pp. 5–15.
2. For the history of Canadian–Latin American relations, see J.C.M. Ogelsby (1976) *Gringos from the Far North: Essays in the History of Canadian–Latin American Relations* (Toronto: Macmillan). For more on recent developments, see James Rochlin (1994), *Discovering the Americas: The Evolution of Canadian Foreign Policy towards Latin America* (Vancouver: University of British Columbia Press), especially pp. 75–202; J. Haar and E. Dosman (eds) (1993), *A Dynamic Partnership: Canada's Changing Role in the Americas* (Coral Gables, FL: North–South Center Press); and P. MacKenna (1995), *Canada and the OAS* (Ottawa: Carleton University Press).
3. Griffith (1993), pp. 217–42. See also L. Schoultz (1987), *National Security and US Policy in Latin America* (Princeton, NJ: Princeton University Press), pp. 15–16. For background on the inter-American reaction to this situation, see F.V. García-Amador (1987), *La cuestión cubana en la OEA y la crisis del sistema interamericano* (Coral Gables, FL: University of Miami Press).
4. Much of this is discussed in H. Klepak (ed.) (1993), *Canada and Latin American Society* (Montreal: Méridien).
5. For a fascinating analysis of the impact of culture and communications on this context, see the excellent work of D.V.J. Bell (1993), 'Global Communications, Culture and Values: Implications for Global Security', in D. Dewitt *et al.* (eds), *Building a New Global Order: Emerging Trends in International Security*, (Toronto: Oxford University Press), pp. 12–39.
6. Some potential areas of cooperation were set out in a joint Canadian Foundation for the Americas (FOCAL)–Instituto Tecnológico Autónomo de México (ITAM) workshop on Mexican and Canadian views on international security held in Mexico City in May 1994. See H.P. Klepak, (ed.) (1996), *Natural Allies? Canadian and Mexican Perspectives on International Security* (Ottawa: Carleton University Press).
7. See the highly critical articles by Marci MacDonald in the *Toronto Star*, 12–13 October 1993, entitled 'NORAD and Drug Cop', and 'Canada's Role in the Rebirth of Star Wars'.

8. This author has discussed this issue in his 'Confidence-building Measures and a Cuba–United States Rapprochement' (1995), in A. Ritter and J. Kirk (eds), *Cuba in the International System: normalization and integration* (London: Macmillan), pp. 226–36.
9. For one of the few good treatments of the special circumstances of the Dominican military, see P.A. Mariñez (1988), 'Las fuerzas armadas en la República Dominicana: profesionalización y politización', in A. Varas (ed.), *La autonomía militar en América Latina* (Caracas: Nueva Sociedad), pp. 365–85.

References

Andean Commission of Jurists (1993) *Drug Trafficking Update* (July) (Lima: Andean Commission of Jurists).

Bell, D.V.J. (1993) 'Global Communications, Culture and Values: Implications for Global Security', in D. Dewitt *et al.* (eds), *Building a New Global Order: Emerging Trends in International Security* (Toronto: Oxford University Press).

Cuff, R.D. and J. Granatstein (1975) *Ties that Bind: Canadian–American Relations in Wartime from the Great War to the Cold War* (Toronto: Hakkert).

Ecclees, W.J. (1972) *France in America* (Vancouver: Fitzhenry & Whitehead).

Finan, J.S., and S. Flemming (1995) 'Public Opinion and the Policy Process', in D. Dewitt and D. Leyton-Brown (eds), *Canada's International Security Policy* (Toronto: Prentice-Hall).

García-Amador, F.V. (1987) *La cuestión cubana en la OEA y la crisis del sistema interamericano* (Coral Gables, FL: University of Miami Press).

Garrié Faget, R. (1968) *Organismos militares interamericanos* (Buenos Aires: Depalma).

Granatstein, J. (1989) *How Britain's Weakness Forced Canada into the Arms of the US* (Toronto: University of Toronto Press).

Griffith, I.L. (1992) 'The RSS – a Decade of Collective Security in the Caribbean', *Round Table* no. 324 (October).

Griffith, I.L. (1993) *The Quest for Security in the Caribbean* (Armonk, NY: Sharpe).

Haar, J. and E. Dosman (eds) (1993) *A Dynamic Partnership: Canada's Changing Role in the Americas* (Coral Gables, FL: North–South Center Press).

Jamieson, A. (1992) *Drug Trafficking 1992: A Special Report* (Southampton: Research Institute for the Study of Conflict and Terrorism).

Klepak, H.P. (1990) *Canada and Latin America: Strategic Issues for the 1990s*, extra-mural paper no. 54 (Ottawa: Operational Research and Analysis Establishment).

Klepak, H.P. (1991) 'Hard Times Ahead for Havana', *Jane's Defence Weekly*, vol. 12 (October).

Klepak, H.P. (1992) 'The Use of the Military against the International Drug Trade', *Jane's Intelligence Review*, vol. XX, p. 4 (November).

Klepak, H.P. (ed.) (1993) *Canada and Latin American Security* (Montreal: Méridien).

Klepak, H.P. (1994a) 'Les Forces armées et l'armement au Canada', in S.J. Kirschbaum (ed.), *La Sécurité collective au XXLe siécle* (Québec: Presses de l'Université Laval).

Klepak, H.P. (1994b) 'The Impact of the International Narcotics Trade on Canada's Foreign and Security Policy', *International Journal*, vol. XLIX, pp. 66–92.

Klepak, H.P. (1995) 'Confidence-building Measures and a Cuba-United States Rapprochement', in A. Ritter and J. Kirk (eds), *Cuba in the International System* (London: Macmillan).

Klepak, H.P. (ed.) (1996) *Natural Allies? Canadian and Mexican Perspectives on International Security* (Ottawa: Carleton University Press).

Lafeber, W. (1983) *Inevitable Revolutions* (New York: Norton).

Lanctot, G. (1965) *Canada et la Révolution américaine* (Montreal: Presses de l'Université de Montréal).

Lemaitre, E. (1974) *Panamá y su separación de Colombia* (Bogota: Planeta).

MacDonald, M. (1993) 'NORAD as Drug Cop'. *Toronto Star* (12–13 October).

MacDonald, M. (1993) 'Canada's Role in the Rebirth of Star Wars', *Toronto Star*, (12–13 October).

MacKenna, P. (1995) *Canada and the OAS* (Ottawa: Carleton University Press).

Mariñez, P.A. (1988) 'Las fuerzas armadas en la República Dominicana: profesionalización y politización', in A. Varas (ed.), *La autonomía militar en América Latina* (Caracas: Nueva Sociedad).

Merle, M. (1991) *La Crise du Golfe et le nouvel ordre international* (Paris: Economica).

Morton, D. (1990) *A Military History of Canada* (Edmonton: Hurtig).

Nye, J.S. (1990) *Bound to Lead: The Changing Nature of American Power* (New York: Basic).

Ogelsby, J.C.M. (1976) *Gringos from the Far North: Essays in the History of Canadian–Latin American Relations* (Toronto: Macmillan).

Ornstein, J. (1992) 'Foreign Policy and the 1992 Elections', *Foreign Affairs*, vol. 71 (Summer).

Preston, R.A. (1967) *The Defence of the Undefended Border: Planning for War in North America, 1867–1939* (Montreal: McGill-Queen's University Press).

Queuille, P. (1969) *L'Amerique latine, la doctrine Monroe et le panaméricanisme* (Paris: Payot).

Rochlin, J. (1994) *Discovering the Americas: The Evolution of Canadian Foreign Policy towards Latin America* (Vancouver: University of British Columbia Press).

Schoultz, L. (1987) *National Security and US Policy in Latin America* (Princeton, NJ: Princeton University Press).

Serbin, A. (1993) *El Caribe ¿zona de paz?* (Caracas: Nueva Sociedad).

Serbin, A. (1993) 'Cultura y tensión regional en el Caribe', in F. Jácome (ed.), in *Diversidad cultural y tensión regional: América Latina y el Caribe* (Caracas: Nueva Sociedad).

Sokolsky, J. (1994) 'Canada's Bilateral Defence Relationship with the United States', in D. Dewitt and D. Leyton-Brown (eds), *Canada's International Security Policy* (Toronto: Prentice-Hall).

Soward, F.H. and A.M. MacAulay (1948) *Canada and the Pan American System* (Toronto: Ryerson).

Stanley, G. (1960) *Canada's Soldiers: The Military History of an Unmilitary People* (Toronto: Macmillan).

Suárez Salazar, L. (1990) 'Cuba: respuestas a un mundo cambiante', in H. Muñoz (ed.), *El desafío de los '90: anuario de políticas exteriores latinoamericanas 1989–90* (Caracas: Nueva Sociedad).

5 A Regional Approach to Sustainable Development in the Caribbean: Applying the Test of Common Sense (TOCS)

Patricia A. Lane

While many disciplines strive to define the Caribbean–Canadian relationship of the 1990s and beyond, the single point on which scholars can readily agree is that any foundation for the relationship should be based upon common sense. Few relationships can survive an absence of this precious constituent.

Common sense addresses the problem of what is sensible and practical: what is going to work to achieve expected goals. Clearly, common sense is highly desirable for the Caribbean–Canadian relationship of the 1990s. Yet, how can we ensure that this relationship passes the test of common sense (TOCS)? There needs to be agreement on the test format and content, although an extensive review of the literature has failed to reveal a single published example of a TOCS despite the universal use of the concept. It also appears that the TOCS is apparently applied informally, with vague criteria for passing and failing. In examining, therefore, the Caribbean–Canadian relationship of the 1990s and beyond, it became necessary to devise a TOCS solely for this purpose. It is here focused upon the concept of sustainable development.

THE DEFINITION AND RELEVANCE OF SUSTAINABLE DEVELOPMENT

Definition

The World Commission on Environment and Development has defined sustainable development as:

development that meets the needs of the present without compromising the ability of future generations to meet their own needs. The
concept of sustainable development does apply limits...not absolute
limits but limitations imposed by the present state of technology and
social organization of environmental resources and by the ability of
the biosphere to absorb the effects of human activity...Sustainable
development is not a fixed state of harmony, but rather a process of
change in which the exploitation of resources, the direction of investments, the orientation of technological development, and institutional change is made consistent with future as well as present needs.
(1987, pp. 8–9)

Sustainable development is a difficult concept in theoretical and practical terms (Redclift, 1992, p. 2, pp. 199–201). Although in essence it
should be very practical, to date, it has not been operational.

Sustainability, in its most optimistic sense, means providing for the
present generation while maintaining our ecological–economic options
open for the future development of all generations. It is a strategy for
human survival at many interlocking levels. It involves introducing ethics
and rationality into the interrelationship between the economy and the
environment and into management of ecological resources to foster ro-
bust economies and stable, fulfilling human societies within richly
diverse, healthy ecosystems. The opportunity for a dependable future
must also be there. Sustainable development means trying to use the
environment to fuel the economy for development, while assuring that
development options are left open for future generations by minimising
irreversible damage.

Relevance

The relevance of sustainability to the Caribbean–Canadian relationship
is taken as a valid assumption, as most people would agree. To conclude otherwise would be to fail the TOCS a priori before it could be
applied to the relationship. Thus, we can begin with two assumptions.
First, the Caribbean–Canadian relationship of the 1990s should pass
the TOCS. Second, sustainable development should be a goal of the
relationship.

Since the Caribbean–Canadian relationship is essentially of a
regional nature, the focus of achieving sustainability in this relationship
should be regional as well. Scholars such as J. Rogozinski (1992) have
provided a history of the Caribbean region. He traces the key events

shaping current regional economic and environmental realities that provide a baseline for considering sustainability. Numerous initiatives for sustainable development for the Caribbean region have been undertaken (see, for example, Ali, 1990; Alleyne, 1994; Castro, 1992; Geoghegan, 1985; Griffith, 1994; Pantin, 1994; Thomas, 1990; and the US Department of State, 1986), and Canada has substantially redirected its priorities.[1] Development and aid policies are also being rethought in regard to the developing world (CIDA, 1992, 1995; Dube [1988] 1990; Harrison [1979] 1990; IDRC, 1993). At the global level, a successful approach to sustainability will require a holistic understanding and meaningful integration of all nations and regions in the creation of a functional blueprint for sustainable development. To achieve overall planetary sustainability, attention must be given to the local, national and regional levels as well since all countries are bound by a common geography and ecology needed to cooperate in achieving sustainability. Five questions have been carefully prepared to underline the rationale for promoting sustainable development for the Caribbean.

TOCS QUESTION No. 1: IS SUSTAINABLE DEVELOPMENT SOME SORT OF ACADEMIC RUSE FOR ENVIRONMENTALISTS TO TAKE OVER THE WORLD?

The short answer is no. The question fails the TOCS.

The Increasing Role of Transnational Corporations

As we move into the twenty-first century, there is no evidence supporting the idea that tree huggers will form a global dynasty and control IBM or General Motors. It is more likely that prevailing economic entities will continue their relentless onslaught on their associated environmental systems. Many have predicted that multinational companies will become more important than the nation itself.[2] R.J. Barnet and J. Cavanagh summarised the new world order as follows:

> The emerging global order is spearheaded by a few hundred corporate giants, many of them bigger than most sovereign nations. Ford's economy is larger than Saudi Arabia's and Norway's. Philip Morris's annual sales exceed New Zealand's gross domestic product. The multinational corporation of twenty years ago carried on separate operations in many different countries and tailored its operations to

local conditions. In the 1990s, large business enterprises, even some smaller ones, have the technological means and strategic vision to burst old limits – of time, space, national boundaries, language, custom, and ideology ... These institutions we normally think of as economic rather than political, private rather than public, are becoming the world empires of the twenty-first century ... The balance of power in world politics has shifted in recent years from territorially-bound governments to companies that can roam the world. (1994, 14)

And Drucker (1993) has described how money, information, environment, terrorism and militarisation can no longer be controlled by nation states, which he believes have become obsolete in many ways.

Explaining in detail why the nation-state is no longer the most appropriate unit for organising domestic and external affairs, P. Kennedy concluded, 'The key autonomous actor in political and international affairs for the past few centuries appears not just to be losing its control and integrity, but to be the wrong sort of unit to handle the newer circumstances ... Transnational players such as the large corporations and banks ... are largely outside the control of individual governments' (1993, p. 130). The powerful role of transnational corporations also directly affects the ability of nation-states to control their natural resources and protect their environments. For example, Blaikie (1985) explained how these companies can dictate the contractual terms of forest exploitation in ways that neither suit the economic nor environmental needs of the local people in poor developing countries or their national governments. The environmental costs of these poorly negotiated contracts often outweigh the economic benefits. Soil loss alone, for example, can be irreversible, as can the diminished biodiversity, which, on a sustainability balance sheet, would produce a net negative result. This is not sound development.

The Distinction between Growth and Development

As the economic onslaught continues, many options for future economic prosperity are being destroyed for large areas of the world. The concept of sustainable development is presumably a way to put some degree of balance back into this reckless destruction of the earth. Economists, however, often use the word 'sustainable' inappropriately and devoid of common sense. For them, a sustainable economy is a vehicle for continuous, sustainable growth, which contradicts the essence of sustainability. Sustainable development does not mean that economies can grow endlessly. Wackernagel and Rees (1996, p. 2) pointed out that in reading the second part of the World Commission on Environment and Development (1987) definition carefully, the only limitations that the Brundtland Commission recognised were social and technological.

There are many more limitations, especially on economic growth bounded by the physical constraints of our small planet. No physical system can grow without limits. According to H. Daly:

> In its physical dimensions the economy is an open subsystem of the earth's ecosystem, which is finite, non-growing, and materially closed. As the economic subsystem grows it incorporates ever more of the total ecosystem into itself and must reach a limit at 100 percent, if not before. Therefore, its growth is not sustainable. The term, sustainable growth, when applied to the economy is a bad oxymoron – self-contradictory as prose, and unevocative as poetry. (1991, p. 260)

Daly also illustrated the difference between wealth and growth:

> That all problems are easier to solve if we are truly wealthier is not in dispute. What is in dispute is whether growth, at the current margin, is really making us wealthier. As growth in the physical dimensions of the human economy pushes beyond the optimal scale relative to the biosphere it in fact makes us poorer. Growth, like anything else, can cost more than it is worth at the margin. Growth, which we have habitually come to refer to as 'economic growth' while we were below the optimum scale, becomes 'anti-economic growth' once that optimum has been passed. (1990, p. 5)

Sustainability Concerns Everyone's Survival

In 1950, the world's population was 2.5 billion, and approximately 5 billion in 1987. Between 1960 and 2025 it is expected to triple (Pickering and Owen, 1994, p. 283), and between 2030 and 2040 there will be nearly 10 billion people on earth. Thomas Malthus recognised that the environment, and especially food supply, are finite, whereas the growth of the population is exponential. What is closer to the truth in the 1990s, however, is not only exponential population growth but the exponential environmental decline of ecologically productive lands.

Many of the insults that humans inflict on their environment are multiplicative, not simply additive, and, unfortunately, most of this multiplication is negative. Common sense would tell us that these two realities will come into serious conflict.

Proponents of sustainable development recommend that we live off of the ecological 'interest' and not touch the 'principal' (Pearce, 1989, p. 598). While this indeed passes the TOCS, in some areas of the world there is little or no interest in the future; therein lies the problem. There is also little opportunity for growth. Small island states are especially vulnerable both environmentally and economically. Haiti, for example, has suffered serious environmental degradation and only 2 per cent of its forests remain. Forests can be important economic resources of a country not only for the commercial products they provide but also the ecosystem services they perform, such as water and air purification, soil retention and biodiversity maintenance. Haiti is an extreme case of forest destruction because it has had such extensive loss of topsoil that many of its land's agricultural uses are severely constrained (Head, 1991, p. 103), and there is now no quality topsoil left (Ponting, 1991, p. 228).

The concept of sustainable development is critical to much of the way that the Caribbean–Canadian relationship will be forged in the 1990s and beyond. All of the countries involved in this relationship have advocated sustainable development as a national priority, but it should also be a regional priority as well. The cost of not achieving sustainable development is exorbitant and will become unattainable for many poor countries (Davidson and Dence 1988, p. 54). Lane *et al.* (1989, pp. 3–30) estimated the cost of poor or non-existent environmental management on Jamaica after Hurricane Gilbert in 1988 for both natural and managed ecosystems. The losses, many directly attributable to ineffective environmental management, were high and could have been avoided at relatively low cost. Jamaica has spent less than 1 per cent of its federal government budget on the environment, and it has been encouraged by international financial institutions to engage in agricultural and forestry practices especially in coffee and pine production, needed to quickly generate the most export dollars.

Sustainable development means maintaining the environment in good enough condition to be able to continue its development in perpetuity. Maintaining the global environment as it was at the dawn of recorded history or even in the 1950s is not the issue, rather enabling an overly large population of humans to survive with dignity is.

TOCS QUESTION No. 2: IS THE WHOLE EQUAL TO THE SUM OF ITS PARTS, AND IS THE REGION EQUAL TO THE SUM OF ITS NATIONS?

The short answer is no. This question also fails the TOCS.

Two Examples of Wholes and Parts

Complex-system thinkers, using sagacious judgment, would always reply that the whole is not more than the sum of its parts but is different from the sum of its parts. Furthermore, whole systems have properties that cannot be deduced from knowing their parts. Many such as T.F.H. Allen and B. Starr have used the term 'emergent properties' to identity the unique characteristics of whole systems (1982, p. 38). Emergent properties differ from collective properties, which are merely a set (or collection) of properties belonging to the individual parts.

Let us consider two examples. First, at the biosphere level, J. Lovelock's Gaia Hypothesis (1991) requires that:

> The atmosphere and surface sediments of the planet Earth be taken as a whole. This hypothesis, in its most general form, states that the temperature and composition of the Earth's surface are actively regulated by the sum of life on the planet – the biota. Major aspects of the Earth's surface are dynamically maintained in frantic stability. That is, as changes in the gas composition, temperature, or oxidation state occur, the biota regulates these changes through growth and metabolism. (Margulis and Lovelock, 1989, p. 1)

The Gaia Hypothesis has tremendous ramifications in contemplating our future potentialities. In the last two hundred years, we have begun to toy with the key homeostatic mechanisms that enable life to exist on the planet. Although the Gaia Hypothesis has not been tested, no one has been able to explain the composition of the earth's atmosphere based solely on the principles of physics and chemistry. These are only parts of the whole.

Second, at the physiological to ecological levels, there have been many cases where the appropriate level of understanding and management have gone unrecognised, with unexpected, often disastrous results. For example, scientists realised that DDT could kill insects in laboratory bottles, a physiological truth rigorously proven by means of the scientific method. And when DDT was first introduced into nature, scientists believed that our strongest competitor, the insect, would be immediately annihilated. Quite the opposite occurred, unfortunately. The pesticides wiped out their natural predators, and the number of pests increased. The ramifications of this simplistic assumption were more than the obvious environmental consequences. Large multi-national chemical firms developed, trade regulations were implemented, and foreign policies changed (Norgaard, 1994, pp. 23–8). The resulting social, political and economic consequences of the dilemma have been enormous. While it was a physiological truth that poison kills insects, it was an ecological falsehood that poison can control them in nature. We cannot continue to maintain this mentality if we expect to have sustainable development. Common sense dictates that the scale of the relationship has to be inherently recognised.

Sustainable Development as a Holistic and Hierarchial Concept

The whole is not better or worse than the collection of its parts; it is fundamentally different. To understand the Caribbean–Canadian relationship in a sustainable development context is to realise the importance of the regional scale. There are key holistic properties of the interactions of its member nations both economically and environmentally at this scale that are non-existent at others.

If we ignore the interconnections controlling the behaviour of these systems, we will not be able to understand them, much less manage them (Haila and Levins, 1992, p. 103). By definition, sustainable development centres on the interaction between environment and economy. It stresses how to manage an interaction rather than just characterise isolated parts. The belated conclusion has been reached, in fact, that environment and economy are one coevolving system (Norgaard, 1994, pp. 82–5). Many recent initiatives have been undertaken to form regional trading blocs, such as the North American Free Trade Agreement (NAFTA) and agreements of the European Union (EU). These regional units, however, have been based almost exclusively upon trade and other economic considerations; they do not directly consider the economy–environment interaction, or sustainability as central to the dynamics of each regional system. Thus, important linkages are severed.

The Need to Achieve Sustainability at the Regional Level

To be successful, sustainable development has to work at the local, national, regional and global levels, although the regional level has normally received little attention. This observation is important for the Caribbean–Canadian relationship since it is this regional level that is of direct concern. All levels operate in a hierarchy where there is both knowledge and ignorance at each level. Local communities often become fervently involved in nearby environmental and development issues. National governments establish sustainable development goals, environmental legislation to protect their territories, and policies to exploit their resources. A number of international agencies, such as the World Bank and United Nations (UN), set global priorities through such vehicles as the Global Environment Facility, whose priorities include global climate change, ozone depletion, international water pollution, and loss of biodiversity. The regional level, on the other hand, often has no effective institutional and jurisdictional bodies that can ensure that the regional system's properties are considered a whole system. In addition, national interests often preclude successful regional approaches.

When we speak of the Caribbean–Canadian relationship, we imply regional dynamics; the relationship is certainly more than a collection of bilateral relationships between Canada and each Caribbean country. This regional dynamic requires a corresponding regional approach to sustainable development planning that is specific for this level of complexity. This essentially has never occurred, and yet continuing in the old bilateral, piecemeal fashion does not pass the TOCS.

Overview of Regional Efforts to Enhance Sustainability and Environmental Protection

There have been many attempts at considering the Caribbean Region an integral unit in regard to its environmental management, and, more recently, with sustainability as a goal of various initiatives. Generally, these efforts have been fragmented and under-resourced, and national interests have usually prevailed over planning processes. The greatest problem, however, has been of a conceptual nature because there has been little work on the idea of a regional ecosystem and its interaction with its regional economic subset. Neither the theory nor the practical implementation of true regional-level thinking has yet been possible, and major environmental problems have been poorly managed. There has been no cumulative effects assessment of problems at the regional level, although there are many such problems in the Caribbean region (Caldwell, 1990, p. 160).

In 1979, a key conference sponsored by the United Nations Environmental Programme (UNEP) and the Economic Commission for Latin

America and the Caribbean (ECLAC) on 'Environmental Management and Economic Growth in the Smaller Caribbean Islands' was held
in Barbados. In 1981, the Plan of Action for the Programme on the
Environment of the Caribbean (CEP) was formalised in Montego Bay,
Jamaica. UNEP has since been successful – after a decade of endeavour – in securing agreement from some 27 nations, territories and
dependent islands of the Greater Caribbean to protect the regional
environment. In March 1983, in Cartagena, Colombia, 13 Caribbean
nations signed the Convention for the Protection and Development of
the Marine Environment of the Wider Caribbean Region. To date, 19
countries have ratified or acceded to the Convention.

The Caribbean Action Plan, the most comprehensive approach
taken to the regional environment, has attempted to describe the state
of the environment, create and maintain databases to assist in regional
environmental planning and management, and prioritise problems of
coastal zone management, physical-ecological degradation (especially
related to tourism and fishing), depletion of resources, pollution from
land-based sources, pollution from marine dumping and transport, climate change, and environmental accidents and natural disasters. It
includes 66 projects of mutual interest, such as guidelines for the management of watersheds, improvement of environmental health services,
protection of coastal marine resources, renewable energy production,
environmental education, contingency planning for combating oil
spills, and prevention of the negative environmental impacts of tourism
(Caldwell, 1990). Regional coordination for the Action Plan was established in Kingston, Jamaica, in 1987.

Protocols have been added to the Cartagena Convention, the first
dealing with oil-spill contingency planning, the second with specially
protected areas of wildlife, and a third on land-based sources of pollution which is to be finalised in 1997. There have been several sub-
programmes, including Specially-Protected Areas of Wildlife (SPAW),
Integrated Planning for Industrial Development (IPID), Control and
Evaluation of Marine Pollution (CEMPOL), Information Systems for
Management of Coastal and Marine Resources (CEPNET), and Education, Training and Awareness (ETA). Because these initiatives are
greatly underfunded, progress has been hampered.

In 1996, The Caribbean Environmental Programme issued its report,
'The Status of Protected Area Systems in the Wider Caribbean'. Based
on the Protocol Concerning Specially Protected Areas and Wildlife in
the Wider Caribbean (SPAW) to the Cartagena Convention, also termed
the Kingston Protocol, it called for the creation of protected areas to

manage threatened and endangered species. David Freestone, Managing Editor of the *International Journal of Estuarine and Coastal Law*, concluded:

> The Kingston Protocol is arguably the most comprehensive regional wildlife protection treaty in the world – it is certainly the most comprehensive of its kind ... Its provision on environmental impact assessment, planning and management regimes, and buffer zones, as well as the range of protection measures it envisages (including species recovery plans), reflects much of the best in modern thinking on wildlife protection and management. (Caribbean Environment Report, 1996, p. iv)

Guidelines, manuals, databases, species recovery plans, training programmes and methodological development and standardisation have been created and implemented in accordance with this protocol.

The CEP Technical Report no. 36 on the SPAW describes the biodiversity-protected area status of each of the 37 member countries and territories, with associated legislation and implementation. There are a total of 1307 protected areas with 20 per cent encompassing marine and coastal resources. In analysing the recommendations of this document, however, it is clear that the effort is largely a collection of national initiatives, with some common training, institutional development, and so forth. The programme is not regional in the sense of understanding the environment on this level and then devising an environmental management plan based upon the regional dynamics of species, their ecosystems, and threats to them.

A Caribbean Trust Fund was established in 1982, with US$1.5 million to be provided regional governments and $1.38 million to be administered by the UNEP. There is a nine-country monitoring committee that directs the operations and activities of the Action Plan. Over the following ten years, this fund was resourced at just under $7 million, which is less than one million dollars per year. From 1988 to 1991, there has been some counterpart funding of approximately $8 million, with the United Kingdom, Venezuela, France and the United States participating in this funding effort. Altogether, this is a small sum of money for the work that clearly needs to be done.

The Canadian International Development Agency (CIDA) has three bilateral programmes in the Americas: the Caribbean, Central America and South America. These programmes include government-to-government funding in several countries, scholarships, food aid and humanitarian assistance. Through its Partnership Programme, there is a sector that includes non-governmental organisations and institutions, such as universities, unions and professional associations, whose volunteer base is quite strong. The Partnership Branch also supports the Industrial Cooperation Programme, which focuses on human resource development, training, technology transfer, environment, and women in development, and generally promotes commercial links with Canada and countries in the region. Canada also funds multilateral organisations, and these contributions find their way into a number of Caribbean initiatives with UN agencies – Development Programme (UNDP), Environment Programme (UNEP), Food and Agriculture Organisation (FAO), International Children's Fund (UNICEF), Higher Commission for Relief (UNHCR), among others, including the Pan-American Health Organisation, OAS, World Food Programme, and such international financial institutions as the World Bank and the Inter-American Development Bank (IDB).

One important multilateral initiative supported by Canada is the Global Environmental Facility (GEF) managed by UNDP, UNEP and the World Bank. It addresses global environmental problems, essentially key forms of cumulative effects, identified by the Brundtland Commission (UNCED, 1987) as having global significance. The impact of many of these problems is also regional, and several GEF projects have been funded in the Caribbean Project. One is a large project on the northern archipelago of Cuba, involving the Sabana–Camagüey ecosystem, an important area for biodiversity for the whole Caribbean region and one that is threatened by an array of cumulative effects, especially from large-scale tourism development. The International Development Research Centre (IDRC) in Ottawa has funded many research projects in the Caribbean region that contribute to each country's overall development. Long-term marine research has been undertaken in Jamaica. The IDRC has also assumed a key role in Canada in regard to the Rio Earth Summit in 1992 and Implementation of Agenda 21, a global action plan on sustainability that emerged from the Summit that specifically addresses the relationship between environment and development – thus focused on achieving global sustainability.

In addition to the these efforts, the ministers of the environment of Latin America and the Caribbean meet periodically to evaluate and follow up on regional cooperation efforts on environmental matters within the context of sustainable development. Their eighth and ninth meetings were held in Santiago, Chile, in 1993, and in Havana, Cuba, in 1995, respectively. The ministers attempted to coordinate regional positions within UNEP (1995). One of their stated objectives is, 'to achieve greater effectiveness and coherence in the regional planning and implementation of the environmental agendas of international agencies' (UNEP/LAC.IX, p. 4). Several recommendations made at the ninth meeting included regional initiatives, such as the acceptance in principle of UNEP's Regional Cooperation Programme to Contribute to the Implementation of Agenda 21 in Latin America and the Caribbean, which enhances the regional Environmental Training Network coordinated by UNEP and strengthens the Regional Seas Programme, also coordinated by UNEP, among others.

Another more recent initiative has involved the formation of the Association of Caribbean States in 1995, based in Trinidad and Tobago. The first meeting of the Special Committee for the Protection and Conservation of the Environment and of the Caribbean Sea was held in Caracas in November 1996, several delegations (Barbados, Cuba and Guatemala) presented their views on how to manage the regional Caribbean environment in the future. Barbados suggested that the Caribbean Sea be recognised internationally as a specially protected habitat. Cuba provided the rationale for a Regional Environmental Strategy that became part of the Committee's work plan. Guatemala proposed the establishment of a technical committee and special foundation for sustainability in the Caribbean, and Jamaica provided an excellent discussion on environmental problems presently facing the Caribbean. Interestingly, one of the participants, Lennox Ballah of the Institute of Marine Affairs of Trinidad and Tobago, concluded:

With the possible exception of Guyana, Jamaica, Trinidad and Tobago and the continental mainland countries, the single major resource to be developed is the resource that is the environment. Paradoxically, therefore, development equates with the protection and preservation of the environment. (Association of Caribbean States, 1996, p. 1)

TOCS QUESTION No. 3: IS ACHIEVING SUSTAINABLE DEVELOPMENT AT THE NATIONAL LEVEL SUFFICIENT FOR THE CARIBBEAN REGION?

Again, the answer is no. It does not pass the TOCS.

When the World Commission on Environment and Development laid out the initial rationale for sustainable development in 1987, they did so by categorising large-scale patterns of environmental deterioration across the planet. They documented many types of deterioration, including water pollution, soil loss, habitat fragmentation, loss of biodiversity, deforestation and acidic deposition (acid precipitation or rain), among others. In essence, the Commission described cumulative effects, which are regional patterns of environmental degradation extended in time and space.

Cumulative effects are the results of the multiple activities of humans within a region, and these activities can be both large and small. Perhaps up to 85 to 90 per cent of global deterioration can be attributed to cumulative effects (Roberts, 1994, p. 20), which often work in a multiplicative fashion with unpleasant surprises. The rationale for sustainable development, therefore, was established based upon the chronicle of cumulative effects. In contrast, most of our environmental management tools, such as environmental impact assessment, are applied to the local ecosystem and single projects, yet another example where the scale of the problem and its solution are not commensurate.

Cumulative effects do not respect geopolitical boundaries. For small island states in the Caribbean, regional environmental deterioration can be overwhelming, and an individual state can often do little by itself to reverse these trends. Many island environments are exceedingly fragile and too small to accommodate the ecology of species that live on the mainland or lack the habitat diversity needed to support the mainland's biodiversity.

The environment is a dynamic, as many organisms and their reproductive products move considerable distances over island archipelagos. Some animals spend their lives in different places, migrating between them. Ocean currents and flotsam carry other species passively from one location to another. There is a whole subdiscipline in ecology termed island biogeography. It focuses on patterns of distribution and abundance of species living on islands (Simberloff, 1988, p. 473), which are examples of meta-populations or a population of populations (Hanski and Gilpin, 1991). Rather than the usual population parameters of density, age-specific survivorship values, birth rates, death rates and growth rates, island biogeography uses the immigration and emigration rates of populations on islands, the size of islands and distances between them, and local colonisation and extinction rates as the main parameters of interest.

Island biogeography has been successful in explaining many of the ecological patterns observed for island archipelagos (Myers and Giller

[1988] 1994). Much of the ecology of island states can only be understood in a regional context (Edwards, May and Webb, 1994 p. 111), which holds many practical aspects in regard to conservation, biodiversity management, environmental protection, monitoring, contingency planning in general, and sustainable development planning specifically. Given these realities, it appears impossible for the Caribbean archipelago to achieve sustainable development without progress at the regional level in the areas of both enhanced environmental and economic understanding and management.

Canada is a vital part of the Caribbean region; it shares common aspects of environment and economy. The relationship between the Greater Caribbean Region and Canada extends far back into their history of trade and exchange (see, for example, Ponting, 1991). Ecologically, the two areas have always been linked through the Gulf Stream, which is vitally important to fisheries, and the migrations of large populations of birds and mammals that exhibit a mixed strategy of living in both the Caribbean and Canada. According to Head, the forests in Canada and the United States depend greatly on these migrating bird populations to feed on the insect populations that destroy the forests. The well-being of these birds depends on their entire habitat in both the North and the South:

> Some 250 species of North American birds migrate regularly to the neotropics. The migrants constitute as much as 85% of the local populations. Once in their winter habitats, these birds become fully integrated members of the local communities, often altering both diet and behavior to conform...Canadian songbirds from the eastern part of the country fly deeply into the Caribbean and Central America...Deforestation in any of these southern destinations is of considerable significance. Sadly, those regions that most suit people (often mountain slopes between 500 and 2000 meters altitude), and are therefore under the most intense attack from human exploitation, are those most favored by birds. Any decrease in the numbers of songbirds visiting Canada has both ecological and economic implications. (1991, p. 107)

Head concluded that the destruction of Canadian forests is directly related to the destruction of forests in the Caribbean.

Both the Caribbean and Canada are also part of a unique biogeographical gradient in tropical to temperate ecosystems, with species ranges overlapping throughout the gradient. Many of the same gene pools and benefits of the associated biodiversity are shared, and thus there is strong mutual interest in the well-being of Caribbean and Canadian ecology. In a fundamental way, we share this ecology and the management of a common environment. Brown (1985) has made a compelling argument for the development of 'macroecology' as the best way to understand many of the current theoretical and practical ecological dilemmas. He has outlined why some of the key environmental questions at the end of the twentieth century, including those related to species abundance, distribution and biodiversity can only be answered with a spatially and temporally extended approach.

Economically, Canada and the Caribbean region are linked in many ways, and both areas depend heavily on their natural resources. There are strong parallels in fisheries, aquaculture, forestry, agriculture, mining and tourism. Many environmental and economic opportunities lie right here in this hemisphere: Canada manufactures many of the products and provides the raw materials needed by the Caribbean, and vice versa. Both share the same fear of witnessing their economies and cultures overshadowed by the proximity of the now sole superpower of the world.

Cumulative effects are best managed by anticipatory environmental planning, which is essentially planning them away before they occur (see Lane *et al.*, 1988). It involves anticipating the future so that as our environmental and economic systems coevolve, they will do so in mutually supportive ways. In contrast, the current overall global coevolution, with a positive exponential population increase and negative exponential environmental deterioration, exacerbated by the activities of transnational corporations, is mutually destructive. Likewise, the concept of sustainable development a priori embodies the notion of anticipating the future, in that needs of future generations are to be considered now as the present generation is taking its requirements for survival from the earth. To be able to anticipate accurately is as rare as common sense, but anticipating a future of environmental deterioration is a fairly straightforward activity. There is so much documentation on the human impacts on local ecosystems that the consequences of particular actions usually can be predicted. At the regional level, however, cumulative effects have often become too far advanced before they can be fully identified. How to foresee a future of successful regional sustainable development is much more difficult, and for the Caribbean it will require more cooperation and more creativity than has been previously possible.

The main problem with managing cumulative effects through anticipatory environmental planning is related to innumerable jurisdictional and institutional barriers that exist within and between nation-states (Lane *et al.*, 1988, pp. 2–5). These barriers, exacerbated by reductionist thinking, often render the management of cumulative effects impossible even when the underlying science and cause–effect relationships are totally understood. For example, the acidic deposition problem between Canada and the United States was well-understood scientifically, but jurisdictional and institutional barriers effectively thwarted implementation of effective management measures. In the Caribbean, and even within Canada, disparate languages, histories, cultural traditions and national and provincial boundaries have formed barriers. Likewise, the foreign policies and alliances of a large number of countries within and outside the region have served to etch geopolitical fracture lines that are counterproductive to the well-being of the region and to the Caribbean–Canadian relationship. These barriers do not pass the TOCS.

TOCS QUESTION No. 4: WILL APPLICATION OF THE NORTHERN MODEL ENSURE SUSTAINABLE DEVELOPMENT IN THE CARIBBEAN–CANADIAN RELATIONSHIP OF THE 1990s?

This also does not pass the TOCS.

The Northern Model (rich northern countries where the per capita ecological footprint exceeds the world average by 2–3 fold), as defined here, includes both environmental and economic components of sustainable development: (1) common environmental management tools, such as impact assessment, regulatory frameworks, and environmental protection planning and monitoring; (2) heavy reliance on science and technology; and (3) even more reliance on Adam Smith's invisible hand of the marketplace. The latter two components developed at a time when most people in the North subscribed to a frontier mentality and believed natural resources, energy supplies and waste disposal areas were unlimited. Essentially the Northern Model will not function in the Caribbean–Canadian relationship because there are not enough resources in the developing world to support this wasteful approach. Nor will the Northern Model eventually even work in the North, as the following discussion of ecological footprints illustrates.

Many Northern societies have vastly misappropriated the ecological footprints of others; this practice cannot continue indefinitely. The concept of the ecological footprint was developed by Marthus Wackernagel and William Rees (1996). It is essentially the inverse of the more familiar carrying capacity: how many organisms such as human beings can be supported by a given area or volume of biosphere. In this analysis, everything that society uses is included and transformed into ecologically productive land, imports are added to national production, and exports are subtracted, to get a measure of total consumption. Thus, the ecological footprint analysis is a way to calculate certain meaningful bounds for sustainability. According to Wackernagel and Rees:

> The ecological footprint is not about how bad things are. It is about humanity's continuing dependence on nature and what we can do to secure Earth's capacity to support a humane existence for all in the future. Understanding our ecological constraints will make our sustainability strategies more effective and livable. (1996, p. 3)

At present, there is an average 1.5 hectares per person of total available ecologically-productive land. With the projected increases in population and assuming no further land deterioration (which is not a realistic assumption), it is predicted that in our near future there will only be 0.9 ha/person available as a planetary average. Given current levels of soil loss, this figure of 0.9 is an optimistic value. Canada and the United States have the largest footprints per capita in the world, at 4.3 and 5.1 hectares per capita, respectively. Wackernagel and Rees calculated the national ecological deficits of the most developed countries. On a per capita basis, some of the highest values were Japan (730 per cent), South Korea (950 per cent), Belgium (1400 per cent), Netherlands (1900 per cent), Germany (780 per cent) and Great Britain (760 per cent) (1996, p. 97). Australia and Canada are the only two developed countries that exhibit high consumption patterns but consume less than their 'natural income domestically' because of their low populations relative to their national territories.

The consumption habits of northerners, however, require average ecological footprints of about 4.5 ha/capita; therefore, simple arithmetic poses more questions than answers. Biological resources are being turned spontaneously into profit, without replacement for future generations even when replacement would be ecologically possible. How will these finite limits finally impact the Northern Model? More importantly, how will this excessive consumption by the North impact the South? Twentieth-century rates of consumption and resource-use by the North can be shown to be unsustainable, if not physically impossible, for the next century. Ivan Head, former President of the International Development Research Centre in Ottawa, concluded:

> It is the industrialized North that has been responsible so far for the major share of carbon emissions, for the greatest percentage of toxic effluents wasted into rivers and streams. It is the industrialized North that has benefitted historically – and still benefits – from its greedy assumption that it enjoys 'drawing right' on the atmosphere, waters and soil of this planet of a kind and extent that it is far from willing to share with the developing South. (1991, p. 110)

Briefly, consider the three components of the Northern Model. First, most environmental management tools are directed towards local problems such as the location of a power plant or protection of a particular forest. The Northern Model has been exceptionally inadequate in dealing with cumulative effects, whose recognition is barely acknowledged in existing environmental legislation. There are sophisticated tools for modelling the effects of hot water drainage from a power plant into a river, for example, but what if there are a dozen power plants on a single river? What are the cumulative effects of heat, chemical additives, impingement and entrainment of these power plants on a single river? How should other human activities, such as agricultural runoff, shoreline alteration, chemical dumping, acidic deposition, hydrocarbon pollution, habitat fragmentation and loss of biodiversity be evaluated in association with power plant effects? It has been calculated that all of the Hudson River passes through power plants more than once per year, while every power plant is within regulatory requirements. The jurisdictional and institutional barriers to even recognising cumulative effects, let alone managing them, are often insurmountable in the North.

The need to successfully manage cumulative effects will eventually lead to worldwide changes in social, economic and political systems. Environmental-impact assessment has been touted as the way to manage the environment successfully, but it has had many inappropriate applications due to scale problems. Since most environmental deterioration occurs as cumulative effects over regional levels, there need to be management tools that will be effective at the regional level. The concepts of private property and individual rights embedded in the Northern model also impede successful regional management.

Second, science and technology are praised as the universal panacea, but they cannot save us. This has been a long-term myth that has been perpetuated by successes in certain areas, such as transportation, communications, chemical industry (plastics), nuclear energy, computer science, medicine and genetic engineering. Most of the successes have had both positive and negative repercussions on the environment, however.

Much of today's environmental management is focused on cleaning up the environmental impacts of yesterday's technology, and, at best, science can be considered neutral in the overall struggle to achieve sustainable development. Even when a positive form of technology exists, many poor countries do not have access to it because of cost and human resource requirements. But, many authors still stress the importance of achieving sustainable development in the struggle against underdevelopment and poverty (see, for example, Gupta, 1988). Much of the way we apply science and the scientific method constitute exceedingly narrow human endeavours. Weinberg (1976, p. 22) concluded that the apparent success of science is due more to asking the right questions than providing answers to the most important ones.

Changes are occurring too fast and often at geological time scales that are essentially irreversible (McKibben, 1990, p. 133). Most of this failure to manage our planet has been a failure to manage whole systems and especially their interconnections (Haila and Levins, 1992, p. 103). For the last few hundred years, there has been an arrogant belief that through science and technology humans can control nature. Why, if we are in control, are most of our lakes turning into cesspools? Why is there DDT in pristine Arctic environments? Why are more species becoming extinct than at any other time in human history? Why are there holes in the ozone layer? Why is the sea level rising? Gerald Weinberg described our so-called control of nature as more like insidious creeping slavery of the human species (1976, p. 22). We naively mislead ourselves into believing that if we can understand the 'bug in the bottle', we can control its relatives in nature by simple extrapolation of a poison.

Third, anyone who advocates that an invisible hand of the market economy will ensure environmental protection and sustainable development certainly lacks common sense. There is no evidence to support this premise and a great deal to invalidate it. Where was the invisible hand when Lake Erie died or the passenger pigeon became extinct?

Transnational corporations unfettered by national control – both economic and environmental – will make their decisions based upon short-term profits. This is not because they are ignorant or evil, but simply because they want to survive. The essence of sustainable development is that we must share better and in a more far-reaching way than ever before. We must find new ways to interact with our planet that are not self-destructive. Central to this concept is the rapidly changing notion of economy (see d'Arge 1989; Daly and Townsend, 1993; Pearce, 1989; and Redclift, 1987). There are many valuable requirements for the survival of man and the ecosystem that are not sold on markets. Schumacher said that people should matter in an economy and that northern economics has become self-destructive ([1979] 1989, p. 114). The old forms of capital that Adam Smith addressed are being challenged by new ones, such as ecological and information capital, and the old market-based economic premises are becoming as obsolete as their environmental counterparts.

Environments are not static and neither are economic and political systems; change is the rule, not the exception. Given the interaction between environment and economy, these systems are coevolving: how one changes will affect how the other changes in an iterative fashion. The invisible hand has led to the present unsustainable world; it does not pass the TOCS to be able to rely on it in shaping the Caribbean–Canadian relationship of the 1990s.

TOCS QUESTION No. 5: SHOULD THE CARIBBEAN–CANADIAN RELATIONSHIP OF THE 1990s HAVE A MORE REGIONAL FOCUS ON SUSTAINABLE DEVELOPMENT?

Yes, this is the first question in the test that passes the TOCS.

There has to be more focus on the quality of life and less on material gain for all parties to this relationship. Fighting poverty would be much more difficult without growth. Development can help, but a serious reduction in poverty will require population control and redistribution aimed at limiting wealth inequality. These two implications of sustainable development are too radical to be openly affirmed, and to evade them a bit of self-contradiction must seem to politicians a small price to pay for remaining in office. They cannot be 'sustainably' evaded, however (Daly, 1991, p. 5).

The emphasis on a new Caribbean–Canadian relationship should be on building a strong regional approach to sustainable development, which necessitates tearing down as many geopolitical barriers as possible. These barriers and outdated mind-sets hinder development on both sides of the divide. There are many areas of sustainable development that are inherently regional. Examples are:

- Joint management of common ecological resources and cumulative effects in regard to the shared ocean, fisheries, biodiversity, habitats, fragile ecosystems, endangered species, transboundary pollution, as well as shared contingency planning for natural disasters (hurricanes, earthquakes) and pollution events, such as oil spills, that are common in the region. This will require an understanding of regional ecology and trends of environmental deterioration. Mooney, Fuentes and Kronberg (1993) have provided excellent examples of the contrasting ecology of North and South America and how these ecosystems are expected to respond differently to regional and global change.
- The enhancement of regional self-sufficiency by helping each other in the division of labour, agriculture, technology-sharing, education and health so that insularity works for sustainable development and not against it. For example, some islands can produce cattle while others are too small. Rationalisation of what each can do best can improve life for everyone.
- Assisting one another with particular public and agricultural health problems with regional ecological and epidemiological dynamics. There are many diseases (human and agricultural), and pests do not recognise national island borders.
- Development of a joint approach to the rest of the world so that the vulnerability of individual countries to external events beyond the region will be reduced and economies of scale can be realised. This is a time when large trading blocs are forming worldwide, and small island states cannot afford to be further disadvantaged economically. They need to be regionally integrated in ways that promote, not diminish, their collective and individual sustainability. This may also be one of the best ways to escape the economic domination of transnational corporations.
- Sharing, enjoying and promoting cultural and political diversity, which enhances regional richness.
- Helping each other develop environmentally sound technologies and businesses, including the areas of biotechnology, pollution abatement, alternative energy generation, reuse and recycling, environmental services and ecotourism.

- Promoting the identification of those problems that are uniquely regional and that, if left unsolved, will thwart achievement of sustainable development. Cooperative approaches must be developed to deal with those problems and ensure that all barriers to their solution are removed. Some barriers are so obsolete that no one even remembers why they are there.
- Helping to support and build new regional bodies that can successfully work at the appropriate scales to promote sustainable development. The recent formation of the Association of Caribbean States is a notable example.

Canada working in partnership with all of the countries of the Caribbean region could help provide a new regional paradigm for sustainability, with a new conceptual basis focused on the emergent properties of the economy–environment interface. It would take much innovation and creativity to move from a 'collection of states' mentality to a 'set of interacting states' approach. Canada would have to look beyond its own Northern Model to one that is cognisant of sustainability limits, such as that provided by ecological footprint analysis, and which includes social justice for both the present and future generations of the Caribbean region. Reaching a genuine regional level of sustainability will involve a radical refocus of Canadian foreign policy and funding priorities. This is a big challenge, but not to continue fostering the Caribbean–Canadian relationship in a regional context is to not pass the TOCS.

CONCLUSION

Traditionally, the Caribbean Region has not been coherent. Geopolitical affiliations and fracture lines have historically fragmented both the insular and mainland states. History is useful in understanding what has happened to a region that has resulted in its present condition. Given the unprecedented rate of global change, however, the past is no longer a good predictor of the future (McKibben 1990, p. 133). History should not be used as an excuse to continue pursuing non-sustainable, fragmented approaches to development in the Caribbean region and Canada's involvement there. Relationships and priorities need to be radically restructured. Coevolution between environment and economy must be allowed to proceed unfettered by obsolete, counterproductive mind-sets. Although several aspects of sustainable development can only be achieved within a regional framework, this does not negate the need for local, national and global initiatives. It does call attention to the fact, however, that although sustainable development as a concept is inherently regional, it is the level that has received the least attention.

Canada has an unprecedented opportunity to promote wise sustainable development practices at the regional level, but this cannot be carried out successfully by imposing the Northern Model. New models have to be created that will focus on the regional level. The Caribbean–Canadian relationship also needs to be based upon the full partnership of all countries in the area. Aspects of all relevant models, including the Cuban Model (see Lane, 1996, 1997), need to be analysed and integrated into a new regional approach. It is time to use sagacious judgment in anticipating the future and ensuring that sustainable development is made possible. The relationship has to pass the TOCS, and so much in the past has not.

Notes

1. See Boardman (1992) for a description of the changes in Canadian environmental policy over the past 20 years.
2. Cavanagh and Clairmonte (1982) have discussed in detail the growing dominance of transnational corporations and the inability of nation-states to control them.

References

Ali, D.A. (1990) 'Science, Technology and Sustainable Development in the Caribbean', in J. Cox and C. Embree (eds), *Sustainable Development in the Caribbean* (Ottawa: Institute for Social Research).

Allen, R.E. [1964] (1990) *The Concise Oxford Dictionary: Thumb Index Edition* (New York: Oxford University Press).

Allen, T.F.H. and T.B. Starr (1982) *Hierarchy: Perspectives for Ecological Complexity* (Chicago: University of Chicago Press).

Alleyne, F.E. (1994) 'Environment in Development', *Caribbean Affairs*, vol. 7, no. 2, pp. 94–105.

Association of Caribbean States (1996) *Final Report of the First Meeting of the ACS. Special Committee for the Protection and Conservation of the Environment and of the Caribbean Sea. Caracas, Venezuela; November 21–22, 1996* (Havana, Cuba).

Barnet, R.J. and J. Cavanagh (1994) *Global Dreams: Imperial Corporations and the New World Order* (New York: Touchstone Books, Simon & Schuster).

Barry, T., B. Wood and D. Preusch (1984) *The Other Side of Paradise. Foreign Control in the Caribbean* (New York: Grove Press).

Bartlett, J. [1855] (1968) *Bartlett's Familiar Quotations* (Canada: Little, Brown & Co. (Canada) Ltd.).

Blaikie, P. (1985) *The Political Economy of Soil Erosion in Developing Countries* (New York: Longman).

Boardman, R. (1992) *Canadian Environmental Policy: Ecosystems, Politics and Process* (Toronto: Oxford University Press).

Brown, J.H. (1995) *Macroecology* (Chicago: University of Chicago Press).

Caldwell, L.K. (1990) *International Environmental Policy*, Duke Press Policy Studies (Durham, NC: Duke University Press).

Canadian International Development Agency (CIDA) (1992) *CIDA's Policy for Environmental Sustainability*. Supply and Services Canada, cat no. E94–29/9–1.

Caribbean Environment Programme (1996) *Status of Protected Area Systems in the Wider Caribbean*, United Nations Environment Programme, CEP Technical Report no. 36.

Castro Ruz, F. (1992) 'Message by Fidel Castro Ruz, President of the Councils of State and Ministers of the Republic of Cuba', United Nations Conference on the Environment and Development, Rio de Janeiro, June.

Castro Ruz, F. (1994) Untitled address. Global Conference on Sustainable Development of Small Island Developing States, Barbados, 5 May.

Castro Ruz, F. (1995) 'Speech at International Youth Festival. August 6, 1995', *Granma International* (Havana, Cuba).

Cavanagh, J. and F. Clairmonte (1982) 'The Transnational Economy: Transnational Corporations and Global Markets', *The Transnational Institute for Policy Studies. NCTAD Review* no. 4.

CIDA (1994) *Report of Canada to the United Nations Commission on Sustainable Development*. Supply and Services Canada, cat no. E2-136/1994.

CIDA (1995) *Canadian Cooperation in the Caribbean* (Hull, Quebec: CIDA).

Daly, H.E. (1990) 'Toward Some Operational Principles of Sustainable Development', *Ecological Economics*, vol. 2, no. 3, pp. 1–6.

Daly, H.E. (1991) 'Sustainable Growth: An Impossibility Theorem', *National Geographic Research and Exploration*, vol. 7, no. 3, pp. 259–65.

Daly, H.E. and K.N. Townsend (eds) (1993) *Valuing the Earth: Economics, Ecology, Ethics* (Cambridge, MA: The MIT Press).

d'Arge, R.C. (1989) 'Ethical and Economic Systems for Managing The Global Commons', in D.B. Botkin (ed.), *Changing the Global Environment – Perspectives on Human Involvement* (San Diego, CA: D.B. Academic Press).

Davidson, A. and M. Dence (1988) *The Brundtland Challenge and the Cost of Inaction* (Ottawa: The Royal Society of Canada).

Drucker, P.F. (1993) *Post-Capitalist Society* (New York: Harper Business).

Dube, S.C. [1988] (1990) *Modernization and Development: The search for alternative Paradigms* (London: Zed Books).

Edwards, P.J., R.M. May and N.R. Webb (eds) (1994) *Large-Scale Ecology and Conservation Biology* (Cambridge: Blackwell Scientific).

Ehrenfeld, D. (1993) *Beginning Again: People and Nature in the New Millennium* (New York: Oxford University Press).

Elliott, J.A. (1994) *An Introduction to Sustainable Development – The Developing World* (London: Routledge).

Fodor. (1994) *Guide to the Caribbean* (New York: David MacKay).

Geoghegan, T. (1985) *Proceedings of The Caribbean Seminar on Environmental Impact Assessment* (St Michael, Barbados).

Gore, A. (1992) *Earth in the Balance* (London: Earthscan Publications).

Griffith, M. (1994) 'A Chance for Island States', *Caribbean Affairs*, vol. 7, no. 2, pp. 131–42.

Gupta, A. (1988) *Ecology and Development in the Third World* (London: Routledge).

Haila, Y. and R. Levins (1992) *Humanity and Nature: Ecology, Science and Society* (London: Pluto Press).

Hanski, I. and M. Gilpin (1991) 'Metapopulation Dynamics: Brief History and Conceptual Domain', *Biological Journal of the Linnean Society*, vol. 42, pp. 3–16.

Harrison, P. [1979] (1990) *The Third Revolution: Population, Environment and a Sustainable World* (London: Penguin).

Head, I. (1991) *On a Hinge of History. The Mutual Vulnerabilities of the South and the North* (Toronto: University of Toronto Press).

Horgan, J. (1996) *The End of Science. Facing the Limits of the Knowledge in the Twilight of the Scientific Age* (Reading, MA: Addison-Wesley).

International Development Research Centre (IDRC) (1993) *Agenda 21, Green Paths to the Future* (Ottawa: IDRC Books).

Kennedy, P. (1993) *Preparing for the Twenty-First Century* (New York: Random House).

Lane, P.A. (1996) 'Establishing, Supporting and Sustaining the Legacy of José Martí, the Cuban Model: Past, Present and Future. A Global Model for Sustainable Development from an Ecologist's Viewpoint', *Proceedings, Jose Martí and the Challenges of the 21st Century*, Conference, Santiago de Cuba, 15–19 May 1995 (Havana: Center for Studies of Marti).

Lane, P.A. forthcoming, 'Four Intersecting Observations on Revolution: Science, Sustainability, Cuba and the 21st Century', *Proceedings, International Conference on Environment and Society* (Havana, Cuba), 10–14 February 1997.

Lane, P.A., J.J. Harrington, G.A. Shea and J. Douglas (1989) 'Jamaica 1988: Hurricane Gilbert – The Relationship between Environmental Degradation and the Severity of Natural Disasters', chapters 1, 2, 3, unpublished report.

Lane, P.A., R.R. Wallace, R.L. Johnson and D. Bernard (1988) *A Reference Guide to Cumulative Effects Assessment in Canada*, vol. 1.

Lovelock, J. (1991) *Healing Gaia: Practical Medicine for the Planet* (New York: Harmony Books).

Margulis, L. and J.E. Lovelock (1989) 'Gaia and Geognosy', *Global Ecology* (Boston, MA: Academic Press).

McKibben, B. (1990) *The Death of Nature* (Harmondsworth: Penguin).

Mooney, H.A., E.R. Fuentes and B.I. Kronberg (eds) (1993) *Earth System Responses to Global Change: Contrasts between North and South America* (San Diego, CA: Academic Press).

Myers, A.A. and P.S. Giller (eds) [1988] (1994) *Analytical Biogeography: An Integrated Approach to the Study of Animal and Plant Distributions* (London: Chapman & Hall).

Norgaard, R.B. (1994) *Development Betrayed: The End of Progress and a Coevolutionary Revisioning of the Future* (London and New York: Routledge).

Pantin, D. (1994) *The Economics of Sustainable Development in Small Caribbean Islands* (Trinidad: Eastern Specialist Printers).

Pearce, D. (1988) 'Economics, Equity and Sustainable Development', *Futures*, vol. 20, no. 6, pp. 595–7.

Pearce, D. (1989) 'Sustainable Futures: Some Economic Issues', in D.B. Botkin (ed.), *Changing the Global Environment – Perspectives on Human Involvement* (San Diego, CA: Academic Press).

Pickering, K.T. and L.A. Owen (1994) *An Introduction to Global Environmental Issues* (London: Routledge).

Ponting, C. (1991) *A Green History of the World. The Environment and the Collapse of Great Civilizations* (New York: Penguin).

Redclift, M. [1987] (1992) *Sustainable Development: Exploring the Contradictions* (London: Routledge).

Roberts, N. (1994) *The Changing Global Environment* (Cambridge, Mass.: Blackwell).

Rogozinski, J. (1992) *A Brief History of the Caribbean* (New York: Facts on File).

Schumacher, E.F. [1979] (1989) *Small is Beautiful, Economics as if People Mattered* (New York: Harper & Row).

Simberloff, D. (1988) 'The Contribution of Population and Community Biology to Conservation Science', *Annual Review of Ecology and Systematics*, vol. 19, pp. 473–511.

Thomas, C.Y. (1990) 'Economic Policy and Sustainable Development in the Caribbean: Introduction', in J. Cox and C. Embree (eds), *Sustainable Development in the Caribbean* (Ottawa: Institute for Research on Public Policy).

United Nations Environment Programme (UNEP) (1995) *Final Report of the Ninth Meeting of Ministers of the Environment of Latin America and the Caribbean* (Havana, Cuba, 21–26 September 1995, UNEP/LAC-IG.IX/4.

US Department of State (1986) *Proceedings of the Interoceanic Workshop on Sustainable Development and Environmental Management of Small Islands*. US Man and the Biosphere Programme (Washington, DC: US Department of State).

Wackernagel, M. and W. Rees (1996) *Our Ecological Footprint* (British Columbia: New Society Publishers).

Weinberg, G.M. (1976) *Introduction to General Systems Theory* (New York: Simon & Schuster).

World Commission on Environment and Development (WCED) (1987) *Our Common Future* (Oxford: Oxford University Press).

World Conservation Union (IUCN), United Nations Environment Programme (UNEP), and World Wide Fund for Nature (WWF) (1991) *Caring for the Earth, A Strategy for Sustainable Living* (Gland, Switzerland: Gland).

6 Emerging Linkages: New Brunswick, Nova Scotia and the Caribbean

M.C. Ircha

INTRODUCTION

Linkages between the British Commonwealth communities of Canada and many of the Caribbean nations developed over several centuries of mutually beneficial trade. Seaborne trade between the Caribbean and Eastern Canada was reinforced with the incursion of Canadian banks and other trading facilities into the Caribbean in the nineteenth century, while the continued favoured trading status of Caribbean nations in the Canadian context was reinforced through development aid (Canadian International Development Agency [CIDA] and other sources), emergency assistance (following disastrous hurricanes), and preferential trading arrangements with Canada through CARIBCAN.

Economic globalisation and the North American Free Trade Agreement (NAFTA) have affected trade development and continental transportation systems in the Caribbean and indeed other Latin American nations. This chapter examines the impact of economic globalisation and current trends in trade between Canada and the Caribbean, with a special focus on the links between the Caribbean and the two Canadian Maritime provinces of New Brunswick and Nova Scotia, followed by specific initiative to develop a Canada–Caribbean trade consolidation centre in New Brunswick. Current revival of this concept, the growing tendency for Canadian shippers to look southward, and the emergence of several shipping lines offering direct services to the Caribbean and Central America contribute to growing optimism about this north–south trade link.

ECONOMIC GLOBALISATION

There is little doubt that we now live in the global village that Marshall McLuhan first defined decades ago. Information technology and the development of global transportation systems are fundamentally changing the way business is conducted. The critical success factors for sustainable national economic development have changed dramatically. Efficiency, innovation, upgrading, clustering, strategic alliances, joint ventures and partnering are but a few of the keys to success in our increasingly competitive global economy.

The structure of the world's economy is undergoing several major transformations, which are generated by:

- Advances in information technology that are shrinking our concepts of 'time' and 'distance'. People can communicate over long distances with affordable and accessible communication networks. Firms operate branches and subsidiaries effectively throughout the world. Transactions and documents are handled by electronic data interchange (EDI). Delays and overheads are reduced and productivity improved.
- The growing importance of knowledge to the creation of wealth. We are now in the midst of the 'knowledge era', where knowledgeable workers are the primary resource used by many firms. The rapid growth of information technology is contributing to the knowledge-base of firms such as those in Canada.
- Technological changes that have led to financial, production and marketing systems operating at local and national levels are increasingly being linked on a global basis, resulting in the integration and interdependence of national and regional economies.
- Trade liberalisation under the former General Agreement on Tariffs and Trade (GATT) and now the World Trade Organisation (WTO), which has contributed to more open trade among nations. International trade depends on effective and efficient transportation systems. The trend towards increased trade liberalisation at the regional level is reflected in the expansion of the European Community (EC) and the European Free Trade Area, the Canada–US Free Trade Agreement (CUSFTA) and NAFTA, and Caribbean trade liberalisation through the Caribbean Community and Common Market (CARICOM).

The effect of these economic forces has been a significant increase in world trade. Between 1970 and 1992, the real US dollar value of world trade had increased 179 per cent (GATT, various years). Similarly, as the activities of multinational firms expanded rapidly in the 1980s, the flow of foreign direct investment grew even faster than world merchandise trade. During the period 1980–96, world gross domestic product (GDP) grew by approximately 47 per cent (International Monetary Fund, various years). Such rapid growth trends are expected to continue in the 1990s, particularly following the successful conclusion to the Uruguay Round of GATT and its replacement with the WTO. As far as Canada is concerned, the growth of global trade should lead to significant changes in its economic environment and international trading relationships.

In 1989, resource-related exports accounted for about 51 per cent of the Canadian total, compared to about 35 per cent in the United States and the EC (United Nations, 1992). Resource-based manufacturing includes food, beverages and tobacco, wood, paper products, primary metals, non-metallic minerals and refined petroleum. Over time, however, Canadian exports have shifted from resources to manufactured end products. Table 6.1 shows that exports of end products increased by almost 52 per cent during the 1980s. Thus, Canada is no longer merely a supplier of raw materials to other nations.

Table 6.1   Composition of Canadian imports and exports (percentages)

	1980	*1988*	*1992*
Exports			
Food/agriculture	10.9	8.4	9.4
Raw materials	19.4	12.8	12.5
Manufactured materials	38.8	35.7	29.5
End products	30.6	42.5	46.4
Special transactions	0.3	0.3	0.6
Imports			
Food/agriculture	7.0	5.4	6.6
Raw materials	16.4	5.7	8.8
Manufactured materials	18.4	18.8	14.9
End products	57.1	68	67
Special transactions	1.1	2.1	2.7

Source: J.A. Finlayson and S. Bertasi (1992), 'Evolution of Canadian Postwar International Trade Policy', in A.C. Cutler and M.W. Zacher (eds), *Canadian Foreign Policy and International Economic Regimes* (Vancouver, British Columbia: UBC Press), pp. 19–46; and Statistics Canada, *Preliminary Statement of Canadian International Trade – December 1992* (Ottawa: Statistics Canada, 1993), tables 3 and 4.

In 1990, Canada was the world's eighth largest exporting nation, accounting for 3.8 per cent of total global exports. It was also the ninth largest importer that year, with 3.3 per cent of global imports (Finlayson and Bertasi, 1992, pp. 19–46). In 1994, the United States accounted for 75 per cent of Canada's total trade (exports 82 per cent, and imports 68 per cent) (Statistics Canada, 1996, tables 3 and 4). Although Canada maintains both a multilateral (supporting the WTO and seeking other trade partners) and a bilateral (entering the FTA and NAFTA) trade policy, its primary economic success is the product of its bilateral trade with the United States.

What role will transportation play in the emerging global economy? One outcome is the growth of new transportation service concepts. Global networks are being formed through a variety of strategic alliances aimed at creating 'seamless transportation' – moving people and goods from origin to destination in an integrated, sometimes, intermodal system. Carriers and shippers will be working together on the design of innovative logistics systems to create competitive advantages. Information technology itself will play a key role in the highly integrated transportation systems of tomorrow.

As industries are restructuring to cope with the changing global economy, so too are the flow patterns of goods and services changing. In the Canadian context, the traditional East–West flow of goods is increasingly being reoriented on a North–South axis.

TRANSPORTATION ASPECTS OF THE FTA AND NAFTA

Because a number of trade-related elements were not included in the FTA, in particular the important issue of transportation, Canadian negotiators conducted several studies to determine the nature of transportation competitiveness within the scheme (for example, see Transport Canada, 1987; and Yee, 1987). In the marine mode, US cabotage restrictions under the 'Jones Act' apply to domestic coasting trade, including shipping to offshore states and protectorates such as Alaska, Hawaii and Puerto Rico, to US flag vessels operated by US companies, with US crews, and built in US shipyards. Canada also has cabotage restrictions on its coasting trade, albeit more liberal. Foreign flag vessels may be used if no suitable Canadian flag vessels are available, but they must meet Canadian construction standards and pay a 25 per cent import duty. Also, Canadian flag vessels can be built in offshore shipyards, and there are no ownership regulations on the domestic trades, enabling US firms to own and operate Canadian fleets.

Several alternatives were discussed during the FTA negotiations, including the provision of full cabotage rights in the other country's coastal trade, cabotage rights limited to specified ports of call, and opening up ownership/investment opportunities in each country (Cubukgil, Soberman and Yee, 1988, pp. 257–71). With full cabotage rights, Canadian and US vessels would be able to carry cargo between any two ports in each other's country. By restricting ports of call for Canadian and US carriers, this would help them to secure backhaul traffic and improve operating performance. Permitting Canadians to own and operate US flag vessels would have eliminated some inequity, as US investors can own Canadian ships.

Despite the benefits for both nations of modifying the Jones Act and other cabotage restrictions, the transportation section was deliberately excluded from the FTA. In fact, final negotiations were placed in jeopardy by an extensive effort on the part of the US maritime lobby. As Robert Burns of *World Wide Shipping* pointed out during the final stages of the FTA negotiations:

> In a rare display of unity, America's disparate maritime interests assert that the Jones Act is not negotiable. American domestic carriers would be driven out of business because they cannot meet the lower cost Canadian competition . . . Without Jones Act protection, it is feared that the Canadians would eventually dominate America's [Great] Lakes domestic trades also. (1987, pp. 45–6)

On the Canadian side, Burns's arguments were echoed by Adil Cubukgil and others who argued, 'The US lobby in support of the Jones Act proved to be too powerful to overcome during the trade negotiations' (1988, pp. 257–71). And as subsequently pointed out by an outspoken proponent of removing cabotage restrictions, Frederic Pitre, then President of Canada Steamship Lines (a major Great Lakes shipping line), 'It is hard to believe that the Berlin Wall fell before the Jones Act did' (1990).

NAFTA opened up a freer trading market with a continental population of 360 million, a total GDP of $7 trillion and a trilateral trade flow of approximately $500 billion (Finlayson, 1993). The agreement addresses transportation (primarily surface modes), and three years after it was signed, US and Canadian trucks were allowed to enter Mexican border states. A further phased approach to non-Mexican ownership of trucking companies engaged in international service is also included. In the railway mode, US and Canadian railroads continue to be free to market their services in Mexico, operate their own unit trains, and construct and own terminals. From a maritime perspective, NAFTA liberalises port activities, and Mexico now permits 100 per cent Canadian and US investment in port facilities (Government of Canada, 1992, pp. 11–12). However, NAFTA is silent on the matter of opening cabotage privileges among the countries involved. In fact, Pierre Sauvé, Canadian Deputy Senior Negotiator for NAFTA, claimed that the US interests would 'go nuts' and leave the room whenever maritime shipping was raised during the negotiations (1993). Cathcart and Kakoschke pointed out that 'Canada and Mexico [were] anxious to having [*sic*] maritime services included in the NAFTA negotiations. The position of the US [was] quite clearly on the opposite side' (1992, pp. 27–9). However, the mere fact that transportation is included in NAFTA may permit future discussion on cabotage restrictions.

The issue of continuing Jones Act protection in the US domestic trade was discussed in Vice-President Al Gore's *National Performance Review* (Office of the President, 1993). His panel's early draft called for opening US domestic trade to foreign competition. Although this dramatic reversal of US maritime policy was toned down in the final report, it may emerge in the recommended 'independent commission'. As pointed out by William A. McGrudy Jr., logistics and commercial counsel for Dupont Corp., 'This country's maritime interests must learn – as the rest of US industry is learning – to compete in the new emerging global marketplace' (Vail and Bonney, 1993, pp. 15–17).

Inclusion of transportation in NAFTA does not imply ready access to Mexican markets by Canadian carriers. Modern highways are scarce, the railway system is incapable of handling significantly increased traffic, and the country's 24 ports are outmoded. Furthermore, ports on Mexico' eastern coast are over 400 miles from the main centres of commerce, rendering intermodal transport uneconomic compared to the traditional North–South surface routings (Brennan, 1993). Mexico is trying to overcome some of these transportation problems by privatising many facilities and welcoming foreign investment to upgrade them. The reorientation of Canadian trade and transportation in a north–south direction may not be totally the result of the FTA and NAFTA. Economic deregulation in the United States and subsequent regulatory reform by Canada have also contributed to the shift in trade patterns.

Given the length of the Canadian–US border, much of the trade between the two nations is by surface (rail and truck). In terms of tonnage, marine transport dominates, accounting for 51 per cent of total bilateral trade, rail follows at 32 per cent, and trucks at 17 percent. However, despite the low tonnage carried by the two surface modes (road and rail), in 1993 they accounted for 86 per cent of the total value of transborder trade (US Department of Transportation, 1994).

Canada's two national railways have focused on developing continental networks. Table 6.2 shows that transborder railway tonnage increased during the past decade, with North–South movements being the main growth traffic lanes for Canadian railways. In the 12-year period between 1980 and 1992, transborder traffic with the United States grew by 14.5 per cent, as compared to a 1.4 per cent increase in total Canadian railway tonnage. The importance of North–South movements is even more apparent in the FTA period (1989–92), where transborder traffic increased by more than 20 per cent and overall Canadian tonnage remained constant. The transborder component of Canadian railways' total tonnage increased from 22 per cent in 1980 to more than 29 per cent in 1992 – a significant shift in trade.

The significance of North–South trade was reflected in the investment decisions of the two railways, Canadian National Railways (CN) and Canadian Pacific Railways (CP). CN consolidated its US subsidiaries (the Grand Trunk Western, the Duluth, Winnipeg and Pacific Railway, and the Central Vermont Railway) into a fully integrated continental CN North America. Similarly, CP consolidated its US subsidiaries (the

Table 6.2   Canada–US trade by rail (millions of tons)

Year	Canadian exports to US	Canadian imports from US	Total north– south	Total CN/CP[*]	North– South as % of CN/ CP
1980	30.8	8.9	39.7	181.5	21.9
1986	29.3	11.5	40.8	182.9	22.3
1989	33.0	12.1	45.1	183.5	24.6
1992	40.2	14.0	54.2	184.1	29.4
% change 1980–92	30.5%	57%	14.5%	1.4%	
% change 1989–92	21.8%	15.7%	20.2%	0.3%	

[*]CN = Canadian National Railways; CP = Canadian Pacific Railways.
Source: National Transportation Agency, *Annual Review, 1991 and 1992* (Ottawa: Minister of Supply and Services, 1991 and 1992).

Soo Line and the Delaware and Hudson Railway) into its CP Rail System. CP also established a joint service with Conrail to move containers between Montreal and Toronto and the Port of New York and New Jersey; entered into a seven-year agreement with Norfolk Southern to service a Buffalo to Chicago route; and established a joint container service with Burlington Northern Railroad between Montreal and Toronto and markets in the US midwest and south. CN also established alliances with US and Mexican railways (National Transportation Agency, 1992, pp. 58–9).

CANADA–CARIBBEAN TRADE

What do Canadian transportation trends mean for trade between the Caribbean and Canada? Following approval of the FTA and NAFTA, Canadian shippers have increasingly looked southward for trade opportunities, with their primary focus on the United States and then Mexico. Recently, however, there are signs that other nations within the Americas are also being evaluated for potential trade. This is partly the result of the overall trade liberalisation taking place in other American nations, as former trade protection practices are rapidly being dismantled in favour of freer trade. Both New Brunswick and Nova Scotia have mounted trade missions to Latin America and the Caribbean. The feasibility of developing a Canadian–Caribbean consolidation centre at the port of Saint John has been considered, and, in recent years, the port of Saint John has sent trade missions to Mexico, Cuba and Jamaica. The 1993 annual Saint John Port Days was devoted to the theme 'NAFTA and Saint John' and included speakers from Costa Rica and Mexico, along with a delegation of businesspeople from Mexico seeking trade opportunities in New Brunswick.

Trade between Canada and the Caribbean has been sporadic and relatively small. As shown in Table 6.3 in terms of their dollar value, exports to major Caribbean nations declined by 6 per cent between 1984 and 1995, while imports from these Caribbean countries increased by 62 per cent during the same period. Although the dollar value of trade provides useful information on the degree of interaction between nations, it does not reflect the problems caused by varying exchange rates and inflation, both of which could lead to more conservative estimates in the amount of actual trade between Canada and the Caribbean.

More accurate, but difficult, data to obtain are on tonnage movements between the Caribbean and Canada. Table 6.4 outlines exports

Table 6.3   Canada–Caribbean trade (millions of dollars)

	1984 Exports	1984 Imports	1988 Exports	1988 Imports	1995 Exports	1995 Imports
Bahamas	41.3	127.5	39.0	20.9	38.8	16.8
Barbados	41.0	19.0	43.4	6.6	34.0	17.2
Cuba	337.7	62.7	226.2	87.2	274.3	320.9
Dominican Republic	32.8	31.9	60.6	36.5	78.1	71.1
Jamaica	76.4	138.7	131	150.2	103.1	200.2
Puerto Rico	–	–	[233.6]*	[226.9]*	–	–
Trinidad & Tobago	140.4	19.0	58.1	56.4	102.1	19.0
Total	669.6	398.8	558.3	357.8	630.4	645.2

*Trade data on Puerto Rico is difficult to obtain as it is included in US data. The trade value recorded is for 1987.
Source: Statistics Canada, *Exports by Commodity*, Catalogue 65-004 (Ottawa: Statistics Canada, various years); and, Statistics Canada, *Imports by Commodity*, Catalogue 65-007 (Ottawa: Statistics Canada, Ottawa, various years).

Table 6.4   Canada–Caribbean trade (millions of tons)

	1984 Exports	1984 Imports	1988 Exports	1988 Imports	1992 Exports	1992 Imports
Bahamas	66	666	61	141	206	181
Cuba	1325	252	833	156	389	440
Dominican Republic	20	27	12	3	131	3
Jamaica	107	508	129	555	173	721
Puerto Rico	132	33	193	3	353	1
Trinidad & Tobago	51	610	44	348	55	220
Total	1701	1496	1272	1206	1307	1566

Source: M. Clouthier (1994), 'North/South Trade – Transportation Trends between Canada and the Rest of the Americas', *Proceedings*, 29th Annual Canadian Transportation Research Forum, Victoria British Columbia, May 1994, pp. 798–812.

and imports in terms of tons between various important Caribbean countries and Canada. Canadian exports to these Caribbean nations declined by 23 per cent between 1984 and 1992, with the most decline registered in exports to Cuba, which reflects a significant decrease in this nation's purchases of Canadian wheat. Imports from these Caribbean nations increased only slightly, by approximately 5 per cent.

In an earlier study of Canada–Caribbean trade based on 1987 data, it was found that many Caribbean exports were produced by Eastern Canada, primarily Ontario, Quebec and the Atlantic provinces (see Ircha *et al.*, 1989). In 1987, in dollar-value terms, Eastern Canada exported to the Caribbean some 69 per cent and imported 94 per cent of the national total. Food and paper products dominated exports to the region when tonnage was considered, while manufactured products and food dominated in terms of dollar value. The primary origin of Caribbean exports from Eastern Canada was the Atlantic region, even though, flour and wheat produced by Nova Scotia were, for example, transhipped from the Canadian prairies. Major imports in 1987 from the Caribbean to Canada included manufactured products, food and aluminum ores, with the primary destination of those imports being Central Canada (Ontario and Quebec).

A comparison of trade between New Brunswick and the Caribbean and Nova Scotia and the Caribbean in 1987 is shown in Table 6.5. Nova Scotia primarily provided bulk service to the region, while New Brunswick provided a more diversified trade in the form of neo-bulks and break-bulk cargoes. The value of exported goods and their tonnages from each province helps to reinforce the findings. Although Nova Scotia ships more tons of cargo to the Caribbean than New Brunswick (209 000 tons versus 138 800), the actual dollar value is considerably lower (54.7 million versus 82.4 million for New Brunswick commodities).

The principal origin of Canadian trade to the Caribbean is Eastern Canada, and among the Atlantic provinces, New Brunswick and Nova Scotia are the primary exporters and importers of Caribbean commodities. This can be expected, given geographical and transportation imperatives. Transportation from Eastern Canada to the Caribbean must include either a water- or an air-borne leg, and in the case of most commodities, the water-borne service is dominant. The Canadian ports of Montreal (decreasing in use due to distance and US intermodal competition), Halifax and Saint John can provide service. Alternative ports lie along the eastern coast of the United States, in particular the port of Miami which is rapidly becoming a major 'hub' for the Caribbean and Latin America. Improved continental intermodal connections (both truck and rail) have resulted in an ever-increasing share of Canadian

Table 6.5   New Brunswick and Nova Scotia trade with the Caribbean, 1987

	New Brunswick	*Nova Scotia*
Exports		
Tonnage (thousand tons)	138.8 (30% of Atl Cdn*)	209.0 (45% of Atl Cdn)
Dollar value (millions)	82.4 (43% of Atl Cdn)	54.7 (28% of Atl Cdn)
Major commodities (tonnage)	paperboard (33%) newsprint (19%) potatoes (16%)	flour/wheat (63%) dimensioned stone (19%) sand (11%)
Major commodities ($ value)	paperboard (26%) newsprint (22%) vegetables (15%)	preserved fish (38%) flour/wheat (33%) milled cereals (18%)
Imports		
Dollar value (millions)	18.6 (36% of Atl Cdn)	23.4 (45% of Atl Cdn)
Major commodities ($ value)	raw & refined sugars (48%) fish (25%) fuel oil (22%)	crude petroleum (85%) steel bars (8%)

* Atl Cdn = Atlantic Canada
Source: M.C. Ircha *et al.* (1989), *Feasibility Study: Consolidation Centre Concept Canadian–Caribbean Trade* (Fredericton, New Brunswick: The Transportation Group, University of New Brunswick, December), Appendix B.

shipments to and from the Caribbean and Latin America being handled through US ports (Clouthier, 1994, pp. 798–812).

CANADIAN–CARIBBEAN CONSOLIDATION CENTRE

In 1989, the Transportation Group at the University of New Brunswick was asked by External Affairs Canada, Atlantic Canada Opportunities Agency, the New Brunswick Department of Commerce and Technology, and the Saint John Port Corporation to evaluate the feasibility of consolidating Canadian–Caribbean traffic at the port of Saint John as a means of combating the growing trend towards commodity diversion through US ports. The study concluded that a consolidation centre was feasible, particularly if additional traffic to and from other Central or South American countries could be brought through Saint John. This facility would enable reasonable volumes of general cargo and other commodities to be assembled easily for shipment. Consolidation could make Saint John attractive to Caribbean-bound carriers using larger vessels (resulting in economies of scale and lower freight rates), with improved service frequency. An essential ingredient for success is marketing Saint John as Canada's primary Caribbean and South American connection.

The port of Saint John has traditionally served as a major Canadian point of entry/exit for Caribbean and other Central and South American trade. In recent years, an increasing volume of Caribbean-bound general cargo has been diverted through southern US ports, as improved intermodal systems have resulted in lower freight rates and improved service, with a concomitant erosion in the viability of the allwater route from Canada to the Caribbean.

The consolidation centre analysis was limited to examining commodity movements to and from Eastern Canada (the four Atlantic provinces of New Brunswick, Nova Scotia, Prince Edward Island and Newfoundland, as well as Quebec and Ontario) and seven Caribbean countries (the Bahamas, Barbados, Cuba, the Dominican Republic, Jamaica, Puerto Rico, and Trinidad and Tobago). The evaluation included Canada–Caribbean trade movements, potential opportunities for enhanced Canadian export trade, transportation system needs, including all relevant modes, consideration of the perspectives of eastern Canadian shippers' on trade with the Caribbean, and consolidation centre operating requirements and options.

Concept

An effective consolidation centre depended upon efficient intermodal transportation. Upon arrival, individual freight packages could be consolidated into full container loads (FCL) for shipment to the Caribbean. Similarly, import shipments could either be transported inland as FCLs and full truck loads (FTLs), or stripped into less than truck load (LTL) size for delivery to nearby destinations. A review of several existing intermodal terminals in Canada, the United States and Sweden revealed that few, if any, served the proposed role of the Saint John facility, that is, consolidation of a wide range of commodities for a specific geographic destination. Normally, such facilities limited the range of goods handled (for example, those specialising in neo-bulk forest products) and distributed them globally.

In the Canadian context, inland consolidation facilities play an important role in the operation of port consolidation centres, permitting containers to be stuffed or stripped at a location closest to their point of origin or destination. As suggested by Brian Slack, inland consolidation centres are typically spaced between 800 and 1400 kilometers apart (1988, pp. 26–30). Trucks serving a 400 to 700 kilometer radius could be used to deliver goods to and from the inland facility; unit trains carrying FCLs on flatcars or on double-stack container trains could then be used to transport the consolidated commodities to the port consolidation centre.

Eastern Canada–Caribbean Trade Analysis

Information provided by Statistics Canada (1987) as well as a special tabulation on exports by water on a tonnage basis were used to determine the extent of commodity movement between Canada and the seven selected Caribbean countries. As previously shown, in 1987 Eastern Canada exported 30 per cent of total Canadian tonnage of products to the Caribbean, which on a dollar-value basis accounted for 70 per cent of all Canadian goods shipped to the region. In 1987, while Cuba was the main recipient of Canadian exports (primarily wheat) per ton, on a dollar-value basis Puerto Rico was the main Caribbean destination of eastern Canadian exports, with 38 per cent of exported goods (primarily manufactured commodities).

The four Atlantic provinces contributed 79 per cent of Eastern Canadian exports to the Caribbean per ton, and 35 per cent on a dollar basis. Major 1987 exports from the Atlantic provinces to the Caribbean on a tonnage basis included:

> flour and wheat (28 per cent)
> newsprint (16 per cent)
> chemicals (13 per cent)
> paperboard (10 per cent)
> potatoes (9 per cent)
> dimensioned stone (9 per cent)

On a dollar value basis, major exports included:

> preserved fish (21 per cent)
> newsprint (21 per cent)
> vegetables (13 per cent)
> other food (13 per cent)
> paperboard (11 per cent)
> flour and wheat (9 per cent)

In 1987, total Canadian imports from the Caribbean were valued at $522 million, compared to $800 million worth of exports. Puerto Rico was the main Caribbean exporter of goods to Canada, with its commodities valued at $217 million, or 43 per cent of total Canadian imports. The major commodities imported by Canada were:

manufactured goods (23 per cent)
aluminum ores (18 per cent), primarily from Jamaica
other foods (17 per cent)

Eastern Canada accounted for 94 per cent of imported Caribbean commodities, with the Atlantic provinces importing some 11 per cent, or approximately $51 million worth of goods.

To establish the potential amount of Caribbean-bound throughput, the vast array of commodities exported from Eastern Canada were examined to determine the amount that could be diverted from current trade routes through the United States and other Canadian ports by means of the Saint John consolidation centre.

Caribbean Trade Analysis and Country Profile

Despite the locational advantage to Canada of Caribbean countries, they have often been overlooked relative to other larger export markets (such as Western Europe and the Far East). As individual island nations, each Caribbean country offers little opportunity, but, as shown in Table 6.6, taken as a whole, the Caribbean Basin provides a relatively large potential market for Canadian exporters. Potential export opportunities for Canadians in the Caribbean were identified by examining the current market-share of Canadian exporters within each sector of the local market, the economic trends and structure of each country, and specific country projections provided by External Affairs Canada. Detailed country-by-country analyses of specific Canadian export opportunities were undertaken in the consolidation centre study.

The Caribbean countries examined have initiated national 'value-added' policies, such as the establishment of import quotas and tariffs along with currency devaluations, to stabilise and enhance their local economies. The primary objective of these policies was to shift from a single commodity-based economy to a more diversified structure. The Caribbean countries' value-added policies provide opportunities for Canadian exporters, as major shipments to the region are raw or unprocessed commodities and machinery equipment – both designed

Table 6.6   Caribbean market size

Country	1994 population (thousands)	GDP (1993) (US$ billions)	GDP per capita (US$)
Bahamas	257	4.4	17 120
Barbados	256	2.2	8 594
Cuba	10 938	13.7	1 253
Dominican Republic	7 948	23.0	2 894
Jamaica	2 574	8.0	3 108
Puerto Rico	3 685	25.3	6 866
Trinidad & Tobago	1 271	10.4	8 183
Total	26 929	87.0	3 231

Source: *The World Almanac and Book of Facts – 1996* (Mahwah, NJ: Funk & Wagnalls, 1995); and *The Europa Yearbook – 1995* (London: Europa Publications 1995).

to bolster the development of indigenous local economies. In addition, as tourism expands and the younger population of the Caribbean continues to grow, the need for construction materials and food will also increase. Canada is in a good position to supply this rising demand from the Caribbean.

Other potential Canadian exports to the Caribbean include semi-processed and finished goods, such as textiles, pharmaceuticals, electronics and transportation equipment. Enhanced Canadian export trade to the Caribbean would further increase potential traffic flow through a Saint John consolidation centre.

Potential Export Traffic through Saint John

To determine the range of potential export traffic through the port of Saint John, optimistic and conservative scenarios were developed, based on existing and potential traffic to the Caribbean. The optimistic scenario assumed that the Saint John consolidation centre could capture 100 per cent of Caribbean-bound bulk commodities from all of Eastern Canada (primarily grains). The conservative scenario limited the potential capture of bulk commodities to 50 per cent.

All 1987 commodities exported from Eastern Canada through all ports (including the United States) were evaluated to determine whether or not they could be diverted through Saint John. Based on the analysis, the potential increase in existing export traffic (including general cargo in the form of containers, neo-bulk forest products, and dry/liquid bulk) at the port of Saint John varied from 104 000 to 170 000 tons, depending on the scenario used. In addition, the potential growth in the Caribbean market based on identified opportunities for Canadian exporters increased the range of total additional exports that could come through Saint John from 140 000 to 207 000 tons. This represents an increase of between 86 and 127 per cent of 1987 Caribbean-bound exports through the port.

Transportation System Analysis

Five transportation system alternatives for the movement of commodities to the Caribbean were evaluated. These included inland transportation from Toronto/Montreal to each of five major ports (Montreal, Saint John, Halifax, New York and Miami), and the subsequent ocean carriage from each of these ports to the Caribbean.

The estimated average transit time for the inland transportation leg to each port is: Saint John/Halifax, one to two days (rail); New York, one day (truck); and Florida, three to five days (rail/truck). The ocean leg of the journey – a variety of ocean shipping services are available – involves the additional time to destination in the Caribbean. The total transportation time for Central Canadian commodities to the Caribbean from Montreal on scheduled services is seven to eight days; Saint John, six to ten days; Halifax, seven to ten days; New York, six days; and Florida, four to eight days (AGB Consultants, 1989) Thus, Saint John/Halifax is one to two days closer to the Caribbean than Montreal, and roughly equal to New York and Florida.

In addition to these improved ocean connections to the Caribbean, initiatives were undertaken to establish a consolidation/distribution centre in Kingston, Jamaica, that would complement the proposed facility in Saint John. The Kingston facility would use Kingston Container Terminals, the port's Free Trade Zone, and enhancement of regional shipping services to various Caribbean and Latin American ports (Ircha and Deans, 1990)

Shippers' Perspectives

A 1989 survey of Eastern Canadian shippers who ship to the Caribbean sought input on their preference of port of export and why Saint John was not being used. It was found that Saint John, Halifax, and Miami were roughly equivalent in terms of preference, attracting about a third of the shippers. Montreal was clearly the port of choice, with 65 per cent of the respondents using it for their Caribbean exports. Many shippers indicated that Montreal was used because of convenience, minimum ground transportation and frequent sailings. The main reasons indicated for not using Saint John were the cost of inland transport to the port, freight forwarders determining optimal routings, and the limited port service. In terms of shipping service, most exporters desired weekly sailings to the Caribbean. Over half of the exporters surveyed (59 per cent) used FCLs for their shipments to the Caribbean; a further 37 per cent exported part loads in LCL shipments.

To change the perceptions of Eastern Canadian shippers, the port of Saint John has to market its function as a Caribbean consolidation centre aggressively and establish itself as the primary Canadian–Caribbean/Latin American connection.

Consolidation Centre Requirements

Using operating data from existing consolidation centres and inland facilities to determine minimum viable throughputs, the cargo handling infrastructure at the port of Saint John was found to be more than adequate to handle the additional traffic generated from Caribbean trade. The annual traffic volumes required for a viable inland load centre and port consolidation centre are 20 000 TEU (twenty-foot unit) and 6000 TEU respectively. Using the conservative scenario for the current and potential Caribbean container and neo-bulk exports through the port of Saint John, the traffic through the consolidation centre could amount to 3800 TEU from Ontario and Quebec, and 17 500 TEU from the maritime provinces. Only a small portion of these containers will require consolidation, as many shippers would use FCLs from their factory gate.

The volume of goods shipped from the maritime provinces may be sufficient to justify a consolidation centre at the port of Saint John. If one-third of the volume required consolidation, the annual throughput in the centre at Saint John would be 5800 TEU, close to the 6000 TEU estimated for economic viability.

The analysis considered only Canadian exports to the Caribbean. However, if imports from the Caribbean to the Atlantic provinces, amounting to about one-third of the region's exports to the Caribbean, were included, such important import data (if available on a tonnage basis) would enhance the overall viability of the proposed consolidation centre. Similarly, if additional traffic destined to other Caribbean and

Central and South American countries were consolidated in Saint John, the operation's viability would be ensured further.

Synopsis

The Canadian Atlantic exports a number of commodities to the Caribbean, mainly food and paper products. Bulk wheat and flour normally are shipped from Halifax and neo-bulk paper products from Saint John. Quebec and Ontario normally ship manufactured goods to the Caribbean. The Atlantic region ships 79 per cent of the export tonnage to the Caribbean, much of it low-value commodities. Quebec and Ontario ship 65 per cent of the exports by value.

In 1987, Eastern Canada exported 12 per cent more products by value to the Caribbean than it imported, with a net trade balance of $61 million. The Atlantic region exported more than three times the amount it imported by value, with a net trade balance of $141 million.

Significant opportunities exist in the Caribbean market for Eastern Canadian exporters, as major exports to the region are raw/unprocessed commodities and machinery equipment (desirable for the 'value-added' policies of Caribbean countries). To thoroughly tap into this important market in several small countries, Canadian exporters will have to completely understand the nature of each individual market within the Caribbean Basin. Many of these nations require small, but frequent, commodity shipments; a consolidation centre in Saint John would satisfy some of this demand. The development of a complementary consolidation–distribution facility in the Caribbean (as proposed in Jamaica) should contribute to developing Canadian–Caribbean trade.

RECENT NEW BRUNSWICK–NOVA SCOTIA INITIATIVES IN THE CARIBBEAN

Whereas, traditionally, there has been a tendency for Canadian exporters to look first to the United States, many are now reconsidering investment opportunities in the Caribbean. Trade liberalisation in the area after the 1989 adoption of CARICOM has made many Caribbean nations an attractive location for Canadian firms. Locating in the Caribbean enables firms (often in joint venture partnerships with indigenous firms) to serve the Caribbean market and explore opportunities for exporting their goods and services to Latin American countries.

The Halifax branch of the World Trade Centre initiated a pilot project in 1993 to determine the feasibility of creating joint ventures between Atlantic Canadian firms and similar organisations in the Caribbean (see Connor, 1994). Eleven Atlantic Canada firms active in a wide range of goods manufacturing and services participated in the pilot project. Company profiles were produced and distributed in the Caribbean, which were followed up with visits to like-minded Caribbean firms, particularly in Trinidad and Barbados. As a result, eight Canadian firms formed joint ventures with Caribbean partners to provide a wide range of goods and services, including computer training, consulting engineering, software development, food equipment manufacturing, foundry services, telecommunications and value-added food processing. Four of these Canadian firms are located in Nova Scotia, three in New Brunswick, and one on Prince Edward Island.

The Caribbean partners sought the export expertise offered by their Canadian partners, who helped them export their goods to other Caribbean nations and to Latin America and provided them with components and services to improve efficiency and competitiveness. The pilot project was a success, and the Canadian participants were themselves surprised at the new business generated by their involvement in the Caribbean. Additionally, the growth in inter-firm relations should lead to increased trade between the Canadian Maritimes and the Caribbean.

In the early 1990s, New Brunswick's Department of Economic Development and Tourism focused on Mexico (see McQuire, 1994). Several trade missions were mounted, the port of Saint John actively sought a direct shipping service between New Brunswick and Mexican ports, and, by 1994, some 50 New Brunswick firms were actively involved in selling goods and services or pursuing opportunities in Mexico. The Province's next target was Latin America and the Caribbean.

The port of Saint John has promoted north–south trade. Kent Lines, the shipping subsidiary of New Brunswick's Irving Corporation, now operates a liner service to Latin America. Using two vessels, Kent Lines offers a biweekly container service from Saint John to Puerto Rico, the Dominican Republic, Jamaica and Central American ports. An additional vessel is used in a three-week container and break-bulk service from Saint John to Puerto Rico, Barbados, Trinidad and Tobago and Venezuela. The port's private sector terminal operators have noted an increase in cargo to and from the Caribbean and Latin America. Brunterm, the port's container terminal facility, handles between 10 000 and 12 000 containers per year to and from the Caribbean (approximately 100 000 to 120 000 tons), and traffic is still growing. There is apparently a Canadian port being developed that specialises in southbound commodities – a successful conclusion to the earlier Canadian–Caribbean consolidation centre study.

Shipping commodities to and from Cuba poses problems for shipping lines. In October 1992, the United States passed the Cuban Democracy Act to strengthen its existing trade embargo against Cuba. Like the contemporary Helms–Burton Law, it also extended US law to other nations. Under Helms–Burton, subsidiaries of US companies in Canada and other nations can be prosecuted if they trade with Cuba. In addition, ships carrying cargo to or from Cuba are prohibited from visiting US ports for a six-month period after visiting the island. Obviously, this causes a serious concern for Canadian coastal vessels that serve both the United States and the Caribbean. In addition, the limitation imposed by the United States on free trade in the Caribbean has forced various shipping lines to discontinue services to Cuba.

CONCLUSION

It is apparent that opportunities for Canadian businesses exist in the Caribbean, which has been a neglected market for some time. Canada's southward trade tendencies are now bringing this region back into focus for many export-oriented Canadian firms. Undoubtedly, historical trade links, particularly between New Brunswick and Nova Scotia and the Caribbean, will encourage increased trade in the contemporary era of trade liberalisation and economic globalism.

In examining the emerging linkages between Canada's Maritime Provinces and the Caribbean, a number of potential research topics have emerged. These include:

1. Emerging trade and joint venture links between Canadian and Caribbean companies, determining obstacles and barriers and uncovering elements necessary for success.
2. Prospects for trade growth not only to the Caribbean but to other Latin American countries, which will help develop strategies that will provide them with adequate services from both Canadian and US ports.
3. The impact on Caribbean trade and economic development of an eventual thaw in relations between Cuba and the United States.

Will the Cuban government in exile in Florida cause a significant shift in trade relations, leaving Canada out of the equation?
4. Opportunities for both Canadian and Caribbean companies to form partnerships, joint ventures or other strategic alliances to mount competitive campaigns to export goods and services to other Latin American countries.
5. The feasibility of further consolidation/distribution services for South–North-bound goods at the port of Saint John.

References

AGB Consultants (1989) *Survey of Eastern Marine Services to Major Caribbean Destinations*. Prepared for the Transportation Division, External Affairs Canada, Ottawa.

Brennan, J. (1993) 'Changing Transportation Patterns', paper presented at Crossroads at the Borders: Trade and Transportation Issues of the Americas, Joint Conference of CIT and ICHCA–Canada, Ottawa, June.

Burns, R. (1987) 'The Effects of a U.S.–Canada Free Trade Agreement', *World Wide Shipping*, vol. 50, no. 7 (October).

Cathcart, P.G. and Q.C. Kakoschke (1992) 'From the North of the Border', *Portus*, vol. 7, no. 2 (Spring).

Clouthier, M. (1994) 'North/South Trade – Transportation Trends between Canada and the Rest of the Americas', *Proceedings*, 29th Annual Canadian Transportation Research Forum, Victoria, British Columbia, May.

Conner, D. (1994) Private communication, Nova Scotia World Trade Centre, Halifax, Nova Scotia, 1 June.

Cubukgil, A., R. Soberman and P. Yee (1988) 'Implications of Free Trade for the Canadian Transportation Industry', from *Proceedings* of the Canadian Transportation Research Forum, 23rd Annual Meeting, Minaki Lodge, Ontario, May.

Europa Publications (1995) *The Europa Yearbook – 1995* (London: Europa Publications).

Finlayson, J.A. (1993) 'Market Opportunities and Limitations', paper presented at Crossroads at the Borders: Trade and Transportation Issues of the Americas, Joint Conference of CIT and ICHCA–Canada, Ottawa, June.

Finlayson, J.A. and S. Bertasi (1992) 'Evolution of Canadian Postwar International Trade Policy', in A.C. Cutler and M.W. Zacher (eds), *Canadian Foreign Policy and International Economic Regimes* (Vancouver: UBC Press).

Funk and Wagnalls (1995) *The World Almanac and Book of Facts – 1996* (Mahway, NJ: Funk & Wagnalls).

GATT (various years) *International Trade – Trends and Statistics* (Geneva: GATT).

Government of Canada (1992) *North American Free Trade Agreement: An Overview and Description* (Ottawa: Government of Canada).

International Monetary Fund (IMF) (various years) *World Economic Outlook* (Washington, DC: International Monetary Fund).

Ircha, M.C., B.G. Bisson, F.R. Wilson and J. Christie (1989) *Feasibility Study: Consolidation Centre Concept for Canadian–Caribbean Trade* (Fredericton, New Brunswick: Transportation Group).

Ircha, M.C. and E. Deans (1990) 'Proactive Port Marketing: Saint John, New Brunswick and Kingston, Jamaica', unpublished paper prepared for *Portus* Award competition. National Transportation Agency (1992) *Annual Review – 1992* (Ottawa: Minister of Supply and Services).

McQuire, F. (1994) 'New Approaches to Doing Business in the Americas', Remarks to the Conference on Hemispheric Trade Liberalization: Assessing the Opportunities', University of New Brunswick, Fredericton, New Brunswick, May.

Office of the Vice President (1993) *National Performance Review* (Washington, DC: National Printing Office).

Pitre, F. (1990) 'To Be or Not to Be: The Impact of North America's Legislative and Regulatory Environment on the Marine Industry', paper presented to the 1990 Joint ICHCA–Canada and ICHCA–USA Conference, Ottawa, September.

Sauvé, P. (1993) 'Trade Policies and Prospects – the Future of NAFTA', paper presented at Crossroads at the Borders: Trade and Transportation Issues of the Americas, Joint Conference of CIT and ICHCA–Canada, Ottawa, June.

Slack, B. (1988) *Locational Determinants of Inland Load Centres* (Ottawa: Transport Canada, Economic Analysis Directorate).

Statistics Canada (1987) *Canadian Export Statistics by Destination Country and Province of Loading*. Special Tabulation (Ottawa: Statistics Canada).

Statistics Canada (1993) *Preliminary Statement of Canadian International Trade – December 1992* (Ottawa: Statistics Canada).

Statistics Canada (1996) *Imports by Country* Catalogue 65–003 (Ottawa: Statistics Canada).

Statistics Canada (1996) *Imports by Country* Catalogue 65–006 (Ottawa: Statistics Canada).

Transport Canada (1987) *A Study of the Competitiveness of Canadian and U.S. Transportation under Free Trade* (Ottawa: Transport Canada).

United Nations (1992) *World Investment Report* (New York: United Nations).

US Department of Transport (1994) *Assessment of Transborder Crossings for North American Trade: A Report to Congress*. Federal Highway Administration, no. FHWA-PL-94-009, Washington, DC.

Vail, B. and J. Bonney (1993) 'A (White) House Divided', *American Shipper*, vol. 35, no. 10 (October).

Yee, P. (1987) *The Competitive Position of Canadian and U.S. Coastal Fleets in a Free Trade Environment* (Ottawa: Transport Canada, International Shipping Policy Branch).

Part III
Caribbean Views

7 Canada–CARICOM Relations since the 1980s: An Overview

Harold Robertson

Relations between Canada and the Caribbean Community and Common Market (CARICOM) countries – Commonwealth Caribbean – are well-established and centuries old. They originate in the years immediately following the American War of Independence, which resulted in the creation of the United States of America as an independent nation when the rejected colonial power, Great Britain, attempted to punish the new nation by excluding it from the lucrative West Indian trade. Imperial policy after 1788 essentially focused on the development of the remaining North American colonies under British control as a replacement for the Untied States as supplier of essential inputs to West Indian islands specialising in the production of sugar.[1]

Since that time, Canada–CARICOM relations have tended to be influenced more by the dynamics of the international environment than by inherent factors salient to either party. This perhaps has been inescapable, given the circumstances surrounding initiation of the relationship, with both regions as colonies and thus subject to a larger design. Another result was an overemphasis on the economic aspects of the relationship: political considerations were to become manifest only in the post-1960 era when the West Indian islands began to emerge as independent countries.

Early Canadian involvement in the Caribbean revolved around private sector initiatives and religious expeditions, especially those of Canadian Presbyterians who were trying to convert East Indian populations in Trinidad, Grenada and British Guiana, among others. Canadian private investment was in such areas as banking, mining (especially bauxite) and retail trade. The first official effort to establish a formal framework for the development of relations addressed, not surprisingly, trade relations between Canada and the English-speaking Caribbean. In 1898, the Canadian government unilaterally decided to adopt a policy of preferential treatment for certain West Indian products

131

entering the Canadian market, among which was raw and refined sugar.

In 1911, a Canada–British West Indies Economic Conference convened in Ottawa. Out of this conference the Canada–West Indies Reciprocity Treaty emerged, which went into force in 1912. The treaty governed economic relations between Canada and the British West Indies until 1925, at which time a Canada–West Indies Trade Agreement was signed following a Canada–West Indian conference that year. The 1925 agreement elaborated a regime for reciprocal preferential access to each market for selected regional products and served, with amendments and adjustments as needed, as the bedrock for Canada–West Indian relations for some sixty years.

The 1925 agreement extended preferential rates in the Canadian market to such Caribbean products as sugar, rum, angostura bitters, bananas, cocoa beans, cocoa butter, limes, arrowroot, coconuts, grapefruits, pineapples, coffee, spices, nutmegs and mace. Significantly, the East Indies granted preferential treatment to Canadian flour, apples, salted and pickled beef, boots and shoes, butter, cement, cheese, lard, condensed milk, salted or pickled pork, lumber, as well as canned, preserved, dried, salted, smoked and pickled fish.

The first comprehensive review of the agreement was undertaken in 1966 when, at the special Canada–Commonwealth Caribbean Prime Ministers' Conference convened in Ottawa, a protocol to the agreement was adopted, creating a new regime for entry of sugar into Canada and providing for the establishment of a Commonwealth Caribbean–Canada/Trade and Economic Committee to consult on trade, finance and related matters. The protocol proved short-lived. It was unilaterally terminated by Canada in 1970 and replaced by a Canadian $5 million fund for agricultural development. The Canadian decision to terminate the protocol added a sour note to what until then had been a harmonious relationship. Evidence of cordiality had been the immediate establishment of formal diplomatic relations and the exchange of high commissions between newly-independent CARICOM countries and Canada during the 1960s. Canada's membership in the commonwealth and its role in international affairs where it had acquired a reputation for being sympathetic to the aspirations of the developing world combined with its long tradition of interaction with the West Indies to become a valued friend to the new nations. In this context, the 1970 abandonment of the protocol and the manner in which it was implemented were a serious disappointment to CARICOM leaders.

In spite of Canadian generosity towards the Commonwealth Caribbean, relations between Canada and CARICOM in the 1970s declined to possibly their lowest level. For example, during the visit of Canadian Prime Minister Pierre Trudeau to Port of Spain in April 1975, the Prime Minister of Trinidad and Tobago refused to meet Mr Trudeau at the airport and to participate in a joint press conference. Discussions, which were behind closed doors, clearly did not please the Prime Minister of Trinidad and Tobago, who later acerbically commented, 'The simple fact of the matter is that Canada, whose first real economic progress was stimulated by its West Indian connections, has outgrown the West Indies ... Everybody knows this except the West Indies' (Williams, 1975).

Poor relations were accompanied by a decline in trade. While world trade expanded during the 1960s and 1970s, it was natural that with a growing international presence and outlook, the value of Caribbean trade within the overall Canadian trade picture would decline. What was not anticipated, however, was the extent and rapidity of that decline. During the 1950s, Canadian trade accounted for approximately 17 per cent of total Caribbean trade, but by the 1970s that share had shrunk to 9 per cent, and in 1980 Canada accounted for a meager 5 per cent of CARICOM trade (see Basdeo, 1993, p. 12).

At the end of the 1970s, an array of factors began to encourage both Canada and the Commonwealth to take a fresh look at their positions in the world and relations between themselves. The economic decline affected not only the Caribbean, but Canada as well: rising unemployment, declining GDP and increasing external debt buffeted the Canadian economy, bringing in its wake unprecedented political instability. The Liberal Party, led by Trudeau, had been victorious in the 1968, 1972 and 1974 elections, but was defeated in 1979 by the Progressive Conservatives led by Joe Clark. The Clark administration lasted nine months, after which the Liberals returned to office in 1980. Pierre Trudeau resigned as Prime Minister in June 1984, and the Liberal government was voted out of office by the Progressive Conservatives, led by Brian Mulroney, in September of that year. Uncommon instability characterised the period.

Matters in the Caribbean were equally, if not more, unstable. The oil crisis had devastated many economies. Ideological flirtations by Jamaica and the rise of an unconstitutional, revolutionary government in Grenada threatened to enmesh the Caribbean in the sterile Cold War, while the menace of drug trafficking, drug abuse, and, in some cases, drug production had begun to penetrate the social and political fabric of the region. The peculiar vulnerabilities of small states were becoming more evident to a wider, larger world. And as these developments manifested themselves, another element was beginning to gain momentum and to exert influence on the evolution of relations between Canada and the Caribbean. Since the mid-1950s, West Indians had begun to emigrate to several developed countries, including Canada, and the West Indian community in Canada was becoming established at all levels of society, including the corridors of political power and influence. By the 1980s, the West Indian community in Canada totalled some 140 000 (Basdeo, 1993, p. 12). During the decade of the 1980s that figure increased dramatically, and by 1992 was estimated at between 400 000 and 500 000 (Campbell, 1992, p. 3). Indeed, during the 1980s the influx of CARICOM citizens into Canada constituted a point of irritation between Canada and CARICOM. It had become clear by 1979 that new measures were needed to restore Canada–CARICOM relations to former levels of cordiality, and to enable both partners to face what appeared to be a challenging future.

The first initiative was the convening in Jamaica in January 1979 of a Canada–CARICOM conference, the first high-ranking meeting between Canada and the Commonwealth Caribbean since the Ottawa meeting of 1966. The most important outcome of that conference was the signing of the Canada–CARICOM Trade and Economic Cooperation Agreement in 1979, which replaced the 1925 Canada–West Indies Trade Agreement and its 1966 amending protocol. The new agreement was designed to provide a comprehensive framework for trade, financial, technical and industrial cooperation between Canada and CARICOM member states and to prove a more effective vehicle for the conduct of relations in the final quarter of the twentieth century. One major innovation agreed upon at the 1979 conference was the establishment of a Joint Trade and Economic Committee (JTEC), which would form the paramount institutional body to implement the agreement and which would meet at regular intervals to assess progress and implement such changes as agreed.

The second initiative on Canada's part was a review of its policy towards CARICOM. That review commenced in 1980, and the results were highlighted by then Canadian Secretary of State for External Affairs, Mark McGuigan, in a statement to the Second JTEC session held in Kingston, Jamaica, in 1981. Canada's new policy was governed by the realisation that the Commonwealth Caribbean was 'a region of major interest to Canada', making it essential that 'Canada intensify and deepen its economic and political relationships with the states of the Commonwealth Caribbean'. The essential, practical elements of the new policy were:

1. Special priority to be accorded CARICOM within the context of an increase in Canada's global development assistance;
2. a 100 per cent increase in aid flows to the region over the following five years (dependent upon the 'absorptive capacity of the region');
3. emergency balance of payments assistance, to be made available to regional countries with an agreed International Monetary Fund (IMF) remedial programme, such assistance to be additional to regular allocations;
4. greater emphasis on the maintenance of economic, social and political stability and the promotion of sustained economic development and growth;
5. particular attention to the development needs of LDC (least developed country) states of the Eastern Caribbean;
6. consideration to decentralising Canadian International Development Agency (CIDA) operations, to ensure a more rapid disbursement of development assistance funds and to improve the effectiveness of programme development;
7. provision of increased levels of technical assistance concentrated on economic and financial management in the public sector and production areas in the private sector;
8. provision of Canadian $1 million per year, at highly concessional rates, for the engagement of Canadian advisers to assist in industrial development planning and implementation;
9. assistance in computerisation; and
10. readiness 'to do a great deal more to enhance the vital contribution of the private sector to the objectives of our joint trade and economic cooperation'.

Secretary McGuigan also referred specifically to the perceived security needs of the region. He informed the meeting that Canada was:

1. prepared to offer training in civil emergency planning to deal with disasters, such as hurricanes, volcanic eruptions, oil spills and epidemics, either to CARICOM as a whole or to individual countries;
2. prepared to accept a modest increase in the number of candidates for military and police training on a space-available basis at appropriate Canadian institutions; and

3. prepared to accept a modest number of candidates for coast-
    guard training on a space-available basis (McGuigan, 1981).

Later in 1981, during the Commonwealth Heads of Government
Meeting in Melbourne, Australia (a meeting at which the author was a
representative of Trinidad and Tobago), Prime Minister Trudeau himself launched another initiative. At a luncheon with heads of delegation
from the Commonwealth Caribbean, he proposed the convening of a
summit of heads of government of Canada and the Commonwealth
Caribbean states. CARICOM leaders were receptive of the invitation,
after considering the matter at their Jamaica Summit in Ocho Rios in
1982. It may be noted that the proposal was made to CARICOM leaders only after the death of Prime Minister Williams of Trinidad and
Tobago in March 1981.

If the proposal for convening a Canada–CARICOM summit had not
been made and accepted as a separate aspect of the thrust to improve
relations, implementation of the new policy as announced by Secretary
McGuigan would probably have had the same result. CARICOM's disappointment with the policy's practical implementation was soon obvious. In preparing for the summit, one CARICOM high commissioner
in Ottawa lamented 'In general, very slow progress has been reported
in obtaining funding approval from Canada' for projects identified as
important by CARICOM countries. He attributed this difficulty to the
failure of CIDA to institute financing arrangements that could lead to
speedy approval. He went on to note that in spite of 'honeyed words'
about the development of human resources, it was clear that the Canadians were primarily concerned with the development of Canadian
human resources and not those of CARICOM. Promises of assistance
for social development were largely symbolic, since profits were not to
be made there. He went on to say that, instead, the Canadian private
sector was being encouraged both by CIDA and by the Department of
Industry, Trade and Commerce to move massively into the Caribbean,
essentially to trade and invest.

It was to be admitted that, on the CARICOM side, requests for
assistance or the projects submitted for funding were not always models of cohesiveness and appropriate management and follow-through.
The general impression garnered by CARICOM countries was that
Canadian authorities evaded firm commitments, avoided meaningful
involvement in projects determined to be important by CARICOM,
and that in the event a sound proposal was placed on the table, the
response invariably was that it needed further clarification. It was in

this atmosphere of pervasive disappointment that the Summit Meeting of Western Hemispheric Commonwealth Countries was held in St Lucia on 20–21 February 1983. It was the most widely attended meeting of its kind, and included the heads of government of territories such as the British Virgin Islands, the Turks and Caicos Islands and Anguilla, which were not independent countries. The only notable absentee was Guyana. In essence, the meeting was a major disappointment.

At the meeting, Caribbean leaders raised issues of substantial concern. Prime Minister Edward Seaga of Jamaica called for 'a comprehensive program of aid, trade, and investment to guarantee socioeconomic stability in the region' (Seaga, 1983). Chairman of the meeting, Prime Minister John Compton of St Lucia, stated the case for the Organisation of Eastern Caribbean States, lamented the negative responses of major industrialised countries to the crisis, and outlined the role that Canada could play in ameliorating the situation (Compton, 1983a). Prime Minister George Chambers of Trinidad and Tobago surveyed a number of issues affecting trade between Canada and the region (Chambers, 1983), and in reply Prime Minister Trudeau offered 'reflections on the global environment', praised regional leaders for their attention to fundamental rights and freedoms and maintenance of democratic values, and promised to increase Canadian aid to the region to Canadian $250 million by 1987 (Trudeau, 1983).

Pressed for an assessment of the meeting at a press conference following its conclusion, the Chairman, Prime Minister Compton, launched into a semantic monologue, expounding the differences between the Commonwealth Caribbean Community and the Commonwealth Caribbean Common Market, and referred assembled media to the innocuous communique.[2]

Meanwhile, Prime Minister Seaga of Jamaica had been persistent in advocating the need for a mini-Marshall Plan for the Caribbean. Also bringing the suggestion to the attention of US President Ronald Reagan, Seaga saw the introduction of increased capital inflows as a counter to creeping social and political instability in the region. At the JTEC meeting in January 1981, he called for the injection of some US$900 million into the region. The US response was the creation of the Caribbean Basin Initiative (CBI), announced in February 1982 and going into effect on 1 January 1984.

Shortly after assuming power in September 1984, Canada's new Prime Minister, Brian Mulroney, visited the Caribbean in February of the following year. At a summit with CARICOM leaders in Kingston,

Jamaica, Prime Minister Seaga proposed that Canada could develop its own programme for CARICOM along the lines of the CBI. Reaction to the proposal from the new Canadian administration was positive, signalling its intent to introduce its own package during the Commonwealth Summit held in Nassau, Bahamas, in October 1985. The new programme was to supersede both the 1979 Canada–CARICOM Trade and Economic Cooperation Agreement and the CARICOM policy outlined by Secretary of State McGuigan in 1981. The programme has come to be known as CARIBCAN. Coming into effect on 1 June 1986, CARIBCAN was initiated as a non-reciprocal arrangement, allowing a majority of CARICOM exports into Canada free of duty. It was designed to enhance bilateral commercial relations between Canada and CARICOM states; improve the export performance of the Commonwealth Caribbean; promote economic growth, development and new investment in the region; and encourage regional cooperation and integration.

The main feature of CARIBCAN was the extension of preferential duty-free access to the Canadian market for a wide range of CARICOM products, excluding textiles, clothing, footwear, luggage, handbags, leather garments, lubricating oils and methanol. The package also included measures to foster Canadian investment and industrial cooperation with the region, specifically through seminars and workshops for businesspeople as well as those from the state sector connected with trade. Canadian authorities had attached no time limit to the programme, but since CARIBCAN conflicted with Canada's GATT obligations, a waiver had to be obtained for implementation of the programme. The GATT waiver, approved in November 1986, provided for a 12-year duration (until 1998), after which Canada would be required to seek an extension.

Rules of origin were established to determine which CARICOM products would quality for duty-free treatment under CARIBCAN. In order to be eligible, the goods were to have been grown, produced and manufactured in the Commonwealth Caribbean, but they could incorporate materials or components from outside the region if certain conditions were met. A minimum of 60 per cent of the ex-factory price of the goods was to have originated in one of the beneficiary countries or Canada. This amount could include product labour costs, research, development, design, engineering and blueprint costs, and inspection and testing costs. Overhead expenses, profits and export packaging costs were also included. In addition, local value amounts could be cumulated among the countries of the region, thus allowing CARICOM to be treated as a single country for purposes of meeting rules-of-origin requirements.

Transportation provisions were also elaborated. To be eligible for CARIBCAN treatment, products were to be imported directly from the export country or pass in transit through an intermediate country. While in transit, the goods were to remain under customs control and undergo no operations other than reloading, division of loads, or operations required to maintain the products in good condition. Two additional features of CARIBCAN are worthy of mention. First, the programme contained a built-in safeguard provision by which the facility for duty-free entry of any product could be withdrawn or suspended where the product 'caused or threatened to cause injury' to a Canadian product. Second, CARIBCAN also contained a built-in provision for a review after two years of operation, following which provisions were subject to amendment.[3]

The introduction of CARIBCAN drew a welcome, though cautious, response from CARICOM representatives. Concern was expressed regarding several factors that CARICOM leaders felt could negate the optimal operation of the programme. One concern was that products excluded from duty-free treatment were precisely those for which CARICOM had developed production expertise and capacity, and their exclusion severely compromised the stated intent of the programme. Second, preferential treatment did not extend to the waiver of non-tariff barriers, which govern the importation and sale of goods in Canada. Thus CARICOM exporters remained subject to sales taxes, excise duties, packaging and labelling regulations, standards and safety regulations that could be manipulated conveniently, intellectual property regulations, health regulations and other import controls. In spite of limitations, regional leaders placed CARIBCAN in the same category with such pacts as the Lomé Convention and the CBI, which provided CARICOM business with entry into the European Economic Community (EEC) and US markets, respectively.

CARICOM expectations that the CARIBCAN programme would result in a significant increase in exports to Canada were to be answered with serious disappointment during CARIBCAN's initial operation. The trade balance between Canada and CARICOM remained heavily skewed in Canada's favour. CARICOM figures suggested that in 1985 the imbalance totalled EC $175.2 million, in favour of Canada. In 1987 it was $217.9 million, and in 1988 $198.9 million. As the figures would suggest, the majority of CARICOM member-states continued to record negative balances of trade with Canada after the introduction of CARIBCAN. Trinidad and Tobago and Barbados had the largest deficits, while Jamaica and Guyana were the only countries to record favourable balances on their trade with Canada during the period.

Canada's experience was somewhat different. Canadian exports to the Commonwealth Caribbean in 1985 totalled EC$584.7 million. In 1986 there was a drop to $576.3 million, but for 1987 and 1988 the figures increased to $638.8 and $678 million, respectively (CARICOM Secretariat, 1992). CARIBCAN had enhanced Canada's export performance to CARICOM, but as far as its stated intention of encouraging an increased quantity of CARICOM exports to Canada was concerned, CARIBCAN had failed.

The Caribbean's disappointment with CARIBCAN was exacerbated by Canada's development of a hard-line immigration policy. For most of the developing world, the decade of the 1980s was one of economic decline and even marginalisation, a process accompanied by a phenomenal growth in external debt. As CARICOM economies contracted, their citizens increasingly began to seek other outlets for their labour. CARICOM residents were familiar with the strictures of migration to the United States and Great Britain; Canada, however, employed different systems. Caribbean citizens, in the main, did not require visas for entry, and, moreover, the refugee policy was probably the most lenient in the developed world. As CARICOM economies contracted, thousands flocked to Canada, remained illegally, and, when apprehended, claimed refugee status knowing that the deportation process was difficult and time-consuming. In fact, Canadian authorities began to place immigration restrictions on CARICOM citizens, especially from Guyana, Jamaica, and Trinidad and Tobago. In the last case, strict visa requirements were imposed beginning in December 1988.

It was in this atmosphere of declining cordiality that the first review of CARIBCAN was conducted in Ottawa on 7 October 1988. The meeting was attended by representatives from the Canadian Department of External Affairs (Caribbean and Central American Trade Division), individual CARICOM states, and the CARICOM Secretariat. The CARICOM team was well prepared, important issues were ventilated, and agreement was reached on regional positions. CARICOM representatives proceeded to dissect virtually every aspect of CARIBCAN. The first area of discussion were rules of origin. The meeting identified the 60 per cent local content requirement as too restrictive and requested its reduction to 35 per cent, in line with the CBI. It was also suggested that inputs from either Canada or the United

States in the production of CARICOM goods should be included as part of local value-added, in view of the imminence of the signing of the US–Canada Free Trade Agreement. CARICOM representatives pointed out that the establishment of this pact meant that inputs produced in either country could be imported into the other free of duty. Therefore, the rationale for the maintenance of differentiation between Canadian inputs and US inputs would be invalidated by the free trade agreement.

CARICOM then dealt with exclusions, arguing that they constituted a major flaw in CARIBCAN since excluded articles represented a significant proportion of CARICOM production but, regardless, could hardly do injury to Canadian producers. They also observed that the safeguard provisions and the threat of Voluntary Restraint Agreements (VRAs) combined to lessen the effectiveness of CARIBCAN as a stimulus to economic growth in the region. In addition, attention was drawn to items such as phonographic masters, polypropylene ropes and polyethylene bags, which should have been exempt from duty but were not because of problems with customs classification.

The problems surrounding the sale of rum, a major long-standing West Indian export commodity, were again explored. The Canadian system of marketing liquor effectively established a network of non-tariff barriers that severely hampered rum exports to Canada. CARICOM representatives requested an amendment to Canadian legislation and the discontinuance of discriminating mark-ups that rendered CARICOM rum less competitive on the Canadian market.

CARICOM representatives claimed that the investment component of CARIBCAN was dormant. They suggested that Canada consider the introduction of a programme similar to the US 807 special access programme for garments, under which clothing produced in the Caribbean from cloth woven and cut in the United States was admitted free of duty. This type of programme could help to ameliorate chronic unemployment in the region. With regard to direct investment, CARICOM suggested that the Canadian government extend the same conditions to Canadian investors in CARICOM as were extended to those investing in Canada, that a venture-capital fund be created to finance investment in CARIBCAN beneficiary states, and that a soft-window facility for loans to Canadian entrepreneurs willing to invest in CARICOM be created.

CARICOM representatives also expressed their concern that the US–Canada FTA could erode certain preferences, especially on CARICOM rum with the entry of the US Virgin Islands and Puerto Rican

rum into the Canadian market. They requested that CARICOM beneficiaries under CARIBCAN be placed at no disadvantage *vis-à-vis* US
exporters of similar products. Finally, CARICOM representatives suggested that an on-going mechanism for joint review of CARIBCAN's
operation could be established via the JTEC. The JTEC would then have
as one of its mandates the review and improvement of CARIBCAN.

Only one of these suggestions found favour with Canada: that the JTEC
has the responsibility of reviewing the operation of and making recommendations for the improvement of CARIBCAN. The Canadians
undertook to 'review' all other ideas proposed by the CARICOM representatives. The Ottawa meeting thus produced no concrete results
since Canada avoided making a firm commitment (CARICOM, 1988).

At the fifth JTEC meeting, held in Trinidad and Tobago in March
1989, progress was made with regard to one item: rum. Canada agreed
that rum with 98.5 per cent CARICOM content, blended in Canada,
could be labelled as a product of its CARICOM parent distiller. The
practice of differential markups, raised at Ottawa, had been discon-
tinued since 1 January 1989. It was also reported that a new protocol on
rum was being prepared for consideration between Canada and CARI-
COM. With the exception of the breakthrough on rum, the 1988
Ottawa review of CARIBCAN and the 1989 JTEC session produced
precious little. Official-level discussion had failed, and CARICOM representatives came to the conclusion that resolution of difficulties could
only be reached at a higher level. Accordingly, an initiative was taken
up in June 1989, when, at a special meeting to commemorate the
twenty-fifth anniversary of the Group of 77, the question of a minister-
ial-level meeting to review CARIBCAN was broached. Initially, the
Canadian minister responsible for trade appeared to be reluctant to
interfere in the JTEC process. Other events conspired to place the
issue on the back burner.

Concerned about what appeared to be a stalemate in efforts to
improve CARIBCAN, an apparent deterioration in what had for so
long been described as a special relationship, and uncertain continued
aid flows because of a severe depression in the Canadian economy,
CARICOM leaders felt that the time had come for another summit
between Canadian leaders and themselves. Diplomatic initiatives
proved successful when Prime Minister Mulroney agreed to meet with
CARICOM leaders during the first quarter of 1990. It was clear that
this meeting also held attraction for the Canadian leader. Canada's
major trade initiative in the region was already characterised as a
dismal failure; its position in the Caribbean market was in decline,

anti-Canada sentiment was developing over Canada's immigration policies; new issues were emerging on the international agenda, including
the environment, an issue on which Canada needed regional support in
her battle with the United States; and the Uruguay round of GATT had
failed. If CARICOM leaders were the ones to request the meeting,
they might have just beaten Canada in doing so.

The third meeting of heads of government of the Commonwealth
Caribbean and Canada took place in Barbados on 19 and 20 March
1990. In his keynotes address, Prime Minister Mulroney ensured that
the meeting would be a resounding success and would result in restoration of a warm, cordial relationship between Canada and CARICOM
states. Prime Minister Mulroney plunged straight into the heart of the
matter. He announced the establishment of a US$2.5 million Canadian
programme for the enhancement of the operational safety and physical
maintenance of Caribbean airports; a five-year $10 million Canadian
project for the University of the West Indies; an increase in official
development assistance for the Caribbean by 5 per cent annually for the
years 1991 and 1992, giving assurance that the Caribbean would not
suffer from Canada's commitments to Eastern Europe; and cancellation of all outstanding official debt owed to Canada by CARICOM
countries, totalling approximately Canadian $182 million.

In regard to CARIBCAN, Prime Minister Mulroney told his audi-
ence that Canada would permit the bottling in-bond of Caribbean rum
with minimal blending of Canadian spirits, that he would give serious
thought to establishing an 807-type programme for garments, and that
leather luggage and certain vegetable fibre products would be included
on the list of products eligible for preferential treatment in CARIB-
CAN. He also announced that Canada would host two Caribbean
investment conferences, one in Toronto and the other in Montreal, in
April 1991, and would establish a new industrial cooperation office for
the Caribbean in Ottawa at a cost of $1 million Canadian. He acknow-
ledged that further improvements to CARIBCAN were necessary and
promised to continue to seek feasible ways of achieving that end.

In other areas, Prime Minister Mulroney said that Canada would be
undertaking a number of multilateral and bilateral initiatives to expand
cooperation in the fight against drugs; would support a proposal taken
by Trinidad and Tobago before the United Nations for the establishment of an international criminal court; promised to urge Canada's G-7
partners to follow its lead in cancelling official debt owed by developing
countries; and advised regional leaders to begin developing new
regional trade strategies to cope with the challenges posed by the

dynamic events in the international arena.[4] Prime Minister Mulroney's promises represented significant Canadian concessions to CARICOM, particularly the cancellation of its official debt. Improvements in CARIBCAN were not everything that Caribbean leaders wanted, although they did show the progress made from the previous stalemate that had given rise to requests for the summit. Taken as a whole, however, the trade and aid package, as announced, heralded the unveiling of a new Canadian policy towards the fostering of economic development in CARICOM. In the 1990s, Canadian policy would emphasise the primacy of the private sector as the engine of growth and that, in terms of the direction of cooperation with the region, private sector initiatives would replace public sector or government-to-government arrangements.

CARICOM leaders were disarmed by Mulroney's tour de force. Certainly, outstanding issues remained, and they were ventilated, but the Canadian leader's pronouncements had anticipated and preempted many CARICOM concerns. The representatives of Dominica and Antigua and Barbuda called for the formalisation and upgrading of CARIBCAN to the level of a treaty. Proposals made at the 1988 Ottawa meeting for the investment component of CARIBCAN to be enhanced were repeated. Other discussions touched upon Haiti, South Africa, Canadian membership in the Organisation of American States (OAS), and Cuba. At the conclusion of the meeting the leaders issued the Barbados Declaration, by which they resolved to expand cooperation in matters relating to trade, investment and human resources development, and declared their firm intent to maintain and strengthen the special relationship that existed between their governments and peoples.

CARICOM leaders also welcomed Canada's decision to become a full member of the OAS. They viewed this decision as one that would make the organisation stronger and more effective, especially in its efforts to bolster democracy in the hemisphere. Furthermore, Canada could play a pivotal role in softening the often confrontational positions adopted by Latin American countries on the one hand, and the United States on the other. They expressed the hope that Canada and CARICOM countries could cooperate effectively within the OAS. In the main, Prime Minister Mulroney's promises were honoured. The official debt was cancelled with Jamaica, which was the largest beneficiary among CARICOM states, and investment promotion conferences were held in Toronto and Montreal on 23 and 25 April 1991, respectively. No progress has been made, however, on the establishment of an 807-type programme for garments. One analyst has suggested that such a programme could be suicidal for any Canadian political leader in view of the situation in Quebec (Basdeo, 1993, p. 33).

Since the Canada–Caribbean Business Cooperation Office was opened in April 1990, it has been regarded with concern since it was discovered that the office is essentially the brainchild of the Canadian Exporters Association. In view of the already advantageous position that Canada enjoyed in the CARICOM market, an office created by Canadian exporters appeared unlikely to encourage CARICOM exports to Canada.

The decade of the 1980s was the most intense period for Canada–CARICOM interaction, since relations between Canada and the West Indies were launched within the context of the old colonial system. The 1979 Canada–CARICOM Trade and Economic Cooperation Agreement set the relationship on a course that emphasised the role of the states in the conduct of the interaction and established the JTEC, which continues its work, albeit within an amended framework. Significantly, three summit meetings were held during the decade, indicating the concern that problems between the regions aroused among leaders. The elaboration and implementation of CARIBCAN was an attempt at ensuring that the special relationship, especially its commercial component, survived challenges from arrangements initiated by other countries, notably the CBI and Lomé. CARIBCAN represented a certain level of security of access to the Canadian market, crucial to long-term planning for development and growth. As the 1980s drew to a close, the 1990s would open with the collapse of communism, the discrediting of socialism as an economic ideology, and the apparent triumph of the market as the dominant economic theory. Structural adjustment became the order of the period for the majority of developing countries, including CARICOM.

Prime Minister Mulroney's decisions in Barbados were welcome music to debt-stricken CARICOM ears, but, viewed as a package, they revealed a subtle shift in Canadian policy – a shift in keeping with the prevailing orthodoxy – development and growth, fired by the private sector and the magic of the marketplace. But even as this policy was being emplaced and before the Caribbean had time to fashion an appropriate response, a new threat to their hard-won improved access to the Canadian market was emerging in the form of the North American Free Trade Agreement (NAFTA).

In essence, NAFTA proposed to link Canada, the United States and Mexico as a massive free trade conurbation, a linkage that CARICOM immediately realised could erase the potential benefits available under

CARIBCAN. Canada attempted to downplay such concerns, however. The Honorable Mr Michael Wilson, Minister of Industry, Science and Technology, and Minister for International Trade in the Canadian government, assured high commissioners of CARICOM countries in Canada that Canada's membership in NAFTA 'will in no way change the beneficial access arrangement the Commonwealth Caribbean enjoys with Canada'.[5] He pointed out, however, that the government of Canada was of the view that 'trade liberalization, not continuance of various kinds of preferences...will lead more quickly and efficiently to higher levels of prosperity'.

CARICOM governments could not afford such sanguinity. The reality was that while CARIBCAN provided duty-free access to the Canadian market for some 98 per cent of CARICOM products, the problem lay with the 2 per cent that remained excluded. Since that 2 per cent comprised mainly products that CARICOM countries were best placed to produce, NAFTA would provide Mexico with the huge advantage of duty-free access for precisely those CARICOM products that were excluded under CARIBCAN. Thus, the non-exclusionary aspect of NAFTA provided duty-free entry into Canada for Mexican methanol, while Trinidad and Tobago's methanol remained excluded under CARIBCAN. The same observation applied to lubricating oils, textiles, garments, leather goods and footwear. Furthermore, NAFTA threatened to derail CARICOM because of rules-of-origin restrictions. Rules of origin applicable to Mexico under NAFTA were 100 per cent domestic content, defined as of US, Canadian or Mexican origin, or any combination thereof. CARICOM states operated under a 60 per cent threshold, which, while theoretically lower than the Mexican level, was more difficult to achieve. A Mexican manufacturer could import any amount of raw material from the United States or Canada, process it in Mexico and export the finished product to Canada, qualifying for duty-free entry under NAFTA. A comparable CARICOM company could not enjoy entry under the CARIBCAN rules of origin if more than 40 per cent of the product was comprised of raw material sourced from Canada.

CARICOM leaders were acutely aware of these looming problems if only because CARIBCAN, after its inauspicious beginning, had begun to show signs that it could fulfil its mission. Beginning in 1992, the performance of CARICOM exports to Canada recorded a marked improvement over other years. In 1991, CARICOM exported just under Canadian $200 million to Canada, but that figure increased to $300.4 million in 1993 and $513.5 in 1994. What was more encouraging was that the composition of the export product had also begun to change. CARICOM exports to Canada traditionally had been alumina, sugar, rum, petroleum oils, bauxite and inedible molasses. As late as 1990, these commodities accounted for approximately 81 per cent of the region's exports to Canada, but, by 1994, they amounted to only 40 per cent. Other goods – non-traditional goods – were rapidly gaining ascendancy, among them gold (from Guyana), methanol, iron and steel bars and rods, fertilizers (urea), electronic integrated circuits, lamp-holders, plugs and sockets, and fresh foodstuffs. Methanol from Trinidad and Tobago was still excluded from duty-free entry under CARIBCAN but entered Canada via a special arrangement through the United States.

Improvement was not in one direction only. Canadian exports to the region also increased, from Canadian $268.2 million in 1992 to $310 million in 1993 and $317.3 million in 1994. The main commodities imported from Canada consisted of electrical lines, telephone and telegraph equipment, printing and writing paper and paperboard, manufactured fertilizers, fresh or chilled potatoes, medicine, dried, salted and canned fish and wheat. It was this promising scenario that was threatened by the onset of NAFTA and its inherent Mexican dimension. The situation was rendered more unstable by the unprecedented political turbulence that beset all of the major players in the first half of the 1990s.

In the United States, 12 years of Republican government ended in 1992 with the electoral victory of the Democratic candidate, William Clinton. The Clinton administration rapidly made policies that impacted upon trade and political relations in the hemisphere. First, at the Summit of the Americas in Miami in December 1994, the United States proposed, and won agreement for, the formation of the Free Trade Area of the Americas to come into existence by 2005. Then came Congress' passage of the Helms–Burton Act that provided for US extraterritorial jurisdiction over companies that conducted business with Cuba. Its passage was almost universally condemned, not least by both Canada and CARICOM.

Canada, too, was experiencing its own political upheavals. The Mulroney administration had lost popular support, and, in an effort to shore up its waning popularity, the Conservative Party replaced Mulroney with Kim Campbell. Interestingly, Campbell, taking the party almost immediately into a general election, outlined a new programme of action that the party would pursue if re-elected. Among its promises was the establishment of 'a blue-ribbon Commission to study and make recommendations on the issue of enhancing economic relations between Canada and Latin America and the Commonwealth Caribbean' (*The Globe and Mail*, 1993). Campbell's blandishments cut no ice with the Canadian electorate. The Liberals, led by Jean Chretien, recorded a resounding victory, consigning the Conservatives to virtual political oblivion. Prime Minister Chrétien, however, had little time to reflect upon world or even hemispheric matters; his immediate objective was to head off another threat of Québecois separation from the rest of Canada. A referendum on the issue was scheduled for October 1994, feelings on both sides of the long-running issue were extremely high, and, for the new Prime Minister it was a matter of the greatest priority. During the event, the very closely run referendum left the country intact.

In CARICOM, the political winds of change were also manifest. The composition of its leadership by the mid-1990s had changed radically from 1990. Michael Manley in Jamaica retired due to poor health, which ushered in the administration of P.J. Patterson. In Trinidad and Tobago, Patrick Manning emerged as the country's new Prime Minister following the elections of 1991, and the country was to elect yet another Prime Minister, Basdeo Panday, in 1995. In Barbados, Owen Arthur's Barbados Labour Party won power from the Democratic Labourites. In Antigua and Barbuda, the venerable V.C. Bird, into his 80s, handed over power to his son, Lester. In the Bahamas, Hubert Ingraham replaced Sir Lynden Pindling. In Belize, power alternated between George Price and Manuel Esquivel. Dr Cheddi Jagan won the presidency in Guyana, replacing Desmond Hoyte. Dr Denzil Douglas emerged as the new Prime Minister of St Kitts and Nevis. In Dominica, when Dame Eugenia Charles retired as Prime Minister, her party declined, and Edison James assumed office. Similarly, Grenada also elected a new leader in the person of Dr Keith Mitchell.

By the end of 1994, the presence of a host of new leaders, the time that had elapsed since the previous meeting, and the emergence of new issues, such as Helms–Burton, the Free Trade Areas of the Americas, NAFTA and its implication for CARICOM, the formation of the World Trade Organisation (WTO), and new emphasis on matters such as intellectual property served to impel both Canada and CARICOM to another summit. Freed of the threat of Quebec's secession, Prime Minister Chretien took the initiative. In January 1995, he embarked upon a tour of Latin America during the course of which he made an 18-hour stopover in Trinidad and Tobago where he held discussions with Prime Minister Manning. Proposals for the convening of another Canada–CARICOM meeting at the highest level were discussed, and agreement was reached in principle, subject to ratification by other CARICOM heads of government on the one hand and the Canadian Cabinet on the other. The result of such consultation was perhaps a foregone conclusion.

The Fourth Meeting of the Heads of Government of Canada and the Commonwealth Caribbean was held in St George's, Grenada, 3–5 March 1996. In addition to CARICOM heads of government, a number of observers were also present, such as the chief of ministers of the British Virgin Islands, Anguilla, and the Turks and Caicos Islands, the Vice Chancellor of the University of the West Indies and the Assistant Secretary-General of the OAS. Surinam, which became a full member of CARICOM in July 1995, was a first-time participant.

The summit covered a wide agenda. References were made to developments in Haiti, the situation in Nigeria following its suspension from the Commonwealth, the intractable debt problem, the environment and international terrorism. The meat of the discussions concerned Canada–CARICOM issues, with Prime Minister Chrétien reaffirming the value Canada placed on CARICOM countries as long-standing friends and stressed continued Canadian commitment to CARICOM. He noted that such commitment was reflected in the fact that the Commonwealth Caribbean was the highest per-capita recipient of Canadian development assistance and technical cooperation. The summit agreed on the following specific matters germane to the relationship between the participants:

- *CARIBCAN*: Canada agreed to explore incorporation into CARIBCAN of those products that are currently excluded from the arrangement. Canada also confirmed that it intended to seek an extension of the waiver originally granted by GATT for the CARIBCAN agreement. CARICOM agreed to support the Canadian request at the WTO.
- *Trade and Investment*: The summit agreed that cooperation on specific measures to improve the climate for trade and investment was necessary. In that context, Canada identified the need for individual Caribbean countries to conclude relevant bilateral agreements, especially in the areas of investment protection and intellectual property rights. At the time of the summit, Trinidad and Tobago was the only CARICOM country to have signed such agreements with Canada.
- *Small and Medium-sized Enterprises*: Both sides agreed on the important role that small and medium-size enterprises (SMEs) could play in generating employment opportunities and in contributing to

overall economic development. Canada undertook to investigate the possibility of establishing a Centre for Small and Medium-Size Enterprises, which would support and expand the activities of SMEs in CARICOM.

- *CARICOM Integration:* The summit acknowledged the contribution that Canada had made to the integration process and agreed that future efforts in this regard would be directed to human resources development.

- *Drug Trafficking:* Heads of government agreed that drug trafficking, money laundering and related crimes posed serious problems for both Canada and CARICOM. Prime Minister Chrétian agreed to continue Canadian assistance to CARICOM in combating this threat, and also undertook to assist in the strengthening of regional security capacity for interdiction and to provide material for education in prevention of drug use. Both sides undertook to intensify their cooperation in international bodies directed against the drug trade.

- *Free Trade Area of the Americas (FTAA):* The summit reviewed progress made towards the establishment of the FTAA and agreed that there was need for another meeting of hemispheric leaders. They agreed to seek such a meeting at the next session of the Summit Implementation Review Group, which oversees implementation of decisions regarding the FTAA.

- *Helms–Burton Act:* The summit expressed its strongest objection to the extraterritorial provisions of the Helms–Burton Act, which seek to apply US legislation relevant to US–Cuban relations to third countries. Both sides felt that these provisions were inconsistent with the accepted principles of international law and undermined the trend toward liberalisation of trade among countries (Canada–CARICOM Heads of Government, 1996).

Both Canadian and Caribbean leaders came away from the Grenada Summit satisfied. For the Canadians, an old friendly relationship had been strengthened, basically at little cost, while they had cornered some valuable regional support in their battle with the United States over Helms–Burton, which threatened their not insignificant investments in Cuba. For the Caribbean, even if the canker of immigration had been left untouched, the prospect of an extension of the time-frame of CARIBCAN was welcome news. Arrangements on further cooperation in the battle against drug trafficking, money laundering, as well as in the encouragement of further development of SMEs were also gratifying.

As the new millennium approaches, Canada–CARICOM relations appear to be set fair.

Notes

1. For a fuller discussion of this effort to develop the British North American colonies as a collective replacement for the United States, see Harold Robertson (1975), 'The Commercial Relationship between Nova Scotia and the British West Indies 1788–1822. The Twilight of Mercantilism in the British Empire', unpublished MA thesis, Dalhousie University, Nova Scotia.
2. Verbatim report of the press conference given on 21 February 1983 by the Honourable John Compton, Prime Minister of St Lucia and Chairman of the Meeting of Western Hemisphere Commonwealth Heads of Government.
3. Compiled from Basdeo (1993), pp. 17–19, and CARICOM delegation (1998), *Report of CARICOM Delegation on Review Meeting on Caribcan* (Ottawa: CARICOM).
4. Condensed from Records of the Third Meeting of Heads of Government of the Commonwealth Caribbean and Canada, Barbados 19–20 March 1990.
5. Drawn from a letter circulated to CARICOM High Commissioners in Ottawa by the Honourable Michael Wilson on 23 June 1993.

References

Basdeo, S. (1993) *Caribcan: A Continuum in Canada–CARICOM Economic Relations* (St Augustine: Institute of International Relations, University of the West Indies, January).

Campbell, F. (1992) 'Refuelling a Special Relationship: Canada and the Caribbean States', briefing paper prepared for the North–South Institute, Ottawa.

Canada–CARICOM Heads of Government Summit (1996) Official communique, 3–5 March.

CARICOM Delegation (1988) Report on Review Meeting on Caribcan, Ottawa, October.

CARICOM Secretariat (1992) *Review of Trends in Canada/CARICOM Trade, 1984–90*, document presented at the Sixth JTEC Meeting, June.

Chambers, G. (1983) Statement made during the Summit Meeting of Western Hemispheric Commonwealth Countries, St Lucia, 20–21 February.

Compton, J. (1983a) Statement made during the Summit Meeting of Western Hemispheric Commonwealth Countries, St Lucia, 20–21 February.

Compton, J. (1983b) Press conference report, 21 February.

Globe and Mail, The, 30 August 1993.

McGuigan, M. (1981) Statement made to the Canada/CARICOM JTEC meeting, Kingston, Jamaica, 15 January.

Records of the Third Meeting of Heads of Government of the Commonwealth Caribbean and Canada, Barbados, 19–20 March 1990.

Robertson, H. (1975) 'The Commercial Relationship between Nova Scotia and the British West Indies 1788–1822. The Twilight of Mercantilism in the British Empire', unpublished MA thesis, Dalhousie University, Nova Scotia.

Seaga, E. (1983) Statement made during the Summit Meeting of Western Hemispheric Commonwealth Countries, St Lucia, 20–21 February.

Third Meeting of Heads of Government of the Commonwealth Caribbean and Canada, records, 19–20 March 1990.

Trudeau, P. (1983) Statement made during the Summit Meeting of Western Hemispheric Commonwealth Countries, St Lucia, 20–21 February.

Williams, E. (1975) Statement made to the House of Representatives, Port of Spain, Trinidad, 4 May.

Wilson, M. (1993) Personal correspondence, 23 June.

8 Problems and Prospects of CARIBCAN: The Early Years

Sahadeo Basdeo

INTRODUCTION

Canada–Commonwealth Caribbean relations have been a subject of academic interest and enquiry over the years. There is no shortage of information on the subject, as various facets of the topic have engaged the attention of scholars and researchers in North America, Canada and the Caribbean for decades. From the days of mercantilism in the eighteenth century to the end of the Second World War, academic enquiry had concentrated exclusively on the limited issues that defined the nature of the relationship during the period. Commercial relations, preferential trade access, Canadian investment in the Caribbean, and the role of Canadian missionaries among East Indian indentured workers in the southern Caribbean have largely represented the major areas of academic emphasis and focus.

Since decolonisation in the 1960s, however, the orientation of Canadian policy in the region has assumed new dimensions. Interests and concerns now transcend the confines of the traditional relationship to include a host of other important issues, such as immigration, security, development assistance, human resource development, institutional support programmes, police training, maritime training assistance for Caribbean coast-guards, technical and scientific cooperation, investment, industrial cooperation, the environment, and debt-related issues. These constitute part of a new agenda in a modern, renewed Canada–Commonwealth Caribbean relationship in the final decade of the twentieth century and have become areas of contemporary academic interest for a new generation of scholars.

These developments notwithstanding, trade continues to remain the centrepiece of modern Canada–Commonwealth relations. This is clearly borne out by the introduction of CARIBCAN, an economic and trade development assistance programme instituted in 1986, which, by virtue of its character, reaffirms and reinforces in many ways the ongoing 'special relationship' shared between Canada and the British Caribbean over the years. This initiative was a Canadian response to Caribbean economic and social conditions in the critical decade of the 1980s, when Caribbean states were confronting high unemployment, growing inflation, escalating poverty, a severe shortage of capital and investment, low levels of economic activity, heavy external debt and poor export trade performance. It was a package principally intended to allow the British Caribbean export sector to access the Canadian market on preferential terms as a means of earning valuable foreign exchange and generating growth and development in the region.

Given the recent origin of CARIBCAN, limited work has been undertaken to address vital aspects of this policy initiative. Apart from one study undertaken by the Latin American Economic System (Sistema Económico para Latinoamérica – SELA) in June 1992 (see Gill, 1992), very little exists by way of an assessment of CARIBCAN since its introduction. The purpose of this chapter is, therefore, to contribute to the literature on this subject. It will attempt to provide a brief historical background against which CARIBCAN was introduced, provide an explanation of its arrangements, and examine the concerns that have been raised by Caribbean beneficiary states since its introduction. It will also examine the trade performance of CARIBCAN up to 1992 and posit suggestions that could enrich and enhance this useful preferential trade assistance programme to the mutual advantage of Canada and the Commonwealth Caribbean.

BACKGROUND TO CANADA–COMMONWEALTH CARIBBEAN ECONOMIC RELATIONS

Canada's relationship with the Commonwealth Caribbean began in the eighteenth century, when the British North Atlantic colonies traded fish, lumber and other staples for West Indian rum and molasses. This commercial relationship evolved over the years as a result of mercantilism, giving rise to a degree of trade complementarity and economic interdependence between both areas. In the aftermath of the American Revolution, interdependence grew as the Caribbean sugar colonies began to depend increasingly upon the northern Canadian provinces for vital plantation supplies (Basdeo and Robertson, 1981, pp. 54–8). It was this maritime commercial connection that established the foundation of early Canadian–Caribbean cooperation and subsequently became the vehicle through which Canadian missionaries, banking houses, insurance companies, other business interests and tourists entered the region.

The visibility of the Canadian presence in the Caribbean heightened during the nineteenth century and was reflected in the arrival of Canadian missionaries from Nova Scotia and New Brunswick to undertake evangelical and educational work among East Indian indentured workers in Grenada, Guyana and Trinidad; the establishment of banking houses in the region; the growth of Canadian businesses in selected sectors of the regional economy; and the arrival of an ever-increasing number of Canadian tourists to the British Caribbean. Developments brought the Caribbean closer to the Canadian orbit (Tennyson, 1990, p. 29; see also Chodos, 1977, pp. 151–70). It was against this background that, in 1898, Canada granted preferential trade access for the first time to a number of West Indian products, including raw and refined sugar, at a time when the West Indian sugar economy was in the doldrums. This policy decision by the Wilfred Laurier administration in its first term in office (1896–1911) represented the first in a series of preferential accords to be extended to the Commonwealth Caribbean as the years unfolded.

In 1900, sugar, the mainstay of the Caribbean economy, was granted a tariff preference of 33.3 per cent, as Canada became the main market for West Indian sugar. In 1912, a high-level Canada–West Indies Conference was convened in Ottawa, which led to the signing of the Canada–West Indies Reciprocal Treaty extending tariff preferences between the two areas. Similar conferences were held in 1920, 1925 and 1937, resulting in substantial two-way trade flows, an extension by both parties of general tariff preferences for each other's goods, and wider preferences for selected products.[1] The same policy trend continued throughout the post-decolonisation period, when newly-independent Caribbean states sought to consolidate former trade alliances and establish new ones. To this end, a special Canada–Commonwealth Caribbean Conference was held in Ottawa in July 1966, at which a special protocol to the 1925 agreement was signed, granting duty-free entry for West Indian sugar up to a level based on the average quantity of West Indian sugar exports to Canada over the previous five years. This initiative was, however, shortlived. By 1970, Canada terminated the arrangement, replacing it with a US$5 million fund for the development of Caribbean agriculture as it proceeded to purchase sugar in the international market at existing world prices (Guy, 1990, p. 273).

By the beginning of the 1980s, trade between both partners was again characterised by preferential arrangements, as reflected in the 1979 Trade and Economic Cooperation Agreement which provided for a protocol on trade development and industrial, financial and technical cooperation. It was the area of trade, however, that received considerable emphasis in the agreement, in its Articles II and V. Article II, for instance, pledged the signatories 'to apply to goods originating in each other's territories the highest degree of liberalization, which they apply to Third countries in general' (Gill, 1992, p. 4). In like manner, Article V provided that:

> Any member state, which in pursuance of the objective of promoting trade among Developing Countries, enters into a preferential agreement with any developing country is not required under this Agreement to extend similar or comparable treatment to Canada provided such preferential arrangements are entered into in accordance with the provisions of the General Agreement on Tariffs and Trade. (Gill, 1992, p. 4)

The agreement grants, therefore, certain latitude and space to Commonwealth Caribbean nations as they forge trading links with other developing countries.

Today, the Canada–Commonwealth Caribbean trade relationship is also facilitated by other arrangements. Caribbean Community and Common Market (CARICOM) exports to Canada receive special treatment under the Canadian General Preferential Tariff (GPT), Canada's Generalised Preferential Programme for developing countries or GSP, and the British Preferential Tariff (BPT) which applies to all Commonwealth countries. As a recent SELA study shows, these arrangements provide CARICOM goods with additional trade advantages. Under the GPT, preferential entry is granted for most industrial items, and a select list of agriculture products, such as spices, rum, fruit juices and cocoa. Similarly, under the BPT, there are more advantageous provisions for certain agricultural goods than those enjoyed under the GSP, while 'for manufactured goods the tariff rate under either scheme is similar' (Gill, 1992, p. 4).

CONTENT AND CHANGING DIMENSION OF CURRENT RELATIONS

The nature and content of current Canadian–Commonwealth Caribbean trade relations have changed from decades ago. The era when

Canadian cod, lumber and other staples were exchanged for West Indian rum, sugar and molasses has now given way to a new quality of trade, characterised by a more diversified, sophisticated grouping of products. The range of products in recent years has included goods and services, such as machinery, technical and consulting services, telecommunications equipment, agricultural technology, consumer goods, food products and resource commodities, in exchange for such imports as petroleum and petroleum products, steel, textiles, sugar, bauxite, alumina, ores, rum and other alcoholic beverages, molasses, fish, food products, goods and tropical fruits.

Despite this transformation in the character of the age-old trade pattern, there has not been any dramatic increase in the bilateral flow of goods and services between the two areas. In fact, the level of Canadian–Caribbean trade in the 1970s and 1980s has declined proportionately, mirroring a similar trend in Canadian trade with developing countries as a whole over the same period. The fact is that the changing international economic landscape has produced new, more attractive opportunities for Canadian trade. A substantial amount of Canadian trade is now diverted to the Pacific rim states of Korea, Taiwan, Hong Kong, Malaysia and Singapore at the expense of Caribbean and Latin America countries. In fact, at the regional level, Canada–CARICOM trade has not only remained small and relatively insignificant, but by the onset of the 1980s, Canada's share of the CARICOM market had declined compared to that of the European Economic Community (EEC) and Japan. This is in keeping with a trend begun following the Second World War. In the 1950s, Canada's share of Caribbean trade was approximately 17 per cent. By 1970 it had dropped to 9 per cent, and by 1978 to 5 per cent. Indeed, by 1980 Canada had supplied some 5 per cent of CARICOM imports and had only imported some 5 per cent of CARICOM exports (see MacGuigan, 1981).

Outside of trade, Canada–Commonwealth Caribbean relations today encompass a broad spectrum of cooperative activity in other areas. These include aid, tourism, industrial cooperation, transport, regional security, environment, drug trafficking, democracy and human rights. In addition, Canada has supported a number of CARICOM regional projects in recent years, including institutional support for the University of the West Indies, the CARICOM Airports Maintenance Project, the Caribbean Examinations Council (CXC), the Caribbean Maritime Training Assistance Programme (CMTAP), and the Canadian Training Awards Programme (CTAP). Similarly, Canada has contributed generously to the work of the recently concluded West Indian Commission.

Over the same period, Canadian bilateral aid has also found its way in the construction of basic Caribbean infrastructure, such as airports, harbours, bridges, reservoirs, schools, hospitals, university expansion, agricultural research, scholarships, and capital and technical assistance in a host of other areas.

Canada also provides substantial financial aid to the Caribbean through various multilateral agencies in which it enjoys membership. These include programmes and activities of the United Nations Development Programme (UNDP), the World Bank Group, the Caribbean Development Bank (CDB), and the Inter-American Development Bank (IDB). Commensurate with bilateral and multilateral development assistance, Canada has been assisting, through the Canadian International Development Agency (CIDA), the efforts of non-governmental organisations (NGOs) working at the grass-roots level in the region on projects mainly in the sectors of health, agriculture, rural development, education and community development. The Canada Fund for Local Initiatives (or Canada Fund) has been instituted, enabling Canada to become involved with grass-roots groups such as farmers, villagers and refugees by giving accredited Canadian diplomatic missions a means of responding more adequately and quickly to local requests and needs.

Simply, Canadian development assistance programmes have helped to strengthen the Canada–Commonwealth Caribbean relationship. But, so too have other factors. These include the large migrant Caribbean community in Canada; the close educational linkage, which has historically facilitated the training of West Indians at Canadian universities;[2] an agreement on the recruitment of migrant farm labour under the Canada–Caribbean Seasonal Workers Programme; and the injection of high levels of Canadian development aid. Approximately Canadian $600 million, excluding funds from multilateral agencies, were disbursed to the region during the period 1987–91, making the Commonwealth Caribbean the highest per capita recipient of Canadian development assistance.

Another factor consolidating the close relationship has been the role played by Canada as spokesman for CARICOM's interest at the Group of Seven (G7) meeting and the World Bank's board meetings. Equally, the recent initiative taken by Canada to chair the Guyana Support Group, aimed at drawing Guyana back into the international financial community by clearing the arrears of its large debt, has gone a long way in cementing close Canadian–CARICOM relations. In addition, with entry of Canada into the Organisation of American States (OAS) in

1990, a new dimension in closer Canada–CARICOM cooperation has been forged. While Canada and the Commonwealth Caribbean enjoy membership in many multilateral organisations, the former's entry into the OAS has facilitated a closer, more immediate working relationship with CARICOM states on issues of a regional and hemispheric nature that previously had not received priority on Canada's foreign policy agenda. After a four-year tenure in the hemispheric forum, Canada and the Commonwealth Caribbean have been engaged in promoting human rights, democracy, regional peace and stability, and monitoring democratic elections in such places as Nicaragua and Haiti (Dosman, 1992, pp. 543–9). A common British heritage, the English language, democratic values and cultural ties have contributed to fruitful, productive interaction within the OAS and have led Canada and Caribbean countries to make influential contributions to the organisation's policy orientation.

THE ORIGINS OF CARIBCAN

By the late 1970s, CARICOM states were facing serious social and economic problems. These problems, as mentioned, ranged from a rapid decline in economic growth, poor export trade performance, mounting unemployment, increasing poverty and shortage of capital and investment, to low levels of economic activity. The drug trade had also begun to penetrate Caribbean life, making the region vulnerable to threats posed by mercenaries and drug traders. In addition, Jamaica's flirtation with Cuba and, subsequently, Maurice Bishop's relationship with the Castro administration made Canadian officials afraid that 'Cuban activism could provoke a defensive US response and an East–West confrontation in the region' (Baranyi and Dosman, 1990, p. 105). This fear subsequently materialised when the United States invaded Grenada in 1983 following Bishop's assassination. The Caribbean, as Canadian officials feared, had now developed into an arena for international conflict between the United States and Cuba. In an era when the United States had introduced the Caribbean Basin Initiative (CBI) and the EEC had completed the negotiation of the Lomé II Convention to combat regional economic problems, it was expected that Canada would do likewise to prevent the region from becoming increasingly vulnerable to internal and external threats.

As early as 1979, Canada began to view developments in the region with concern. Its own declining trade performance with the

Commonwealth Caribbean led to the establishment of the Joint Trade and Economic Committee (JTEC), which became the main institutional vehicle for dialogue between both partners, aimed at discussing and improving various aspects of the Canada–Caribbean relationship. It was this vehicle that identified the need for the Canadian government to conduct an overall review of Canadian policy in the Caribbean. Indeed, declining trade with the region converged with other domestic, regional and international developments to make such a review necessary. As a close Commonwealth partner, Canada could not remain oblivious to the changing fortunes in CARICOM. Like the United States and the United Kingdom, Canada was expected to address certain features of Caribbean life, particularly at a time when there was not only a general deterioration in regional conditions but also a quickening pace of economic and political crisis that was threatening to envelop the area. It was in this context that, by the early 1980s, the Caribbean found a prominent place in the foreign policy agenda of the United States, Great Britain and Canada.

In January 1981, in a speech to the Canada–CARICOM JTEC in Kingston, Jamaica, Canada's Secretary of State for External Affairs, Mark MacGuigan outlined the Canadian government's new policy towards the region. He promised a renewal of Canadian commitment to the CARICOM relationship, the strengthening of commercial ties between both areas, balance of payments support to CARICOM countries that had concluded remedial programmes with the International Monetary Fund (IMF), and announced Canada's intention to work with CARICOM in maintaining social, economic and political stability in the region. He promised continued Canadian aid, quicker disbursement of development assistance funds, and increased levels of technical assistance to CARICOM (see MacGuigan, 1981). Indeed, it was this statement that not only represented the cornerstone of Canadian official policy towards the Caribbean in the decade of the 1980s, but also provided the framework and context for a new Canadian trade and commercial policy for CARICOM in the 1980s. As John Graham, Canadian High Commissioner to Guyana, confirmed some weeks after MacGuigan's speech in Kingston, the decline in Canadian–Caribbean trade in the 1970s, 'was an important factor which my Government examined and a trend which, with the cooperation of the region, we hope to see reversed' (*Barbados Advocate News*, 7 February 1981).

Canadian policy coincided with a call made by Edward Seaga, then Prime Minister of Jamaica, suggesting that Canada initiate a CBI-type programme for CARICOM. In an address to the second meeting of the

Canada–CARICOM JTEC in January 1981, he called for a mini-Marshall Plan for the Caribbean and Latin America as a means of introducing badly needed capital inflow to counteract social and political stability in the Caribbean. It was a point he had made earlier to US President Ronald Reagan. Seaga suggested that aid flows of some US$900 million were needed to reconstruct West Indian economies. In this regard, Canada's role was vital and called for her assistance in mobilising aid flows to the region. Seaga made a case for greater access for Caribbean products to the US and Canadian markets as a means of enhancing the region's trade and export earnings (see MacGuigan, 1981). When the United States responded with the CBI in 1984, Seaga proposed a similar package to Mulroney in 1985, arguing that such a package was necessary to counteract regional instability.

The Jamaican Prime Minister's proposals received the backing of his CARICOM counterparts in February 1985 in Kingston, Jamaica. At the Kingston summit, heads of government outlined what they envisaged could be the major elements in any Canadian CBI-type package. These included: duty-free access across the board for all products of Caribbean origin; preferential value-added treatment for the region, which would involve a reduction in the current value-added requirement from 40 to 35 per cent and could include all imports originating from any of the participating Caribbean countries as part of the value added in the exporting beneficiary country; and special attention to sensitive products, such as rum, textiles and footwear, to ensure that access would not be impeded by non-tariff barriers. It was also felt that any Canadian initiative of a CBI nature should include a medium-term Canadian investment programme for the Caribbean that would provide financing for industrial development, agroindustry and tourism. In addition, CARICOM leaders felt that Canada should offer special incentives to the private sector to encourage Canadian private investment in the region, since it was believed that the quantum of investment needed could not be adequately provided by official development assistance (ODA) or through multilateral donor agencies (Report of the Third Meeting, 1985, pp. 15–16).

This was the background against which Prime Minister Mulroney announced in October 1985 at the Commonwealth Summit in Nassau, Bahamas, his intention to introduce a trade and aid package akin to the CBI. Such a package, he concluded, would help CARICOM countries export most of their products duty-free to the Canadian market. He anticipated then that the 'arrangement will cover 99 per cent of the goods which the Caribbean currently exports to Canada' (*Barbados*

Advocate News, 22 May 1986). This preferential arrangement was called CARIBCAN.

CARIBCAN

In February 1986, the Canadian government announced the creation of CARIBCAN. Designed as a programme for trade, investment and industrial cooperation, it received legislative approval in June 1986 through an amendment to the Customs Tariff Act. The programme covers 18 countries and dependent territories in the British Caribbean, 13 of which are member-states of the Caribbean Community and Common Market (CARICOM). Programme beneficiaries include Anguilla, Antigua and Barbuda, the Bahamas, Barbados, Belize, Bermuda, the British Virgin Islands, the Cayman Islands, Dominica, Grenada, Guyana, Jamaica, Montserrat, St Christopher/Nevis, St Lucia, St Vincent and the Grenadines, Trinidad and Tobago, and the Turks and Caicos Islands. Since enactment, no other state has so far sought entry into the arrangement.

A statistical profile of beneficiary states, as shown in Table 8.1, reveals not only their extremely small size but also a population of slightly more than 5.8 million, with a combined gross domestic product (GDP) of approximately $4617 million and a per capita income of some $2277. In addition, almost half of these states have populations of less 100 000, with Jamaica the largest beneficiary and accounting for more than 41 per cent of the population of the entire group.

The stated objective of CARIBCAN was to enhance bilateral commercial ties between Canada and the Commonwealth Caribbean. It was specifically designed to enhance existing trade and export earnings, improve the trade and economic development prospects of the region, promote new investment opportunities, and encourage enhanced economic cooperation within the region. The centrepiece of the programme was, nevertheless, its provision for preferential, one-way, duty-free entry into the Canadian market for the vast majority of goods exported from the Commonwealth Caribbean. A few products were excluded from the arrangement, including textiles and clothing, footwear, luggage and handbags, leather garments, lubrication oils and methanol. These products, however, were to continue to be subject to established preferential duties under the GPT and BPT, where these preferential rates existed (*Jamaican Gleaner*, 7 March 1986).

Table 8.1 CARIBCAN beneficiaries: comparative statistics

Country/Territory	Population 1988 (000s)	Area sq km	GDP 1988 $ million	GDP $ per capita
CARICOM members				
Antigua and Barbuda	84	440	274	3 279
Bahamas	249	13 940	2 153	8 649
Barbados	254	430	1 540	6 057
Belize	166	22 960	277	1 673
Dominica	86	750	140	1 629
Grenada	117	340	166	1 423
Guyana	794	214 970	360	454
Jamaica	2 398	19 990	3 416	1 425[*]
Montserrat	10	n.a.	40[*]	3 330[*]
St Kitts and Nevis	49	360	113	2 315
Saint Lucia	132	620	242	1 835
St Vincent & the Grenadines	109	340	136	1 246
Trinidad and Tobago	1 240	5 130	4 280	3 452
CARICOM non-members				
Anguilla	10	n.a	10[*]	850[*]
Bermuda	73	50	1 389	18 931
British Virgin Islands	13	150	131	9 830
Cayman Islands	19	260	70[*]	3 480[*]
Turks & Caicos Islands	9	430	10[*]	780[*]

[*] 1987 GNP and GNP per capita data.
Sources: UNCTAD, *Handbook of International Trade and Development Statistics, 1990*; GDP and GDP per capita data for Nicaragua taken from IDB, *Economic and Social Progress in Latin America, 1991 Report*; GNP and GNP per capita data for Anguilla, the Cayman Islands, Turks and Caicos Islands and Montserrat taken from OECD, *Development Cooperation in the 1990s* (Paris), 1989.

Other features of CARIBCAN included measures to encourage Canadian investment and other forms of industrial cooperation with the region. Among such measures was a programme to strengthen the region's export capability with particular emphasis on the Canadian market, including the holding of seminars for CARICOM diplomatic and commercial personnel, with a focus on ways and means of developing markets in Canada for Caribbean products. A commitment was also made to mount a pilot project to develop a sourcing directory that would provide an inventory of Commonwealth Caribbean manufacturing and export capacity. Funding for the seminars and the pilot project was to be provided by CIDA. In addition, Canada promised to establish a system that would enable Caribbean trade commissioners to receive assistance from the regional offices of the Department of Regional Industrial Expansion in their trade promotion efforts there.

The Canadian government attached no time limit to CARIBCAN. However, because the granting of duty-free access for CARICOM imports conflicted with the provisions of paragraph 1 of the General Agreement on Tariffs and Trade (GATT), Canada had to obtain approval of GATT contracting parties before proceeding with the arrangement. The waiver was granted on 28 November 1986, by virtue of which Canada was exempted from the requirement to extend the same duty-free treatment to similar products of any other contracting party for a period of 12 years (until 15 June 1998).

Like the CBI, rules of origin were established to guide the duty-free entry of goods under CARIBCAN into the Canadian market. In order to qualify for such entry, the goods had to be grown, produced or manufactured in the Commonwealth Caribbean, but could incorporate materials or components from outside the area if certain conditions were met. A minimum of 60 per cent of the ex-factory price of the goods had to originate in any of the beneficiary countries or Canada. This included production costs, overhead expenses, profit and export packaging. The 'cost of production' used to determine the 'origin content' under many other preferential trade systems differs significantly from the ex-factory price of goods as obtained under CARIBCAN. In many cases, the cost of production includes the cost of materials and actual processing costs, including overhead, but does not include profit and export packaging.

Under CARIBCAN's rules of origin as well, local value-added amounts can be 'cumulated' among the countries of the region. In other words, the Commonwealth Caribbean is considered a single country for purposes of meeting content requirements. Goods must also be imported directly from the exporting country or pass in transit through an intermediate country with or without transshipment or temporary storage facilities. In an intermediate country, they must remain under customs transit control; they cannot undergo any operations other than reloading, splitting up of loads, or operations required to keep the articles in good condition; and they must not be traded or consumed in the intermediate country.

CARIBCAN contained other important features. There was, for example, a 'safeguard provision'. Under CARIBCAN, duty-free entry for any product could be withdrawn or suspended, in whole or in part, from a beneficiary country if it threatened injury to Canadian production, and after there is an opportunity for all interested parties, including representatives of beneficiary governments and exporters, to present their views. Another feature dealt with the process of review. Since CARIBCAN was a new experience for both Canada and the Caribbean, it was decided in 1986 that the arrangement should be reviewed after an initial period of two years to determine whether its provisions should be amended or improved (Canadian Department of External Affairs, 1988, pp. 7–17). Another aspect of CARIBCAN was the Canadian government's commitment to addressing the problems faced by Caribbean rum producers in labelling and bottling in Canada as well as securing improved access to the Canadian market. To this end, the Canadian government undertook to add another clause to the 1979 Trade and Economic Cooperation Agreement, permitting the bottling of rum in Canada without blending. In like fashion, commitments were made to negotiate double-taxation treaties with CARICOM states as a means of stimulating Canadian investment in the region.

Although CARIBCAN arrangements provide for duty-free entry of eligible goods, they do not exempt exporters from a range of taxes and regulations governing the importation or sale of goods in the Canadian market. For example, under the Customs Tariff and Excise Tax Act, rum and most alcoholic beverages and tobacco products must pay a special customs duty levied on similar products from any source. Imports from the region, for instance, are subject to federal and provincial sales tax, packaging and labelling regulations, product standards and safety regulations, health regulations, rules on imports of endangered species, and import controls, as specified under the Special Import Measures Act. This means that federal government permits may, therefore, be required for a range of fresh and processed fruits and vegetables as well as coffee and sugar products (Canadian Department of External Affairs, 1988, pp. 7–17).

The introduction of CARIBCAN, though welcomed in the region, did not meet the expectations of Caribbean heads of government. In fact, the Canadian package fell short of the Caribbean's expectations in many respects. Coverage was limited; the method used to compute the origin content differed from the accustomed value-added formula; no special incentive was identified to promote the expansion of Canadian investment in the region; and, while some progress appeared to have been made with respect to rum exports, there were outstanding problems concerning entry of textiles, garments and leather products into the Canadian market. These were problems that CARICOM states continued to identify with CARIBCAN after its introduction; thereafter, they represented a Caribbean agenda for reform.

CARIBCAN'S EARLY YEARS

Despite CARICOM's initial apprehensions, its leaders supported CARIBCAN, anticipating that the opportunity existed under the JTEC to advance the case for early reform. Measures were taken with prompt dispatch both in Canada and the Caribbean for implementation of the arrangement. In Ottawa, a CARIBCAN desk was established within the Caribbean and Central American Trade Development Division of the Department of External Affairs, and a coordinator for the programme was appointed to facilitate execution of the arrangement. In the Caribbean, CARICOM governments, assisted by Canadian diplomatic officials, held seminars in May 1986 to familiarise traders, businesspeople, government officials and members of the CARICOM secretariat with the nature, dimensions and expectations of the arrangement. In 1987, the Canadian government, in consultation with CARICOM, showcased a range of regionally produced goods in Western Canada during the Vancouver Commonwealth Summit to show CARICOM products to buyers and potential investors. This was followed the same week by an investment and tourism promotion conference in Vancouver and another CARICOM trade exposition in Toronto later that month (*Trinidad Guardian*, 15 October 1987).

During CARIBCAN's first two years, meetings of the pre-existing JTEC operational mechanism were held in Canada and the Caribbean to conduct a performance appraisal. In addition, Ottawa-based CARICOM diplomats, government ministers and technicians, and Canadian officials from the Department of External Affairs met to examine the programme's shortcomings. At these meetings, CARICOM representatives sang the same tune: they sought changes in CARIBCAN on the basis of identified weaknesses in the programme. A case was made for revision of the value-added criteria, with CARICOM arguing for its reduction from 60 to 35 per cent, in keeping with CBI levels, in view of the region's limited resource base. It was further argued that inputs from either Canada or the United States used in the production of CARICOM goods should be assessed as part of the local/regional value-added, since the imminence of the Canada–US Free Trade Agreement (CUSFTA) would mean that input for the manufacture of goods in respective countries could soon be imported duty free from either country. Under the circumstances, the rationale for the taxation of inputs from the United States used in the production of CARICOM goods would cease to exist.

CARICOM also objected to the list of exclusions, on the grounds that they prevented the region from exporting a significant portion of its regional output. Moreover, it argued that regional production of the excluded items was too small to threaten domestic Canadian or US industry, a view subsequently endorsed by the *Montreal Gazette*. As an editorial in this newspaper noted, 'If Caribbean industries can compete with Canadian ones in those [sensitive] sectors, they should be allowed to do so ... Protectionism hurts almost everyone. And Canada, of all countries should have sympathy for the plight of small economies dependent on exports of primary products' (*Trinidad Guardian*, 3 January 1990).

Anticipating Canada's rejection of its request for unlimited duty-free access for the excluded items, CARICOM proposed the inclusion of a programme similar to the US 807 Special Access Programme for Garments, which guarantees access to the US market for Caribbean-produced clothing made from cloth woven and cut in the United States. A call was also made for inclusion of an investment component within the arrangement, since CARICOM insisted that Canadian capital investment in the Caribbean could enhance regional economic fortunes. The suggestion was made that such investment could be facilitated if Canadian investors in the Caribbean were granted the same tax credit facility that they had received under the Special Investment Tax Credit Programme for investing in Canada. Likewise, Canada should create a venture capital fund that could be used to finance investment in CARIBCAN beneficiary states. A proposal was also advanced for the creation of a soft window facility, through which loans could be made available to Canadian entrepreneurs interested in CARICOM investment.

Another important matter broached by CARICOM at these meetings dealt with the anticipated impact of CUSFTA on the Caribbean. It was feared that the agreement would erode certain CARIBCAN preferences, particularly on CARICOM rum, especially in the context of Canadian imports from Puerto Rico and the US Virgin Islands. For this reason, Caribbean representatives requested that CARIBCAN beneficiaries be accorded no less favourable treatment than that granted US producers and manufacturers under CUSFTA. The Caribbean Community was concerned that CARIBCAN's benefits would be diminished if Canada's entry into a free trade arrangement with the

United States remained unchecked. Consequently, CARICOM insisted that CARIBCAN should be improved in order to minimise the negative impact that Canada's entry in CUSFTA could have on the region.

The JTEC meetings also heard about problems of CARICOM rum entry into the Canadian market. Caribbean states protested the array of non-tariff barriers existing in Canada that hampered an increase in export sales of this most important traditional CARICOM product. Difficulties included impediments to the bottling of CARICOM rum in Canada, access for CARICOM brand rums, problems of labelling, and problems of listing in systems operated by the Provincial Liquor Boards. An amendment to Canadian legislation was requested to allow CARICOM rum producers to ship their branded rum in bulk for bottling in Canada under their own brand names. A request was also made for the renewal of the Canada–CARICOM Protocol on Rum, which had lapsed in 1979 (Ministry of Foreign Affairs, 1988).

By April 1989, when the fifth JTEC concluded in Trinidad, these issues were still largely unresolved, except for the matter of rum entry into the Canadian market. In November 1986, the Canadian Prime Minister urged Provincial Premiers to grant favourable consideration to applications for listings from CARICOM rum producers. In January 1989, differential markups on rums by provincial boards went into force, and in March 1989 agreement was reached whereby CARICOM rum of 98.5 per cent content and blended in Canada would be labelled as a product of the particular CARICOM distiller. Amendments to the Canadian Food and Drug Act were effected to allow these changes. In addition, the West Indian Rum and Spirit Producers' Association and the Association of Canadian Distillers had reached agreement on revised customs guidelines on the labelling of rum for sale in Canada, allowing rum producers to place their names or logos on bottle labels. The Excise Act distilling regulations were also eventually amended to permit bottling of Caribbean rum in-bond, a demand for which CARICOM had long been pressing. Finally, the Protocol on Rum was ready for signing (Caricom Secretariat, 1989).

The review of CARIBCAN conducted by the JTEC for the period up to April 1989 did not produce any meaningful change in the arrangement. Except for rum access, all major issues raised by CARICOM remained outstanding. Ottawa-based Caribbean diplomats were obviously very disheartened and concluded that it was futile pursuing the JTEC meetings and so advised their home governments. In their opinion, any meaningful review at this stage could only be conducted at the political level. It was felt that regional ministers were better positioned to influence their Canadian counterparts than the JTEC officials. An initiative was therefore taken up in June 1989, when the Chairman of the CARICOM Council of Ministers raised the subject with Canada's Minister of External Affairs in Caracas, Venezuela, where both were attending the special ministerial meeting of the Group of 77. It was subsequently agreed that such a meeting, though desirable, should be held in abeyance until the JTEC completed its review process, which was still in progress.[3] However, before such a meeting could be pursued any further, it was pre-empted by a request from Prime Minister Mulroney for a Canada–CARICOM summit to discuss CARIBCAN. This meeting took place in Barbados on 19–20 March 1990.

THE BARBADOS SUMMIT

The Canada–CARICOM Summit held at Sam Lord's Castle in Barbados was seen by CARICOM leaders as the ideal opportunity not only to resolve both outstanding CARICOM problems, but one that could set the tone for continued good relations into the 1990s. West Indian expectations were high as CARICOM leaders gathered two days ahead of the meeting to prepare an agenda, which would focus on trade, investment, technical and financial cooperation. Also included were international political and economic issues of mutual bilateral interest. CARICOM leaders felt that the opportunity should be used to harmonise Canadian–CARICOM positions on such topics as the environment, foreign debt, drug trafficking, the Haitian crisis, Cuba reintegration into the international economy, and progress in the Uruguay Round of GATT. Yet, it was the existing deficiencies in CARIBCAN that CARICOM Leaders hoped would be addressed by the Canadian Prime Minister.

In addressing the summit, Prime Minister Mulroney covered a number of topics identified for discussion on the agenda. He announced a series of important changes relating to trade, investment, debt and financing, and a revision of CARIBCAN provisions. To this extent, Mulroney's contribution far exceeded the expectations of CARICOM leaders; his proposals certainly turned out to be extravagant. The Prime Minister pledged that under Canada's Official Development Assistance Programme, his government would grant $10 million to the University of the West Indies to spearhead the Canadian Institutional Strengthening Project between Canada and the University, and an additional $2.5 million to enhance the safety of Caribbean airports.

Mulroney also promised to increase Canada's ODA by 5 per cent for 1991 and 1992, respectively, and assured the region that Canada's economic response to events in Eastern Europe would not come at the expense of its responsibility to the developing world, including CARICOM (Report of Commonwealth Caribbean–Canada, 1990).

Mulroney indicated that Canada would forgive the region's entire official debt of $182 million and that aid would in the future take the form of grants (see Table 8.2). This gesture of goodwill was highly appreciated by CARICOM leaders notwithstanding the predictable consternation and condemnation that it caused in Canada, which was caught up in a major economic recession. Prime Minister Michael Manley of Jamaica, whose country was the major beneficiary of Mulroney's announcement, described it as 'a tremendous signal to the international community and to other developed countries...an example of magnanimity we hope other developed countries, the IMF, World Bank, other lending agencies and international commercial banks would follow' (*Trinidad Guardian*, 21 March 1990). It was certainly a measure that provided considerable relief to the region's beleaguered economies.

Improvements in CARIBCAN were also addressed. Duty-free access was extended to leather luggage and certain fibre products, bringing product coverage to 98 per cent of all CARICOM goods, with only two

Table 8.2   Individual country breakdown of official debt written off by Canada (amount of outstanding ODA[*] debt owed to Canada)

Country	Canadian$ 000s
Barbados	23 458
Belize	10 781
Guyana	37 205
Jamaica	93 378
Trinidad and Tobago	7 224
Leeward and Windward Islands	
Antigua and Barbuda	5 175
Dominica	1 679
Grenada	744
Montserrat	632
Saint Lucia	453
St Vincent and the Grenadines	996

[*]ODA: Official Development Assistance.

important items remaining on the list of dutiable products: textiles and methanol. Canada also agreed to permit in-bond bottling of Caribbean rum with minimal blending of Canadian spirits. Mulroney indicated that the Canadian International Trade Tribunal had been mandated to study the issue of entertaining an 807 American-type programme for garments as well.

Other matters were broached by the Prime Minister. During the course of the meeting he committed himself to study the related issues of sea transportation, tourism and rules of origin; promised Canadian cooperation on drug control; and announced his intent to encourage investment flows to the Caribbean. In this latter regard he was prepared to facilitate the establishment of a new Industrial Cooperation Office in Ottawa for the Commonwealth Caribbean at a cost of $1 million. The Canada–Caribbean Business Cooperation Office (CCBCO) would be involved in improving industrial cooperation and promoting linkages between the private sectors in Canada and the CARICOM region through joint ventures, investment, technology transfer, training, licensing, franchising and other forms of industrial cooperation. It was to be funded over a three-year period by CIDA and the Canadian Exporters Association (CEA), with the CEA responsible for its day-to-day operations. In a similar vein, he announced Canada's intent to sponsor two investment conferences in April 1991 in Toronto and Montreal to stimulate private sector contacts between Canada and CARICOM.

While the range of subjects touched upon and proposals made exceeded Caribbean expectations, some of the concerns raised by CARICOM since 1986 with respect to CARIBCAN were not addressed. These included the use of Voluntary Export Restraints, the treatment of inputs from the United States, and, more importantly, the Canadian response to CARICOM concerns about the potential adverse effects of CUSFTA on CARICOM economies. Yet, these did not stand in the way of implementing the announcements made by Prime Minister Mulroney after his departure from Barbados.

In Canada, the CCBCO was opened in April 1990 under the management of the CEA in Ottawa. Unfortunately CARICOM was disappointed at the lack of consultation preceding the staffing and organisational structure of the CCBCO, since regional governments felt that the Caribbean's public and private sectors should have been consulted. This did not impede other decisions taken in Barbados from being implemented, however. The Caribbean Investment Opportunities Conference proposed by Mulroney was convened in Toronto and Montreal on 23–24 March 1991 and was preceded by a mini-investment seminar in Moncton, New Brunswick, on 13 June 1990. The conference and seminar brought together public and private sector representatives from Canada and CARICOM to share information on trade and investment opportunities. Canadian investors initially showed interest in investing in the light-manufacturing sector, agribusiness, high technology industries, tourism and the provision of financial services. Regrettably, more than three years since the Ottawa-based CCBCO was launched, only four projects linking Canadian and Caribbean business interests 'have resulted in signed contracts', with the most successful partnership project so far being one established between producers of snacks in Quebec and Port of Spain (*The Express*, 8 October 1993). In other areas, however, implementation has been very slow: the proposed study on entry of CARICOM textiles into the Canadian market is still incomplete and studies on tourism, sea transportation and rules of origin remain outstanding.

ASSESSMENT OF TRADE, INVESTMENT AND INDUSTRIAL COOPERATION UNDER CARIBCAN

As indicated earlier, it was expected that after the creation of CARIBCAN, the region would experience an improvement in its balance of trade with Canada. It was also believed that CARIBCAN would generate investment flows and encourage industrial cooperation between the two. As of 1991, these expectations had not been met. In the area of trade (considered the centrepiece of CARIBCAN), for instance, there was no dramatic surge in regional exports to Canada. Likewise, was there no marked difference in the pattern of investment flows to the Caribbean nor any industrial linkage of significance between Canada and CARICOM between 1986 and 1992.

The export value of the trade programme remained unexciting after the inception of CARIBCAN. To expect otherwise would have been unrealistic since product coverage under the arrangement was limited. The number of products exported to the Canadian market at the outset of the programme ranged from a high of 20 tariff items for Jamaica, 15 for Trinidad and Tobago, four for Barbados, and one for Bermuda and the Leeward and Windward Islands (Government of Canada, 1988).[4] The arrangement, in fact, only catered to a small percentage of CARICOM goods, which hitherto had not been accorded market access under such preferential arrangements as 'most favoured nation status' (MFN), the BPT and the GPT. Indeed, by 1986, the value of dutiable imports from CARICOM was very small, since 94.8 per cent of all imports had already received zero-tariff access through such programmes as the MFN, the BPT and the GPT.

According to Table 8.3, tariff treatment for 1987 reveals that of the total volume of imports into Canada from CARICOM valued at $264.6 million, some $250.8 million entered duty free, with the majority receiving MFN, BPT or GPT treatment. In fact, of the majority of imports paying zero duty, 83 per cent were accorded MFN and BPT entry, while 16 per cent were accorded GPT entry.

Duty-free imports under CARIBCAN, however, reflect a different scenario. Strikingly less than $4 million of duty-free imports entered Canada in 1987 under this arrangement. This figure was equivalent to 1.6 per cent of all duty-free imports, or 1.5 per cent of overall imports. Of the $4 million duty-free imports, the major beneficiaries were Trinidad and Tobago and Jamaica, registering $2.6 million and $1.2 million, respectively. What the data clearly shows is that for 1987, trade performance under CARIBCAN had a limited impact on CARICOM economies both in general terms as well as for individual CARICOM states. In fact, the impact was particularly negative in the smaller Leeward and Windward Islands where no benefit was recorded. Though the 1987 trade performance proved a disappointment, CARICOM states argued for more favourable terms of trade, which they felt could be improved if adequate attention was paid to non-duty-free imports.

The 1987 trade performance provided the basis for CARICOM states to argue the case for review. It was clear that $13.9 million in imports did not receive duty-free treatment in 1987, a figure equivalent to 5.2 per cent of overall imports. Of this figure, only $2.6 million, or less than 1 per cent of total imports, were excluded specifically under CARIBCAN. What CARICOM officials kept insisting on was that imports valued at $11.2 million that did not qualify under CARIBCAN might have benefitted from the arrangement had the origin requirements, as well as the removal of safeguard procedures and improvements in maritime transport, been addressed. In addition, they argued that the 1987 trade profile could be improved if such products as textiles, clothing, footwear, luggage, handbags, leather products, lubrication oils and methanol were given CARIBCAN coverage, since these were the areas where CARICOM had developed a competitive edge and possessed installed capacity.[5]

Table 8.3   Summary of CARIBCAN tariff treatment, 1987 (figures in Cdn$ 000s)

Beneficiary country	Entered at free rates						Dutiable				
	Total imports ($ 000s)	Under MFN[1] ($ 000s)	Under GPT ($ 000s)	Under CARIB-CAN ($ 000s)	Total free ($ 000s)	Free as a % of total imports	Excluded under CARIB-CAN ($ 000s)	Did not qualify under CARIB-CAN[2] ($ 000s)	Total dutiable ($ 000s)	Excluded as a % of total imports	Total dutiable as a % of total imports
Bahamas	42 178	22 686	14 452		37 138	88.1	–	5 040	5 040	–	11.9
Barbados	21 127	16 649	4 184	157	20 990	99.4	–	137	137	–	0.6
Belize	5 849	5 798	49	–	5 847	100.0	–	–	–	–	–
Bermuda	5 454	3 125	341	25	3 491	64.0	–	2 034	2 034	–	37.3
Guyana	33 777	32 003	1 711	–	33 714	99.8	–	61	61	–	9.7
Jamaica	113 774	100 416	7 113	1 164	108 693	95.5	2 616	2 465	5 001	2.3	4.5
Leeward-Windward Is.	5 525	5 082	58	12	5 152	93.2	–	373	373	–	6.8
Trinidad-Tobago	36 875	22 682	10 457	2 608	35 747	96.9	–	1 131	1 131	–	3.1
Total CARIB-CAN	264 559	208 441	38 365	3 966	250 772	94.8	–	11 241	13 857	–	5.2

[1] Includes imports accorded duty-free treatment under the British Preferential Tariff.

[2] Eligible for duty-free treatment but not granted at time of entry.

Source: Canadian Tariff Treatment for Commonwealth Caribbean Countries, first report of the government of Canada on the trade-related provisions of CARIBCAN, mimeo, 1988.

What had become evident after the inception of CARIBCAN was that traditional commodities, such as fuel oil, bauxite and alumina, sugar, molasses, citrus fruits and spices continued to represent the bulk of CARICOM exports, while non-traditional exports made no significant showing. There were few exceptions in this regard: steel rods from Trinidad and Tobago, which constituted 88 per cent of non-traditional exports; beer, manufactured tobacco extracts and essences, and blouses of textile fabrics from Jamaica; and cordials and liqueurs, cut flowers, hand and machine tools and electrical circuit breakers from Barbados. In any event, except for steel rods from Trinidad and Tobago, the values were almost insignificant in the vast majority of cases.

The 1987 experience was not unique. As the review of trends in Canadian–CARICOM trade conducted in 1991 by the CARICOM Secretariat reveals, there was an adverse balance in merchandise trade with Canada for each year during the period 1988–90, notwithstanding the introduction of CARIBCAN. Overall, Canada maintained a favourable though declining trade balance with CARICOM after 1987, as shown in Tables 8.4 and 8.5. In fact, as far as CARICOM was concerned, there was an adverse balance in merchandise trade for each year during the period 1984–90. Tables 8.6 and 8.7 show that while this situation existed with CARICOM as a whole, the same scenario was reflected with respect to individual countries, with the exception of Jamaica and Guyana (see Table 8.8).

CARICOM's trade balance with Canada in 1984, for instance, was Eastern Caribbean $345.9 million. This improved to $175.2 million in 1985 and to $121 million in 1986. Thereafter, however, it declined to $217.9 million in 1987. There were slight improvements, to $198.9 million in 1988 and $195.9 million in 1989, before declining again to $242.7 million in 1990. Among CARICOM member states, Trinidad and Tobago, with the most highly diversified economy in the entire region, and Barbados recorded the largest negative balance in their trade with Canada and were the main contributors to the overall adverse trade balances that CARICOM experienced with the country. In the case of the former, the balance of trade with Canada moved from EC$316 million in 1984 to $222 million in 1985, $116.3 million in 1986, $145 million in 1987, $76.8 million in 1988, $119.7 million in 1989, and $121.2 million in 1990. For Barbados, the corresponding values were $84.2 million, $70.7 million, $74.6 million, $92.6 million, $94.5 million, $122.4 million and $92.1 million. Jamaica and Guyana, on the other hand, were the only CARICOM countries to record favourable balances in their trade with Canada in each year. Jamaica's trade balance with

Table 8.4   Canada's trade with CARIBCAN countries/territories and the world, 1988–90 (figures in Cdn$ 000s)

Countries/Territories	Imports			Exports		
	1988	1989	1990	1988	1989	1990
Anguilla	117	–	–	509	879	469
Antigua and Barbuda	452	370	181	10 544	8 826	5 605
Bahamas	20 939	32 609	59 042	36 397	27 287	46 501
Barbados	6 577	10 119	15 239	40 074	45 121	32 067
Belize	13 169	13 990	10 606	7 355	5 114	3 494
Bermuda	967	3 091	2 030	38 996	36 916	22 601
British Virgin Islands	71	74	–	6 584	1 596	1 048
Cayman Islands	93	35	4	3 194	2 868	1 977
Dominica	1 065	259	79	3 730	8 257	1 984
Grenada	1 193	886	85	4 225	4 274	3 741
Guyana	15 267	19 999	24 577	5 539	4 393	9 847
Jamaica	150 615	188 663	157 074	126 529	126 075	104 912
Montserrat	389	164	64	865	962	569
St Kitts and Nevis	90	18	34	2 819	3 048	5 040
St Lucia	261	433	9 650	12 786	6 742	6 978
St Vincent & Grenadines	822	661	268	2 885	3 510	3 204
Trinidad and Tobago	52 875	22 255	24 761	51 707	54 123	58 059
Turks & Caicos Islands	8	–	–	673	2 546	523
Total CARIBCAN ($ 000s)	264 970	293 626	303 694	355 411	342 537	308 619
World total ($ 000s)	131 171 696	135 191 139	135 921 739	133 905 153	134 843 430	140 989 301
CARIBCAN/World total	0.20%	0.22%	0.22%	0.27%	0.25%	0.22%
Latin America & Caribbean (LAC)	4 534 070	5 235 370	4 574 837	2 956 388	2 662 759	2 538 159
CARIBCAN/LAC	5.84%	5.61%	6.64%	12.02%	12.86%	12.16%

Source: Statistics Canada, *Summary of Canadian International Trade*, December 1990.

Table 8.5   Canada's trade balance with CARIBCAN countries, 1988–90 (Canadian$ 000s)

	1988	1989	1990
Imports	264 970	293 626	303 694
Exports	355 411	342 537	308 619
Trade balance	90 441	48 911	4 925

Source: Calculation based on figures in Table 8.4.

Canada was $105.4 million in 1984 and $138.8 million in 1985, falling somewhat to $118.7 million in 1986, $74.5 million in 1987, and $42.3 million in 1988. It showed a slight improvement in 1989, to $98.6 million, but fell to EC$19.5 million in 1990. In the case of Guyana, corresponding values were EC$6.0 million, $37.3 million, $43.1 million, $40.7 million, $20.7 million, $35.1 million and $33.0 million, respectively.[6]

In the face of an adverse performance for CARICOM, Canada demonstrated a favourable export performance to the region in the aftermath of CARIBCAN (see Table 8.9). While it is certain that the value of Canadian merchandise exports decreased from EC$720.8 million in 1984 to $584.7 million in 1985, and then to $576.3 in 1986, at an average rate of 10.6 per cent per annum, the picture for the period 1987 to 1990 was different. There was an increase in Canadian exports to CARICOM during those years: from EC$638.8 million in 1987, to $678.0 million in 1988, $682.9 million in 1989 and $741 million in 1990, at an average rate of 5.1 per cent per annum (CARICOM document, 1992).

CARICOM's exports to Canada, on the other hand, rose from EC$479.2 in 1988 to $498.3 in 1990, an increase of approximately 5 per cent. When examined superficially this performance can be deceptive, for although there was an increase in the value of export earnings for CARICOM states, in terms of Canada's overall world trade these figures represented a decline in Canadian imports from the Caribbean from 5.3 to 4.5 per cent. Simply put, Canada–CARICOM trade not only remained small and somewhat insignificant in the 1980s, but declined when compared to that of the EEC and Japan over the same period. Moreover, the major beneficiary of the increase in CARICOM exports over the 1988–90 period were principally Jamaica, accounting for 66 per cent of sales in 1990, Trinidad and Tobago with approximately 15.4 per cent, and Guyana with 11 per cent. The other states experienced either minimal increases or declines. Despite the increase

Table 8.6 Value of Caribbean common market exports to Canada and the world, 1984–90 (EC$ 000s)

Countries	1984	1985	1986	1987	1988	1989	1990
Jamaica	279 701	251 184	257 520	261 431	325 708	365 788	328 125
Trinidad and Tobago	44 024	87 808	107 946	74 778	85 254	44 177	76 908
Guyana	24 567	46 136	52 327	51 694	33 479	45 618	56 896
Barbados	16 953	13 347	31 311	17 098	16 530	14 810	16 802
Belize	5 325	6 987	494	9 489	11 071	9 636	15 345
St Lucia	474	202	526	789	1 044	1 466	1 546
Grenada	1 446	1 037	1 810	2 852	2 597	2 794	1 419
Antigua and Barbuda	823	878	1 471	979	1 909	1 285	419
St Vincent and Grenadines	986	725	871	742	801	576	372
Dominica	58	875	837	448	590	650	203
St Kitts and Nevis	549	256	156	519	124	110	134
Montserrat	26	27	5	10	81	30	90
Total CARICOM	374 932	409 462	455 274	420 829	479 188	486 940	498 259
% of global exports	3.7	4.2	6.0	5.3	5.7	5.1	4.5

Source: CARICOM Secretariat, 1994 (Georgetown, Guyana: CARICOM Secretariat).

Table 8.7 Value of Caribbean common market imports from Canada and the world, 1984–90 (EC$ 000s)

Countries	1984	1985	1986	1987	1988	1989	1990
Jamaica	174 350	112 358	138 855	186 884	283 431	267 192	308 598
Trinidad and Tobago	360 077	309 840	224 208	219 787	162 088	163 841	198 095
Guyana	101 122	84 031	105 879	109 732	111 055	137 185	108 943
Barbados	18 601	8 792	9 220	10 994	12 754	10 521	23 936
Belize	13 396	9 781	13 016	18 247	24 364	24 718	21 649
St Lucia	6 209	4 984	4 787	13 562	10 565	8 737	15 393
Grenada	6 209	4 984	4 787	13 562	10 565	8 737	15 393
Antigua and Barbuda	6 417	7 243	16 933	12 437	11 968	10 171	14 252
St Vincent and Grenadines	6 732	10 632	17 697	15 717	13 528	10 708	13 907
Dominica	12 004	19 115	23 843	23 167	18 660	15 864	13 624
St Kitts and Nevis	8 198	8 197	11 101	14 866	20 126	12 671	13 219
Montserrat	11 970	7 057	8 983	5 667	7 508	19 059	8 044
Total CARICOM	725 285	587 014	579 309	644 622	686 612	689 407	755 053
% of global exports	3.7	4.2	6.0	5.3	5.7	5.1	4.5

Source: CARICOM Secretariat, 1994 (Georgetown, Guyana: CARICOM Secretariat).

Table 8.8   Balance of CARICOM's trade with Canada, 1984–90 (EC$ 000s)

Countries	Trade balances						
	1984	*1985*	*1986*	*1987*	*1988*	*1989*	*1990*
Total CARICOM	-345 859	-175 206	-121 003	-217 928	-198 848	-195 942	-242709
MDCs	-288 905	-116 546	-29 058	-122 396	-108 357	-108 349	-160841
Barbados	-84 169	-70 684	-74 568	-92 634	-94 525	-122 375	-92141
Guyana	5 966	37 344	43 107	40 700 E	20 725 E	35 097 E	32960 E
Jamaica	105 351	138 826	118 665	74 547	42 277	98 596	19527
Trinidad & Tobago	-316 053	-222 032	-116 262	-145 009	-76 834	-119 667	-121187
LDCs	-56 954	-58 660	-91 945	-95 532	-90 491	-87 593	-81868
Belize	-2 873	-1 210	-10 607	-5 377	-9 055	-3 055	2126
OECS	-54 081	-57 450	-81 338	-90 155	-81 436	-84 558	-83994
Antigua & Barbuda	-11 181	-18 237	-22 372	-22 188	-16 751	-14 579	-13205E
Dominica	-11 912	-6 182	-8 146	-5 219	-6 918	-18 409	-7841
Grenada	-5 286	-9 595	-15 887	-12 865	-10 931	-7 914	-12488
Montserrat	-1 689	-2 611	-1 750	-7 687	-1 908 E	-2 182 E	-1218 E
St Kitts & Nevis	-5 660	-4 728	-4 631	-13 043	-10 441	-8 627	-15259
St Lucia	-12 922	-9 579	-12 490	-17 458	-23 320	-23 252	-20103
St Vincent & the G'dines	-5 431	-6 518	-16 062	-11 695	-11 167	-9 595	-13880

E – These balances have been computed from data on Canada's trade with Guyana, Antigua and Barbuda and Montserrat obtained from Statistics Canada, 1990, *Summary of Canadian International Trade*, December.

Table 8.9 Value of CARICOM's imports, Canada, 1984–90 (EC $ 000s)

Countries	1984	1985	1986	1987	1988	1989	1990
				Value of Imports			
Total CARICOM	720 791	584 668	576 277	638 757	678 036	682 982	740 968
MDCs	654 150	515 021	478 162	527 397	569 328	578 742	639 572
Barbados	101 122	84 031	105 879	109 732	111 055	137 185	108 943
Guyana	18 601	8 792 E	9 220 E	10 994 E	12 754 E	10 521 E	23 936 E
Jamaica	174 350	112 358	138 855	186 884	283 431	267 192	308 598
Trinidad & Tobago	360 077	309 840	224 208	219 787	162 088	163 844	198 095
LDC's	66 641	69 647	98 115	111 360	108 708	104 140	101 396
Belize	8 198	8 197	11 101	14 866	20 126	12 671	13 219
OECS	58 443	61 450	87 014	96 494	88 582	91 469	88 177
Antigua & Barbuda	12 004	19 115	23 843	23 167	18 660	15 864	13 624E
Dominica	11 970	7 057	8 983	5 667	7 508	19 059	8 044
Grenada	6 732	10 632	17 697	15 717	13 528	10 708	13 907
Montserrat	1 715	2 638	1 755	7 697	1 989 E	2 212 E	1 308 E
St Kitts & Nevis	6 209	4 984	4 787	13 562	10 565	8 737	15 393
St Lucia	13 396	9 781	13 016	18 247	24 364	24 718	21 649
St Vincent & the G'dnes	6 417	7 243	16 933	12 437	11 968	10 171	14 252

E – Respective values of Canada's exports to Guyana, Antigua and Barbuda, and Montserrat obtained from Statistics Canada, 1990, *Summary of Canadian International Trade*, December.

in CARICOM exports to Canada during this three-year period, however, the region still experienced an imbalance in its trade performance. To this extent, the success of the CARIBCAN trade package became questionable.

In the area of industrial cooperation, the results have not been encouraging. For instance, the Industrial Cooperation Technical Assistance Facility, designed to assist in the development of new export products, was never initiated. For another, the ambitious objectives of the Industrial Cooperation Programme have not been fully met. Under this programme, entrepreneurial and management training, standards development, investment promotion and institution strengthening were to be facilitated. With the exception of the entrepreneurial management programme, which gave rise to the National Development Institutes in most CARICOM states where top and middle-level business managers from the private and public sectors are being trained, other programmes barely got off the ground. This was the case with the standards development programme designed to produce a standardised unit system for the region. None has been established to date. Investment promotion suffered a similar fate. Visits by Canadian businesspeople to the region were few and far between, consequently generating little impact despite the involvement of the Canadian–Caribbean Latin American Association and the Caribbean Association of Industry and Commerce (Gill, 1992, pp. 23–4).

Since introduction of CARIBCAN, there has been, therefore, no marked increase in Canadian investment in the region. In fact, the CARICOM region has not been perceived in recent times as an attractive environment for the Canadian investor. Distance and shipping charges, high labour costs and the current tendency for Canadians to import rather than export investment funds have militated against the attraction of Canadian investors to the Caribbean. As mentioned, both the CCBCO and the Caribbean Investment Opportunities Conferences in April 1991 made little difference in generating investor interest in the region. Despite the heavy attendance – 400 participants, with 300 from the private sector alone – at the Toronto and Montreal Conferences, only four joint-venture projects have taken shape so far (Report on the Caribbean Investment Opportunities Conference, 1991). Undoubtedly, the lack of specific incentives for investing in Caribbean states has worked to some degree against the presence of Canadian investors in CARICOM in the post-CARIBCAN period. Furthermore, the absence of double taxation as well as investment protection agreements between Canada and the majority of CARICOM states has not helped the situation. It is for these reasons that new Canadian investment in the Caribbean is highly unlikely under the present CARIBCAN arrangement.

CONCLUSION

Canadian–CARICOM economic relations clearly represent the major area of bilateral emphasis in the 1990s. CARIBCAN will surely continue to be the centrepiece around which most of these relations would revolve. Unlike the CBI and the Lomé Convention, however, CARIBCAN has not produced significant trade benefits. A review of the arrangement, without which positive results are quite unlikely, must therefore be uppermost in the minds of JTEC officials.

It is important for the JTEC to reconsider the urgent need for a revision of the value-added content for CARIBCAN product coverage, which currently operates under a 60 per cent threshold. Similar review must be accorded to 2 per cent CARICOM products, which remain excluded from the Canadian market. The same applies to existing non-tariff barriers. Even though Canada has not 'instituted safeguard procedures or required voluntary restraints from CARIBCAN beneficiaries', for example, 'there remains the concern that, in the absence of certain guarantees on these questions, investment in production aimed at the Canadian market is possibly being withheld' (Gill, 1992, p. 21). This fear must be removed.

Incentives must be provided to encourage Canadian investment in the region. If the 'special relationship' between Canada and the Commonwealth Caribbean is to be maintained and nurtured, it is incumbent that special effort and attention be given to generating the climate necessary for encouraging the flow of trade and investment. The need for a Venture Capital Fund and a Special Inventive Tax Credit Facility, so often raised by CARICOM as a means of stimulating Canadian investment in the region, cannot be overlooked. Indeed, such incentives can only help to bolster investment and, as a corollary, facilitate trade.

For these proposals to take effect, however, much will depend upon the level of Canadian commitment to CARICOM's development. Reality seems to dictate that the changing Canadian context in recent years is working against the special relationship that has historically existed between both Commonwealth partners. The present downturn in the Canadian economy and Canada's preoccupation with the national unity question and present focus on strengthening international economic alignments with the Far East, the EEC, Eastern Europe, and the United States in particular have all contributed to making the Commonwealth Caribbean peripheral to core concerns in Ottawa. The debate over CUSFTA and NAFTA has clearly demonstrated what Canada's priorities are as far as its foreign economic policy agenda is concerned. In this agenda, CARICOM simply does not feature.

While Canada is preoccupied with NAFTA, it is this very arrangement that ironically represents the greatest threat to CARIBCAN beneficiaries. While assurances have come from the Canadian government that Canada's membership in NAFTA will not affect 'the beneficial access arrangement the Commonwealth Caribbean enjoys with Canada', given the momentum with which trade liberalisation has picked up everywhere, there is little hope that existing trade preferential arrangements would endure in the long run (Wilson, 1993, pp. 1–2). In the short term, therefore, Canada will have to address how best to avoid the erosion of CARIBCAN benefits now enjoyed by CARICOM. In the context of an impending NAFTA, this problem cannot be skirted.

To date, there has been no definitive study of the totality of NAFTA's impact on CARIBCAN beneficiary states. One thing, however, is certain: CARICOM will be placed at a serious trade disadvantage, resulting from a denial of its privileged access position which would be eroded by competing products from the United States, Puerto Rico and Mexico. Tropical products, processed foods and citrus fruits come readily to mind. In addition, because items excluded from CARIBCAN treatment have shown the greatest potential for export growth, NAFTA would now provide Mexico with the advantage of duty-free access for CARICOM products that are currently excluded from CARIBCAN. Under NAFTA, therefore, Mexican methanol, lubricating oils, textiles, garments and footwear would find favour in the Canadian market at the expense of CARICOM.

Likewise, rules of origin restrictions that currently obtain under the CARIBCAN arrangement would undermine CARICOM states. Under NAFTA, for example, Mexican manufacturers could import any amount of raw material from the United States or Canada to produce finished goods for export. As it stands, these finished products will automatically qualify for duty-free entry into the Canadian market. The obvious losers would be CARICOM countries, since they are still restricted under CARIBCAN rules of origin to 60 per cent local value-added for goods exported to Canada, or 40 per cent value-added sourced from Canada.

There is also the psychological dimension to this new economic reality. Since Mexico is about to become a signatory to NAFTA, over time Canadians certainly would become more conscious of Mexican interests. This has already begun. Canadians today have been adopting an aggressive, forward-looking strategy to deal with the largely untapped Mexican market. As this interest in Mexico grows, it could affect Canada's sourcing preferences, investment choices and tourist destinations. Indeed, NAFTA, Canada's membership in the OAS, and its participation in Central American peacekeeping have produced a dynamic change in Canadian–Latin American relations. In this setting, as Edgar J. Dosman has pointed out, 'The Canadian media now treat Mexico as a normal country than merely a nest of problems since the salience of NAFTA has been very successful in focusing attention on Mexico' and this to the point where business, academic and NGO links have changed dramatically since 1989 (Dosman, 1992, p. 550). It is this new development with which CARIBCAN will have to contend if it is to remain relevant to the needs of the Commonwealth Caribbean.

POSTSCRIPT

Since 1992, there has been no major shift in CARIBCAN's structure or performance. The reasons for this have undoubtedly been Canada's preoccupation with its own domestic economy, its greater focus in recent times on Latin American affairs (McCallion, 1995, p. 4), and the concentration of Caribbean energy in the various facets of NAFTA debate. In addition, the delay in convening the seventh meeting of the JTEC in Georgetown, Guyana, in October 1995, held to assess the status of CARIBCAN, and followed in March 1996 by the long-awaited Canada–CARICOM summit held in St Georges, Grenada, did not help in the need for a urgent review of CARIBCAN (*Stabroek News*, 1 September 1995). In fact, it took publication of the *Report of the Foreign Affairs Committee of the Canadian Senate* in August 1995 to generate interest once again in Canada–Caribbean trade relations. This report highlighted, among other things, the need for Canada to consider 'expanding the coverage' of CARIBCAN. It called for an expansion of CARIBCAN as an interim measure to offset some of the trade and investment diversion arising from NAFTA and a renewal of Canada's 'long standing special relationship with the region'. It was not surprising that two months after the publication of this report on Free Trade in the Americas, the seventh JTEC meeting was held at CARICOM headquarters in Guyana. The proceedings of this meeting revealed that, with the exception of two areas where progress could be measured, a continuation of the status quo characterised the CARIBCAN arrangement.

The most heartening development for CARICOM was the news that the balance of trade in favour of Canada between 1984 and 1993 had shifted somewhat in 1994 and 1995 in favour of CARICOM. This change in fortune was largely due to an increase in gold exports from Guyana and methanol from Trinidad and Tobago – a development welcomed by CARICOM and advocates of the arrangement. It was adequate justification for CARICOM heads of state to endorse the request by Jean Chretien, Canada's Prime Minister, for an extension of the waiver granted CARIBCAN by the World Trade Organisation (WTO), which was to come up for review in 1997 (Report of Canada/ CARICOM Seventh JTEC Meeting, 1995, pp. 10–11; and Communiqué on Canada, 1996, p. 4).

The second positive development surrounding CARIBCAN is the renewed interest in promoting Canadian investment in the CARICOM region. Over the last seven years, the CCBCO has proven to be largely ineffective. Recently, it has been resuscitated, however, with joint approaches now being pursued by Canada and CARICOM in designing and implementing a new agenda for its success. New strategies and activities have been drawn up to effect its renewed operation (Communiqué on Canada, 1996, p. 4). Already a CCBCO office has been earmarked for Trinidad and Tobago, with the expectation that others would be established elsewhere in the region.

One advantage of this development for Canadian businesspeople is the opportunity it would provide for their eventual leap into the Latin American market. As Canada's Assistant Deputy Minister for Latin American and Caribbean Affairs, Kathryn McCallion, remarked in October 1995, such a new strategy would help to bring CARICOM and Canadian business interests closer together 'to foster interaction and opportunities for investment' at both the CARICOM and Canadian ends (Report of Canada/CARICOM Seventh JTEC Meeting, 1995, p. 12).

These positive, optimistic signs notwithstanding, CARICOM pleas over the last four years have gone unheeded. Though assurances continue to be given by Canada with respect to addressing such issues as preferential treatment for excluded products (textiles, clothing, leather garments, footwear, lubricating oils and methanol), revision of the rules of origin, establishment of joint ventures, political commitment to assist the region in enhancing its capacity to 'adjust to the evolving global environment' and in 'its preparation for a Free Trade Area of the Americas (FTAA) by the year 2005' (Report on the Twenty-Second Meeting, 1996, p. 3), and Canada's commitment 'to continue dialogue with CARICOM on key issues of mutual interest', very little progress has been made over the last four years with respect to reviewing or revamping CARIBCAN. It continues to be CARICOM's hope that CARIBCAN will be revisited in a fundamental way as to make a difference and that it will become more compatible with Caribbean expectations. In the meantime, the CARICOM region can take respite in the argument made on its behalf by the Foreign Relations Committee of the Canadian Senate in August 1995:

> We wonder whether Canada can really continue to claim a 'special' relationship with the Caribbean if the Canadian government assumes a hard line against modifying CARIBCAN while the United States is prepared to enhance its own preferential trade program, the Caribbean Basin Initiative (CBI), in order to help the region (*Stabroek News*, 1 September 1995).

Notes

1. These conferences also provided for improved transportation and communications between both areas. In fact, it was the conclusion of these meetings that ushered in the era of the 'Lady Boat', which regularly plied the Canadian–Caribbean trade route and which became a regular feature in the communication linkage between the regions in the first half of the 20th century.
2. The most recent evidence of educational cooperation has been the granting of CARICOM scholarships to West Indians under the 1990 Canadian CARICOM Scholarship Programme currently administered by CIDA. This programme, estimated to cost Canadian \$4 074 990, is designed to increase the availability of skilled managers and trainers in public administration, agriculture, industry and tourism.
3. John Crosbie to Sahadeo Basdeo in official letter dated 17 July 1989 (personal correspondence).
4. Data from 'Canadian Tariff Treatment for Commonwealth Caribbean countries', First Report of the Government of Canada on the Trade-Related Provisions of CARIBCAN, mimeo, 1988.
5. These positions were taken at various Canada–CARICOM JTEC meetings.
6. For a comprehensive picture of Canada–CARICOM trade flows over the period 1984–90, see CARICOM Document, 'Review of Trends in Canada–

CARICOM Trade, 1984–90', presented at the Sixth Meeting of the JTEC on 12 June 1992.

References

Baranyi, S. and E.J. Dosman (1990) 'Canada and the Security of the Commonwealth Caribbean', in A.T. Bryan, J.E. Greene, and T.M. Shaw (eds), *Peace, Development and Security in the Caribbean: Perspectives to the Year 2000* (London: Macmillan).

Barbados Advocate News, 7 February 1981.

Barbados Advocate News, 22 May 1986.

Basdeo, S. and H. Robertson (1981) 'The Nova Scotia–British West Indies Commercial Experiment in the Aftermath of the American Revolution, 1789–1802', *Dalhousie Review*, vol. 61, no. 1 (Spring).

Canada Fund for Local Initiatives (1993) *Fiscal Year 1990/1991: America's Branch Annual Review* (Ottawa: Canadian International Development Agency).

Canadian Department of External Affairs (1988) *CARIBCAN: Canadian Programs for Commonwealth Caribbean Trade, Investment and Industrial Cooperation* (Ottawa: Canadian Department of External Affairs and CID).

CARICOM (1992) Document 'Review of Trends in Canada–CARICOM Trade, 1984–1990', presented at the Sixth Meeting of the JTEC, 12 June.

CARICOM Secretariat (1989) Private document (Georgetown, Guyana: CARICOM Secretariat).

Chodos, R. (1977) *The Caribbean Connection* (Toronto: James Lorimer & Co.).

Communique on Canada–CARICOM Heads of Government Summit, held in St George's, Grenada, 3–5 March 1996.

Crosbie, J. (1989) Official letter to Sahadeo Basdeo, dated 17 July.

Dosman, E.J. (1992) 'Canada and Latin America: The New Look', *International Journal*, vol. 47, no. 3 (Summer).

Express, The. 8 October 1993.

Gill, H. (1992) 'Canada and the Commonwealth Caribbean: Evaluation of the CARIBCAN Experience since 1996', paper presented to the XVIII Regular Meeting of the Latin American Council, Caracas, Venezuela, 7–11 September.

Government of Canada (1988) 'Canadian Tariff Treatment for Commonwealth Caribbean Countries', unpublished.

Guy, J. (1990) 'The Caribbean; A Canadian Perspective', in B.D. Tennyson (ed.), *Canada–Caribbean Relations: Aspects of a Relationship* (Sydney, Nova Scotia: Centre for International Studies).

Jamaican Gleaner, 7 March 1986.

McCallion, K. (1995) Report of Canada/CARICOM Seventh JTEC Meeting, held in Georgetown, Guyana, 12–13 October.

MacGuigan, M. (1981) Speech delivered at the Canada/CARICOM Joint Trade and Economic Committee (JTEC) meeting in Kingston, Jamaica, on 15 January 1981, quoted in *Barbados Advocate News*, 17 January.

Ministry of Foreign Affairs (1990) Report of Commonwealth Caribbean–Canada Heads of Government meeting, Barbados, 19–20 March.

Report on the Caribbean Investment Opportunities Conference, held 23–25 April 1991, in proceedings of Twelfth Meeting of Heads of Government of the Caribbean Community, Basseterre, St Kitts and Nevis, 2–4 July 1991.

Report of Canada/CARICOM Seventh JTEC Meeting (1995) Georgetown, Guyana, 11–13 November.

CARICOM Secretariat (1985) Report of the Third Meeting of the JTEC (Georgetown, Guyana: CARICOM Secretariat).

Report on the Twenty-Second Meeting of the Standing Committee of Ministers Responsible for Foreign Affairs and the Related Preparatory Meeting of Officials held in Kingston, Jamaica, 9–14 May 1996.

Stabroek News, 1 September 1995.

Statistics Canada (1990) *Summary of Canadian International Trade*, December.

Tennyson, B.D. (1990) 'Canada and the Commonwealth Caribbean: The Historical Relationship', in B.D. Tennyson (ed.), *Canada–Caribbean Relations: Aspects of a Relationship* (Sydney, Nova Scotia: Centre for International Studies).

Trinidad Guardian, 15 October 1987.

Trinidad Guardian, 3 January 1990.

Trinidad Guardian, 21 March 1990.

Wilson, M. (1993) Personal correspondence, 23 June.

9 Canadian Economic Assistance to CARICOM Countries: Assessment and Future Prospects

Richard L. Bernal and Winsome J. Leslie

INTRODUCTION

Since the 1950s, Canada's historically close trade and investment relationship with the countries of the Caribbean Community and Common Market (CARICOM) has been complemented by an important programme of economic assistance. CARICOM has 15 members: Antigua and Barbuda, the Bahamas, Barbados, Belize, Dominica, Grenada, Guyana, Haiti, Jamaica, Montserrat, St Kitts and Nevis, St Lucia, St Vincent and the Grenadines, Suriname, and Trinidad and Tobago. Haiti is the newest member of the Community; it joined in July 1997.

Cordial relations between Canada and CARICOM have endured for over a century. Because of shared cultural ties fostered by immigration, a common political system and membership in the British Commonwealth, Canada has been viewed by CARICOM as a more 'benevolent' partner than the United States. Canada's affinity for the Caribbean reflects the fact that both Canada and the Caribbean have had to respond to the economic dominance and hegemony in international affairs of the United States.

Over the years, the priorities of Canada's foreign assistance programme have reflected a tension between altruistic objectives on the one hand, focusing on alleviating poverty and promoting sustainable development, and commercial, economic and foreign policy interests on the other (Mundy, 1992, p. 393). Tension has resulted in changing approaches to official development assistance (ODA), coupled with attempts to maintain a sensitivity to the development objectives and strategies of beneficiary countries (Jackson, 1992, p. 96). Initially, the objectives and allocation of Canadian assistance were similar to those of multilateral development institutions, which focused on the promotion

190

of development through funding for infrastructure, rural development and basic human needs. By the late 1980s, Canada's emphasis had shifted towards linking development strategies with broader foreign and domestic policy goals. In addition, as is the case with other Western donors, fiscal considerations and domestic politics adversely affected the level of Canadian aid to the Caribbean resulting in significant decline since the 1980s.

This chapter examines Canadian ODA to the Caribbean, by reviewing past performance, analysing current trends, and looking ahead to possible changes in future assistance. The first section looks at Canadian assistance in historical perspective, highlighting changes that have occurred over the years in Canada's approach to foreign aid. The second section looks at the institutional framework for ODA, with a focus on the Canadian International Development Agency (CIDA), which administers most of the economic assistance programme. This section will also highlight changing trends in the foreign aid programme. Section three examines the aid programme to the Caribbean and, more specifically, discusses the types of assistance that have been extended to the region. The final section provides concluding remarks about the aid programme and discusses future directions given existing budgetary constraints.

HISTORICAL OVERVIEW

The British colonial trade system was a combination of mercantilism and the provision of economic assistance through preferential market access and commodity price support schemes, for example, sugar and bananas. This system extended by Britain and more-developed countries to the developing countries of the Commonwealth provided economic assistance by imposing higher prices on consumers and/or transfers of financial resources. This was the forerunner of financial resource flows, which in the contemporary period have been called foreign aid or development assistance. Canada made economic aid available through trade to small developing economies in the English-speaking Caribbean, or what was then described as the British West Indies.

Canada has traditionally been the Caribbean's third largest trading partner, superseded only by the United States and Britain (see Table 9.1). Trade began early in the eighteenth century and grew steadily, based on increased trade in Canadian salt-cod and cereals. Special trade arrangements commenced in 1925 with the Canada–West Indies

Table 9.1   Distribution of CARICOM* trade, 1896 and 1911–61 (percentages)

	Imports				Exports			
	UK	Canada	USA	Total	UK	Canada	USA	Total
1896	47	6	29	82	38	3	42	83
1911	41	8	33	82	22	23	41	86
1922	31	18	32	81	34	26	27	87
1928	35	19	24	78	28	25	26	79
1933	44	14	13	71	45	24	7	76
1955	40	10	14	64	44	18	8	70
1961	34	7	17	58	26	13	27	66

* Does not include Suriname.
Source: H.R. Brewster and C.Y. Thomas (1967), 'Trade Between the West Indies and Canada', in *West Indies–Canada Economic Relations* (Mona: Institute of Social and Economic Research, University of the West Indies), p. 15.

Agreement and Commonwealth preferential arrangements in the 1930s. Trade with Canada grew rapidly between 1938 and 1963: exports to Canada increased 800 per cent, while imports grew 624 per cent (Brewster and Thomas, 1967, p. 19). In 1963, exports to Canada accounted for 5.9 per cent of gross domestic product (GDP) (*ibid.*, p. 24). The Caribbean only accounted for about 1 per cent of total Canadian imports in 1964, but was still an important source of supply in certain commodities. For example, the region supplied Canada 68 per cent of its bauxite and alumina, 61 per cent of molasses, 42 per cent of unrefined sugar, and 28 per cent of rum, as well as a large share of nutmeg and arrowroot (Jefferson, 1967, p. 77).

Canada has traditionally provided aid through preferential market access. Preferential trade arrangements were first instituted in 1898, when Canada unilaterally provided a 25 per cent tariff preference to a range of imports from the region, including sugar. In 1900, the preference on sugar was increased to $33\frac{1}{3}$ per cent. In 1912, preferential trade arrangements were extended with the signing of the Canada–West Indian Reciprocal Treaty, which was subsequently revised in 1920 and became the Canada–West Indies Trade Agreement in 1925. This treaty provided reciprocal tariff preferences. It was amended in July 1966, when duty-free entry for sugar was provided based on the average quantity of exports the previous five years. In 1979, a Trade and Economic Cooperation Agreement was signed, and, in June 1986, CARIBCAN was established. CARIBCAN provides preferential, one-way, duty-free entry into the Canadian market of the large majority of goods currently being exported to that market by beneficiary countries. The following products were, however, not considered for CARIBCAN treatment: textiles and clothing, footwear, luggage and handbags, leather garments, lubricating oils and methanol. Products excluded from the programme would nevertheless continue to be subject to established preferential rates of duty under the Canadian General Preferential Tariff (GPT).

The expansion of trade attracted Canadian banks into the region, such as the Bank of Nova Scotia (BNS) which opened an office in Jamaica in 1889 (Callender, 1996). Indeed, by the First World War several Canadian banks, including BNS, the Canadian Imperial Bank of Commerce and the Merchant's Bank of Halifax (now the Royal Bank of Canada), had branches throughout the Caribbean. Canada's financial penetration into the Caribbean was important for the economic transformation of both Canada and the Caribbean and helped incorporate them into the global economy.[1] Other than banking (Baum, 1974) Canadian investment was concentrated in the bauxite/alumina sector in Jamaica after the 1950s (Bernal, 1984, pp. 10–12).

Canadian foreign aid to the Caribbean began with a $10 million five-year programme of assistance to the West Indies Federation in 1958 (Levitt and McIntyre, 1967, pp. 107–23), in an attempt to promote economic development by fostering regional integration in the Caribbean region. These efforts continue today and are still part of the current assistance programme. Bilateral development assistance loans commenced in the region in the early 1960s.

The government of Canada has been a sympathetic donor to the Caribbean and has been creative in its lending programmes. For example, in 1990, Canada cancelled all outstanding development assistance debt owed by CARICOM member countries, which totalled Canadian $182 million and represented 1.5 per cent of CARICOM countries' total debt (Bernal, 1991, p. 4). This was noteworthy because at the time industrialised countries were disavowing debt relief through cancellation, except for developing countries which were both the poorest and most indebted.

INSTITUTIONAL MECHANISMS

Canadian ODA is administered by four agencies. CIDA is responsible for 75 per cent of the bilateral aid programme, while the remainder is managed by the Department of Finance (funding for multilateral institutions), the Department of Foreign Affairs, and the Department of Public Works and Government Services. CIDA was created in 1968 out of the External Aid Office set up in 1960 to coordinate Canada's external assistance efforts. That same year, the United Nations (UN) proclaimed its First Development Decade. CIDA's programmes are administered through several 'activities': the Partnership Programme, which directs Canada's assistance to multilateral institutions, including multilateral food aid; the National Initiatives Programme, which administers bilateral aid and a special programme for Countries in Transition in Eastern Europe, which was transferred from the Department of Foreign Affairs and International Trade to CIDA in 1995.

Official development assistance to CARICOM countries is part of the Americas programme, which includes three subregions: the Caribbean, Central America and South America. In addition, CIDA also provides support through regional initiatives as well as the Canada Fund for Local Initiatives. The Canada Fund is available in a number of countries (Jamaica, Belize and Haiti, for example) and consists of a small pool of discretionary resources used to fund Canadian $40000 and $50000 projects. It is administered directly by Canadian high commissions and embassies in the Caribbean, and complements CIDA's bilateral programmes through emphasis on funding small-scale projects that provide technical, educational or social development assistance.

Over the years, CIDA has moved from being an administrator of Canada's aid programme to assuming the larger role of shaping aid policy. During the early years of CIDA's existence up to the late 1970s, CIDA's raison d'être was simply to channel aid to developing countries, with little or no effort to plan for the effective use of those funds, or to rationalise aid allocation based on Canada's foreign policy and commercial objectives (Pratt, 1994, pp. 7 and 159). This was a time when Canada was rapidly expanding its foreign assistance programme and its focus was on widespread dispersal of assistance. In 1961, for example, 33 countries received economic assistance, and, by 1976, this number had grown to 84. By 1989–90, 119 countries were receiving assistance. Bilateral funding from Canada was significant in many countries, including the Caribbean. In 1975, for example, ODA, as a percentage of total aid received, was greater than 10 per cent in 18 countries, 10 of them in the Caribbean. By 1989, however, only seven countries, including Jamaica and Guyana, received aid totalling 10 per cent of ODA (Pratt, 1994, p. 7). One of CIDA's main concerns during these early years was simply using up its foreign aid budget.

During the 1970s, there were pressures for CIDA to concentrate on fewer countries. As a result, a task force was established to develop a five-year aid strategy. The 'Strategy for International Development Cooperation, 1975–80' essentially maintained the status quo in terms of aid policy, reaffirming that most assistance should be extended to the poorest countries. Continued pressures to use the aid programme to promote Canadian business abroad produced the Hatch Report (1980), 'Strengthening Canada Abroad', which advocated for bilateral aid in the 1980s and concentrating assistance in those countries where there was trade potential for Canada. As a result, the Canadian government chose to increase bilateral ODA between 1981 and 1986, at the expense of multilateral assistance, while maintaining a commitment to low-income countries (Morrison, 1994, pp. 125–40).

By the late 1980s, with Canada under fiscal restraints, Parliament undertook a major review of the aid programme. A report released in 1987 entitled 'For Whose Benefit', benefited from input from a wide constituency, including the general public. It made several recommendations for making Canada's aid programme more effective and maintaining its 'constructive internationalism'. While seeking to give CIDA greater control over its development mandate, the report made the following recommendations: CIDA was told to: (a) emphasise poverty-lending; (b) put development priorities first; (c) establish an ODA charter and mandate a minimum level for ODA of 0.5 per cent of GNP; and (d) establish an advisory council.

The government's response came in the form of its 1988 foreign aid strategy report, 'Sharing Our Future', which accepted the first two recommendations dealing with poverty alleviation and the importance of development priorities over other foreign policy goals. Within the overall framework of promoting sustainable development, certain areas of focus for assistance were identified:

(a)   poverty alleviation,
(b)   structural adjustment,
(c)   women in development,
(d)   the environment,
(e)   food security, and
(f)   energy.

With respect to aid levels and targets, 'Sharing Our Future' pledged to gradually increase the ODA/GNP ratio to 0.7 per cent by the year 2000 and to extend all future ODA in the form of grants. Finally, a commitment was made to reduce 'tied aid' from 80 per cent of bilateral assistance to between 60 and 70 per cent (CIDA, 1988, p. 7). By 1991, CIDA had experienced three successive rounds of annual budget cuts, forcing organisational and programme changes. There were also added pressures from both clients and 'stakeholders' in the aid programme. From 1993 to 1994, the International Assistance Envelope, used to fund ODA, was reduced by 10 per cent. While cuts were made across the board in the Americas, Canada's interest in South America meant that cuts were heaviest in the Caribbean (Morrison, 1994, p. 149).

Budget constraints still continue at the present time. While funds for the International Assistance Envelope in 1996–97 remained unchanged from the 1995–96 level, in 1997–98 funds will be reduced by 7.2 per cent and reduced by another 7.3 per cent in 1998–99 (CIDA, 1997–98 estimates, part III). As a result, CIDA has been shifting resources to accommodate a 'strategic' aid programme in keeping with the latest statement on the government's aid strategy, 'Canada in the World', released in 1995. This new approach emphasises the promotion of prosperity and employment for Canada as well as its aid partners, with emphasis on access for Canadian trade and investment abroad. While the focus on sustainable development and poverty alleviation has been reaffirmed, programme priorities now include human rights, democracy and good governance, basic human needs and private sector development, in addition to traditional areas such as infrastructure, women in development and the environment (CIDA, 1995, pp. 10, 42). Nevertheless, CIDA's activities are circumscribed by reduced resources and, to some extent, a refocusing of programming towards countries where there are clear advantages for Canadian business. CIDA's new strategy has affected all regional programmes, including the Caribbean.

AID FLOWS

In 1996, Canada was ranked seventh in the world in terms of total dollars spent on foreign aid. About half of total Canadian ODA consists of bilateral assistance, while the remainder supports initiatives undertaken by multilateral institutions, Canadian non-governmental organisations (NGOs), research institutions and businesses. Canadian aid to the Caribbean has decreased significantly over the years. From 1969 to 1972, for example, Canada was the second major aid contributor to the region after Great Britain, accounting for 20 per cent of total aid flow. For fiscal year 1994/95, CARICOM countries excluding Haiti received

Table 9.2   Canadian Official Development Assistance (ODA) to CARICOM countries, 1982–96[*]

Fiscal years	CARICOM	Americas[**]	Total ODA
1982–83	29.9	111.95	1 672.06
1983–84	45.51	172.31	1 797.08
1984–85	66.93	197.93	2 104.56
1985–86	71.16	175.40	2 247.61
1986–87	90.01	330.02	2 551.77
1987–88	86.08	376.35	2 624.06
1988–89	109.72	398.01	2 946.60
1989–90	120.92	343.30	2 849.87
1990–91	113.63	348.55	3 035.34
1991–92	98.22	400.66	3 182.46
1992–93	83.77	340.05	2 972.70
1993–94	87.17	367.56	3 075.27
1994–95	74.43	310.97	3 092.46
1995–96	47.95	290.92	2 684.31

[*] All amounts are in Canadian dollars.
[**] Includes CARICOM.
Source: CIDA, *Estimates, Table M: Total Disbursements by Country*, CIDA Annual Reports, 1982/83 through 1988/89 and 1995/96 (Hull, Quebec: CIDA); CIDA, *ODA Disbursements to CARICOM Countries*, 1989/90 through 1994/95 (Hull, Quebec: CIDA).

Canadian $74.43 million, or 23 per cent of total assistance of $310. 97 million to the Americas programme. Furthermore, in terms of total ODA, CARICOM countries, excluding Haiti, received only 2.6 per cent of bilateral aid (see Table 9.2).

By CIDA's own estimates, funding for the Caribbean (including Haiti and Cuba) represented 55 per cent of all commitments to the Americas in 1990/91. Caribbean assistance fell to 41 per cent of the Americas allocation in 1995/96, and is expected to fall further to 37 per cent in 1997/98. Furthermore, although CIDA's representation in the Caribbean remains unchanged, resources have been redeployed from Jamaica and three other countries in the Americas (Peru, Colombia and Costa Rica) in order to open new offices in Cuba, Ecuador and the Organisation of American States (OAS) (CIDA, 1996b, chapter II, p. 2).

CIDA's funding programme for CARICOM focuses on assistance for the promotion of self-reliance by increasing the competitiveness of export industries in view of the increasingly liberalised global economy. CIDA also supports projects that promote regional cooperation and integration and facilitate links to other regional markets. There is also a strong emphasis on poverty alleviation and environmental management. The largest percentage of CIDA's funds to the Caribbean is allotted to Jamaica, Guyana, and an Eastern Caribbean programme administered out of Barbados. There are also small bilateral programmes in Trinidad and Tobago, Barbados and Belize. Overall, there is evidence, based on discussions at the March 1996, Canada–CARICOM Heads of Government meeting, that Canada is moving away from ODA and towards a relationship with CARICOM countries based on trade and investment (CIDA, 1996b, chapter I, p. 17).

THE CARIBBEAN DEVELOPMENT BANK (CDB)

At the regional level, Canada has been an important contributor to the Caribbean Development Bank (CDB). The first steps towards establishment of the CDB were taken at a Canada/Commonwealth Caribbean Conference in Ottawa in 1966, where it was decided that a study should be undertaken to explore the feasibility of establishing a financial institution for the Caribbean region. When the CDB was created in 1969, Canada was a founding member, subscribing 2000 shares of the bank's authorised capital stock of 10000 shares. At the moment, Canada holds 10402 shares of CDB's current authorised capital of 115000 shares. Both Canada and the United Kingdom retain the highest non-regional voting share in the bank of 10.27 per cent. Since 1969, Canada has provided US$126 million in paid-up capital subscriptions and other contributions to the bank's resources. Canadian assistance has been particularly important to the bank's Special Development Fund (concessional resources), having contributed 23 per cent of the resources available as of December 1996. The fund has made poverty reduction a central focus of its activities, with an established lending target for poverty of 40 per cent. To assist in this process, CIDA funded the preparation of a framework for poverty assessments in 1994, and subsequently a pilot poverty assessment process for three countries – St Lucia, St Vincent and Belize – was completed in 1995.

Canadian funding for technical assistance has been particularly important to the CDB's activities. The Canadian Agricultural Trust Fund was established in 1971. The Canadian $2.5 million fund, later replenished with $6.88 million, was used to increase agricultural productivity and diversify output in 11 countries. Four years later, the Canadian Commercial Livestock Fund was created, with Canada contributing US$4.3 million (Government of Canada, 1996). In 1992, Canada extended $300000 to the bank for technical cooperation in the areas of poverty alleviation, environment and women in development. In 1994, the two-year agreement was extended to 1994 and assistance increased to $630000.

In October 1996, Canada agreed to establish a US$2.4 million Canadian Technical Cooperation Fund (CTCF) within the CDB to support the bank's work in economic and social analysis, and support project development using Canadian technical assistance. Priority is to be given to activities that coincide with Canada's objectives, such as poverty reduction, human resource development and environmental protection. In addition, the new facility will ultimately be a mechanism with which to support the participation of Canadian consultants in the early stages of CDB-funded projects. Recruitment of consultants will be limited to Canadians residing in Canada, Canadian firms and NGOs located in Canada (*Caribbean Development Bank News*, 1997, p. 4).

As a further indication of Canada's close involvement with the CDB, the twenty-seventh annual Meeting of the bank was held in Toronto in May 1997 – the first occasion in the bank's history that such a meeting was held outside the Caribbean.

JAMAICA

Canada's assistance to Jamaica began in 1963, focusing on infrastructure projects in keeping with the Canadian government's goals. By 1972, however, CIDA began to concentrate on agricultural development. Accordingly, the lending programme in Jamaica began to reflect this orientation. The idea was to increase employment opportunities in rural areas by modernising agriculture, and early projects focused on technical assistance to (a) the cattle and pig industry, (b) improvements in potato production, and (c) improvements in the system of transporting sugar cane from field to factory. This was the period of Michael Manley's efforts to implement democratic socialism in Jamaica, focusing on redistribution of wealth through land settlement schemes, social programmes and government subsidies. Accordingly, CIDA extended technical assistance in agriculture not only to specialised producers, but to government agencies such as the Agricultural

Development Corporation and workers' production cooperatives (Jackson, 1992, pp. 87–9).

By 1976, with the onset of balance of payments problems in Jamaica, CIDA began to extend balance of payments support via lines of credit, consisting essentially of inputs for the agriculture and manufacturing sectors. Edward Seaga's Jamaica Labor party victory in October 1980 was the beginning of what would be a sustained series of structural adjustment programmes in Jamaica and a refocus on the private sector as the engine of growth. CIDA's lending programme was revised accordingly to reflect these new realities. In agriculture, for example, CIDA aimed to assist in the revitalisation of the sector by funding projects that generated employment opportunities for 'vulnerable' groups (women and young people); generated or saved foreign exchange; and increased production, particularly at the level of the small farmer. From 1981 to 1986, CIDA provided Canadian $70 million in agricultural inputs as lines of credit under its revised programme. Commodities were sold either through private companies, such as T. Geddes Grant, or producer organisations, such as the Jamaica Agricultural Society and the All-Island Cane Farmers Association. Part of the counterpart funds generated by these sales were designated for small farmers through a revolving credit fund in the Agricultural Credit Bank (Jackson, 1992, pp. 93–6).

In 1996, Jamaica ended its borrowing relationship with the International Monetary Fund (IMF), and structural reform measures have improved Jamaica's external position. Hence, the government now focuses on poverty alleviation and economic growth. CIDA's current lending programme in Jamaica at the present time focuses on private sector development, environmental management and agriculture.

CIDA has been relatively successful in promoting private sector development in Jamaica through CANEXPORT. The four-year Canadian $4 million project (1993–96) aimed to increase exports to Canada in the following areas: fresh produce, cut flowers and processed foods. Approximately 70 small and medium-sized firms were involved in the project. Executed by Jamaica Promotions (JAMPRO), the project resulted in increases of between 42 and 173 per cent in the following product categories: papaya, citrus/ortanique, sweet potatoes, yams, mangoes, peppers, tilapia, sauces, jams and jellies, coffee and biscuits. Export earnings in these categories totalled Canadian $9 million in 1996, compared to $3.35 million in 1991 before the project's inception. CIDA also provides credit and technical assistance to micro and small-scale enterprises through the National Development Foundation, by funding approximately a third of the cost of a $7.28 million project. The Canadian component is funding the costs of services by Canadian consultants, acquisition of computer and office equipment as well as motor vehicles and spare parts. This project will be completed in March 1998 (Planning Institute of Jamaica, 1996, p. 8).

CIDA is also making a significant contribution in the area of environmental management. The Canadian $2 million Green Fund supports community-based initiatives in natural resources conservation. Fund staff work closely with the Environmental Foundation of Jamaica and other local groups to identify weaknesses in environmental management and design appropriate interventions. The Fund has provided assistance in a number of areas, such as waste recycling, energy conservation, sanitation, and informal sector activities related to environmental management. As of March 1996, a total of 56 projects had been funded through several local NGOs (PIOJ, 1996, p. 26).

The Environmental Action Programme (ENACT) is an eight-year programme designed to strengthen environmental management capacity in Jamaica. The programme provides Canadian $12.4 million in three phases. Phase I, launched in 1994, provides technical assistance to build capacity in the National Resources Conservation Authority (NRCA) to formulate environmental policy. Phase II, which began in January 1997, builds on the work of the NRCA Canadian consultant to implement environmental policies in the public and private sectors, as well as within local community organisations. Emphasis will also be placed on environmental education. Phase III will consolidate the lessons learned from the first two phases and complete Phase II projects, handing over responsibility for ongoing environmental work to Jamaican partners. Canada is also funding a Canadian $350000 Environmental Baseline Study in the Salt River, the site of a proposed power plant. The study will assist the Jamaican government in environmental impact assessment to determine whether such a plant ought to be constructed (PIOJ, 1996, pp. 24–5).

CIDA is funding two important projects in the agricultural sector. First, it is supporting the existing network of rural cooperative banks with a grant of Canadian $4.9 million. The Agricultural Credit Bank is coordinating the project, which also includes technical assistance and training. Second, the project by which CIDA provided bulk fertilizers for balance of payments support (Soil Nutrients for Agricultural Productivity, SNAP), is now in its second phase. The provision of fertilizer for balance of payments support, a Canadian $47.16 million CIDA grant, ended in September 1994. The second phase, or technical assistance component ($2 million), has awarded several research grants to the Banana Board, the Coconut Board, the Citrus Growers Association, and RADA. In April 1996, an additional grant of $2 million was approved for continuation of research activities.

Finally, in the area of technical assistance to the financial sector, CIDA funded the services of a consultant between 1993 and 1996, who ultimately served as Governor of the Bank of Jamaica until 1996.

HAITI

Canada has taken the lead, along with the United States, France and Germany, in Haiti's reconstruction. During the period of military rule (1991–94), the bilateral programme was suspended. However, the Canadian government continued to provide Haiti with humanitarian assistance to Haiti through multilateral agencies and various Canadian NGOs. Following restoration of the constitutional government of Jean Bertrand Aristide in October 1994, Canada, together with other bilateral and multilateral donors, agreed to provide approximately US$1 billion in foreign assistance between October 1994 and April 1996 (CIDA, 1996a, p. 9). A reconstruction plan, the Plan d'Urgence de Reconstruction Economique (PURE), was drawn up which included balance of payments support, funds for reconstruction and humanitarian assistance (36 per cent of the total), infrastructure (21 per cent), governance (9 per cent), social sectors (11 per cent), the environment (4 per cent), and support for the productive sectors (8 per cent). More specifically, Canada agreed to provide US$121.4 million in assistance (see Table 9.3 for breakdown).

CIDA's current priority for Haiti is poverty alleviation. The assistance programme concentrates on three areas: basic human needs, economic growth and democracy/good governance. Therefore, in terms of these development goals, Canada is focusing on (a) reconstruction projects, such as the rebuilding of schools and clinics, and small-scale community projects through the Canada Fund for Local Initiatives; (b) the creation of an Environment Support Fund; (c) technical assistance to the private sector; and (d) training for the police force, court personnel and local judges, as well as institutional support to the Ministry of Justice (CIDA, 1996a, p. 19). In addition, since March 1996, Canada has taken charge of internal security under a UN mandate which was originally due to expire on 30 November 1997.

Table 9.3   Canadian ODA grants for reconstruction in
Haiti 1996–98 (US $ millions)

Sector	Pipeline
Balance of payments support	3.7
Social and health sectors	12.1
Food aid	21.8
Finance	0.7
Justice	22.4
Agriculture	3.7
Environment	8.4
Health	0.4
Education	5.3
Energy	8.15
Water and urban infrastructure	11.05
Private sector development	9.9
Women in development	0.5
Special grants	9.9
Special funds	3.4
Total	121.4

Source: United States Agency for International Development (USAID) (1996), *Haiti: Donor Pipeline and Disbursements* (Washington, DC: United States Agency for International Development), November.

GUYANA

As in the case of Jamaica, Canada has consistently supported Guyana's development efforts since its independence. However, with the launching of Guyana's Economic Recovery Programme in 1988, CIDA's bilateral assistance has increased significantly. Canada led the international 'rescue' effort enabling Guyana to clear its external debt arrears and put structural adjustment measures in place, by chairing the Donor Support Group. Indeed, Guyana was a test case for this new Donor Support Group approach to the debt crisis, which originated with the IMF and World Bank. The idea was that these groups would be chaired by a country considered 'friendly' by the debtor. This country would renegotiate the debtor's Paris Club debts, monitor the debtor's progress in implementing structural reforms, and, finally, arrange bilateral support from Western donors to pay off outstanding arrears, thereby clearing the way for new capital inflows from the World Bank and IMF (Black and McKenna, 1995, p. 65).

Between 1989–90 and 1992–93, Canada was the lead bilateral donor, providing balance of payments support, technical assistance and funding for economic reform projects. For example, the Fertilizer Line of Credit project provided Canadian $36.3 million in balance of payments support to increase agricultural production. The goal was to increase the availability of fertilizers to agricultural producers to increase the productivity of rice and sugar, the country's major export crops. The funds generated from the sale of fertilizers was used to create the Futures Fund, a counterpart fund managed by the Canadian Hunger Foundation to offset the social costs of adjustment by supporting poverty reduction activities. By March 1996, when the project ended, the Fund had provided assistance tor several hundred small-scale community projects geared towards empowering Guyana's most vulnerable groups: the unemployed, single mothers, children, the elderly, and the Amerindian population.

To increase economic competitiveness, the Canadian Executive Service Organisation (CESO) Business Advisory Service focuses on strengthening the operations of small businesses in Guyana. The programme provides volunteer advisers for short-term assignments with Guyanese employers. Phase I of the project ended in 1996. Two hundred and fifty assignments were made, mostly with the private sector. Evaluation impact studies show that most of the clients experienced increases in their productivity. The project has also established the Guyana Volunteer Consultancy Programme, a local business advisory system for micro-enterprises, NGOs and community organisations. Phase II of the project is in progress and will continue until 2001.

Canada is also assisting in the area of governance. The Guyana Economic Management Programme will focus on strengthening the institutional capacity of government institutions by focusing on fiscal planning, budgeting and expenditure management, primarily in the Ministry of Finance.

THE EASTERN CARIBBEAN

CIDA's funding to the Eastern Caribbean is provided on a multi-country basis, through regional programmes such as the Canada Fund for Local Initiatives, Organisation of Eastern Caribbean States (OECS) projects, and Commonwealth Regional programming. Projects focus on human resources development, infrastructure, environmental management and economic management.

More specifically in education, the Eastern Caribbean Economic Reform Project, which was launched in 1995, aims to strengthen the capacity of Eastern Caribbean countries to plan and implement educational reform. An ongoing Training Awards Project, which ended in 1996, focused on increasing the pool of skilled workers in agriculture, forestry, fisheries, small industry and tourism. Overall, 825 long-term scholarships were awarded and more than 10000 people benefitted from short-term training courses.

An Economic Management Programme, which has entered its second phase, focuses on strengthening economic policy analysis and decision-making as well as financial management. To date, the project has developed a new government financial system and tax administration system tailored to the needs of the OECS. The project includes a training component for tax officers and drafting of new tax legislation.

Infrastructure projects have focused on water and sanitation. In Dominica, funding has been provided to improve the delivery of drinking water and sanitation services in ways which are cost-effective, while the Roseau Basin Water Development project in St Lucia provided funding for a dam to meet the needs of households and commercial/industrial users in Castries and the northern part of the island to the year 2025 (CIDA, CIDA and the OECS – March 1997, pp. 3–5).

CARICOM

CIDA administers several regional programmes through CARICOM which also benefit countries, such as Barbados, Belize, Suriname, and Trinidad and Tobago, with small bilateral programmes under the Canada Fund for Local Initiatives. In the area of human resources development, the Canada/CARICOM Scholarship programme provides training for managerial personnel in public administration, tourism, agriculture and industry. Twelve scholarships are awarded each year for study in the Caribbean and Canada. Institutional strengthening is provided both to the University of the West Indies (UWI) through the UWI Institutional Support Project, and to CARICOM through the Caribbean Regional Institutional Strengthening Project (CRISP). Canada is assisting the fisheries industry in the region through a Regional Oceans and Fisheries project, which will provide the region with information on fish stock and how to strengthen institutions that manage fishery resources. Finally, CIDA is working closely with the Pan American Health Organization (PAHO) to help the Caribbean Epidemiology

Centre to start up a project on HIV/AIDS prevention for CARICOM member-states.

CONCLUSION

It is clear that Canada has maintained a very long, consistent involvement in the development of Caribbean countries and has provided aid since the colonial period. In spite of changing foreign policy goals, CIDA has been responsive to the varying needs of recipient countries in the Caribbean, while playing a vital role in cushioning the effects of adjustment in Jamaica in the 1980s and more recently in the ongoing economic reconstruction of Haiti. Canada has maintained a consistent aid programme, regardless of the development strategy pursued by beneficiary countries. For example, the Canadian government continued its support for Jamaica, Grenada and Guyana during periods when these countries declared themselves committed to 'socialist' policies. In spite of US pressure, Prime Minister Pierre Trudeau gave critical support to Grenada during the early 1980s. Speaking at a CARICOM Heads of Government meeting in 1983, Trudeau reiterated Canada's commitment to extending economic assistance to Caribbean countries regardless of their domestic policies (Simmons, 1984, p. 21). As he said:

> States have the right to follow whatever ideological path their people decide. When a country chooses a socialist or even a Marxist path, it does not necessarily buy a 'package' which automatically injects it into the Soviet orbit. The internal policies adopted by countries of Latin America and the Caribbean, whatever these policies may be, do not in themselves pose a security threat to this hemisphere. (1984, p. 3)

In addition to transfers of financial resources, Canada has provided aid through a range of mechanisms, in particular through: (a) preferential trade arrangements, starting as early as 1898 and continuing until the present in the form of CARIBCAN, and (b) debt relief through debt cancellation.

Given declining bilateral aid resources and present global trends, it is clear that the Canada–CARICOM relationship in the future will have to adapt to changing circumstances. There are pressures on CIDA to make aid more effective, and the institution has already begun a shift toward initiatives with 'multiplier effects' in sectors outside that of the original project. The tension between poverty alleviation, the promotion of sustainable development and the pursuit of commercial objectives, which have characterised Canadian aid policy since CIDA's inception, will continue. However, if Canada and the CARICOM countries are to thrive in the current environment of global economic competition, more emphasis will have to be placed on business and investment relations in this partnership. The President of the Caribbean Development Bank (CDB), stated this explicitly at the CDB annual meeting in Toronto, Canada, in May 1997. He suggested that the CDB could be a mechanism for fostering business alliances between Canada and CARICOM. There is also scope for strengthening the Canada–CARICOM trading relationship, and successful projects such as CANEXPORT in Jamaica should be encouraged and duplicated elsewhere in the region.

Note

1. Statement by Sir Neville Nichols, President of the Caribbean Development Bank (CDB), entitled 'Preserving and Strengthening Old Partnerships in a New Dynamic Global Environment', during the Twenty-Seventh Annual Meeting of the Board of Governors of the CDB, Toronto, Canada, 21 May 1997.

References

Anderson, R.S. (1984) 'Jamaica's Development', *International Perspectives* (September/October), pp. 19–22.

Baum, J.B. (1974) *The Banks of Canada in the Commonwealth Caribbean* (New York: Praeger).

Bernal, R.L. (1984) 'Foreign Investment and Development in Jamaica', *Inter-American Economic Affairs*, vol. 38, no. 2 (Autumn), pp. 3–21.

Bernal, R.L. (1991) 'Caribbean Debt: Possible Solutions', *Caribbean Affairs*, vol. 4, no. 2 (April–June), pp. 45–58.

Berry, G.R. (1988) 'The West Indies in Canadian External Relations: Present Trends and Future Prospects', in B.D. Tennyson (ed.), *Canada and the Commonwealth Caribbean* (New York: University Press of America).

Black, D.R. and P. McKenna (1995) 'Canada and Structural Adjustment in the South: The Significance of the Guyana Case', *Canadian Journal of Development Studies*, vol. 16, no. 1, pp. 55–78.

Brewster, H.R. and C.Y. Thomas (1967) 'Trade Between the West Indies and Canada: The Development, Structure and Terms of West Indian Trade with

Canada', In *West Indies–Canada Economic Relations* (Mona: Institute of Social and Economic Research, University of the West Indies).

Callender, V. (1965) *The Development of Capital Market Institutions in Jamaica* (Mona: Institute of Social and Economic Research, University of the West Indies).

Canadian International Development Agency (CIDA) (1990) *What is CIDA?* (Hull, Quebec: CIDA, Government of Canada).

CIDA. *Estimates, Table M: Total Disbursements by Country*, CIDA Annual Reports, 1982/83 through 1988/89 and 1995/96 (Hull, Quebec: CIDA).

CIDA. *ODA Disbursement to CARICOM Countries*, 1989/90 through 1994/95 (Hull, Quebec: CIDA).

CIDA (1995) *Canada in the World*. Government of Canada Statement (Hull: CIDA).

CIDA (1996a) *Haiti: Country Policy Framework for Canadian Co-operation* (Hull: CIDA).

CIDA (1996b) *Equity for Sustainable Growth* (Hull: CIDA).

CIDA (1997) *CIDA and Guyana*, March at <www.acdi-cida.gc.ca>.

CIDA (1997) *CIDA and the Organization of Eastern Caribbean States (OECS)*, March at <www.acdi-cida.gc.ca>.

CIDA (1997) *1997–98 Estimates – Part III – Expenditure Plan for CIDA* at <www.acdi-cida.gc.ca>.

Caribbean Development Bank (CDB) News, (1997) vol. 15, no. 2 (April–June).

Fleming, P. and T.A. Keenleyside (1983) 'The Rhetoric of Canadian Aid', *International Perspectives* (September/October), 18–22.

Gallon, G. (1983) 'The Aid Fix: Pushers and Addicts', *International Perspectives* (May/June), pp. 11–14.

Government of Canada (1996) *Report to Parliament: Canada's Participation during 1995 in the Regional Development Banks*, at <www.acdi-cida.gc.ca>.

Hendra, J. (1987) 'Only "Fit to be Tied". A Comparison of the Canadian Tied Aid Policy with the Tied Aid Policies of Sweden, Norway and Denmark', *Canadian Journal of Development Studies*, vol. 8, no. 2, pp. 261–81.

House of Commons (1981) Standing Committee on External Affairs and National Defense, *Canada's Relations with Latin America and the Caribbean* (December).

Jackson, L.A. (1992) 'Canadian Bilateral Aid to Jamaica's Agricultural Sector from 1972–86', *Social and Economic Studies*, vol. 41, no. 2, pp. 83–101.

Jefferson, O. (1967) 'The Comparative Merits of West Indian Association with Canada, the European Economic Community, the Latin American Free Trade Association and the Central American Common Market', in *West Indies–Canada Economic Relations* (Mona, Jamaica: Institute of Social and Economic Research, University of the West Indies).

Levitt, K. (1988) 'Canada and the Caribbean: An Assessment', in J. Heine and L. Manigat (eds), *The Caribbean and World Politics: Cross Currents and Cleavages* (New York: Holmes & Meier).

Levitt, K. and A. McIntyre (1967) *Canada–West Indies Economic Relations* (Montreal: Centre for Developing-Area Studies, McGill University).

Mahler, S. (1993) 'Foreign Policy and Canada's Evolving Relations with the Caribbean Commonwealth Countries: Political and Economic Considerations', in J. Haar and E.J. Dosman (eds), *A Dynamic Partnership:*

Canada's Changing Role in the Americas (Coral Gables, FL: North–South Center).

Morrison, D.R. (1994) 'The Choice of Bilateral Aid Recipients', C. Pratt (ed.), *Canadian International Development Assistance Policies: An Appraisal* (Montreal: McGill–Queens University Press).

Mundy, K.E. (1992) 'Human Resources Development Assistance in Canada's Overseas Development Assistance Program: A Critical Analysis', *Canadian Journal of Development Studies*, vol. 13, no. 3, pp. 385–409.

Nicholls, N. (1997) 'Preserving and Strengthening Old Partnerships in a New Dynamic Global Environment', statement during the Twenty-Seventh Annual Meeting of the Board of Governors of the CDB, Toronto, Canada, 21 May.

Pratt, C. (1994) 'Canadian Development Assistance: A Profile', in C. Pratt (ed.), *Canadian International Development Assistance Policies: An Appraisal* (Montreal: McGill–Queens University Press).

Planning Institute of Jamaica (PIOJ) (1996) Technical Cooperation Division, *Jamaica/Canada Cooperation Programme* (Kingston: PIOJ).

Rawkins, P. (1994) 'An Institutional Analysis of CIDA', in C. Pratt (ed.), *Canadian International Development Assistance Policies: An Appraisal* (Montreal: McGill–Queens University Press).

Ross, D.J. (1990) 'Aid Co-ordination', *Public Administration and Development* vol. 10, no. 3 (July–September), pp. 331–41.

Rudner, M. (1991) 'Canada's Official Development Assistance Strategy: Process, Goals and Priorities', *Canadian Journal of Development Studies*, vol. 12, no. 1, pp. 9–37.

Simmons, D.A. (1984) 'Legacy of Grenada: Caribbean Militarization', *International Perspectives* (July/August), pp. 21–3.

Tennyson, B.D. (1990) 'Canada and the Commonwealth Caribbean: The Historical Relationship', in B. Tennyson (ed.), *Canadian–Caribbean Relations: Aspects of a Relationship* (Nova Scotia: University College of Cape Bretton, Centre for International Studies).

Trudeau, P.E. (1984) Speech to the Commonwealth Heads of State Meeting, St Lucia, February 1983, and quoted in *Brief on Canada and Central America* (Canada–Caribbean–Central American Policy Alternatives, 29 March 1984), p. 3.

United States Agency for International Development (USAID) (1996) *Haiti: Donor Pipeline and Disbursements* (Washington, DC: United States Agency for International Development) (November).

10 The New Regionalism: The Caribbean–Canada Trade Agenda

Winston Dookeran and Miriam L. Campanella

THE NEW REGIONALISM AND THE NORTH–SOUTH NEW PACT

A Definition for Action

Two powerful and interrelated forces are currently reshaping the world economy. One, the globalisation of business through the spread of multinational companies, is forging increased international interdependence as a growing proportion of production enters trade and as foreign direct investment accumulates. The other, the resurgence of regionalism, certainly in Europe and arguably elsewhere, may point in a somewhat different direction.

Globalisation and regionalism are indeed major topics of discussion in political and scholarly circles in the late 1990s. How will the rise of regional trading arrangements affect the rules and institutions of international trade? Will the new regionalism lead to protectionism and/or deeper trade liberalisation? Would regional trading blocs undermine the multilateral system? The new regionalism/globalisation dichotomy has tended to divert focus from the effects that such trends would have on the internal dynamic of regional arrangements. One of these is the inclusion of developing countries in a North–North (i.e., industrial nations) regional scheme. To what extent will the even greater differentials among members of the regional agreement affect economies of developing countries? How would developing countries cope with the side effects of a core–periphery dynamic that is likely to take place in regional integration? Are export-led policies still suitable in a world of regional blocs?

These questions have grown even more complex as highly industrialised countries view low-wage and non-regulated labour as a competitive threat. It seems obsolete, to a point, to build on the theory of a core–periphery model, or to suggest strategic policies for less-industrialised countries. There is no clear evidence to suggest that developing countries have in fact benefitted from low-wage labour markets. Technological capability, market access, capital availability and production efficiency are essential factor endowments that may not be readily accessible to developing countries, while restrictions on trade and invisible barriers by industrialised nations pose additional constraints. These disadvantages affect non-industrialised economies in the implementation of regional schemes.

A shift, however, is being witnessed in regional integration (De Melo, 1993). The new dimensions include a mix of North–South countries, as is the case of the European Community (EC) and the North American Free Trade Agreement (NAFTA). How to maintain the advantages that have accrued to poorer economies and how to manage the complex process of coordination and sustainable growth are priority issues on the agenda. There are also the questions of how developing countries would be affected by the 'social clause' or 'human rights' requirements, and what solutions may be adopted to ensure independence and autonomy without eroding the new frontier of North–South cooperation. The reasoning for the following discussion basically relies on the following:

- Should one believe that the continental scale of the new regionalism is an enduring trend and that an increasing number of North–South regional schemes will develop?
- Is it plausible to assume that a 'core–periphery' model is likely to emerge, perhaps with different characteristics than those described in the Dependencia theory? (Krugman, 1993)
- Should the management of differentials within regional areas form the basis for a new regional political economy?
- Should a strategic goal of developing countries be to first engage in the process of liberalisation and in the management of selective openness and competition?

Finally, there is the argument that the openness of the global environment via the reinforcement and reform of institutions such as the newly formed World Trade Organisation (WTO) and the setting up of regional arrangements should be viewed as parallel routes rather than alternative mechanisms for small communities such as the Caribbean Community. Commitment to both multilateral arrangements and regional responses may be a strategic path for small economies to benefit from opportunities to which global and regional regimes may be privy.

The New Regionalism and North–South Cooperation

The continental dimensions of the new regionalism in both Europe and North America, seen as an alternative to the traditional deepening and widening of the integration mechanism, add new frontiers to the debate. Integration models must now consider policies of coordination of countries at different stages of growth and take into account the impact of competitive policies on the differing economies in the integration process. The challenge, however, is to convince academic liberals and protectionist schools and those of the North and South political consensus that new analytical approaches may be required to set the framework for the integration policy analysis.

The continental dimension in North America took root in the mid-1980s, following US negotiations with Canada and Israel for free trade arrangements. Subsequently, the United States proposed hemispheric free trade and in so doing launched the Enterprise for the Americas Initiative. NAFTA followed in 1994 between the United States, Canada and Mexico. More recently, efforts have been made to establish the Free Trade Area of the Americas (FTAA). The Summit of the Americas in December 1994 in Miami, convened by US President Bill Clinton, brought all the democratically elected nations of the Western hemisphere together with the primary goal of expanding free trade, strengthening democracy, and advancing economic and social development throughout the Western hemisphere. Simultaneously, European integration enveloped its southern countries (Greece, Portugal and Spain) and was widened to include Sweden, Austria and Finland. The European Union has negotiated agreements with Czechoslovakia, Hungary and Poland.

Opponents to regionalism are hopeful that such interaction will help offset discriminations and exclusions associated with regional arrangements on developing countries (Bhagwati, 1991). Regional schemes now embrace developing countries, in contrast to the earlier regionalism where developed partners held the reins. The unilateral liberalisation of several developing countries and its application to multilateral institutions are evidence of a dramatic turning point in North–South relations. Some argue that the regional integration mechanism of developing countries could be the basis for a new political liberalism (Nogues and Quintanilla, 1993, pp. 278–310).

NAFTA, the association of several developing countries, and the prospect of former socialist states joining the European Union tend to reinforce the success of the free market economy. A shared scale of economic values and rules is making the objective of North–South Cooperation feasible, a goal often avowed but scarcely materialised (De Melo, 1993). Regionalism, it is argued, will irreversibly undermine multilateral institutions, fragment the world economy and, in so doing, throw the globalisation process into recess. The debate on regionalism raises two concerns. The first is the external effects of regional integration viewed as a phenomenon *ad excludendum*, where regional schemes are likely to introduce higher external barriers. The second concern is the probable diverting consequence of state intervention, which might reinforce the diverting effect of free trade schemes harming national as well as global welfare.

The argument derives partly from the theory of hegemonic stability. With US support to regionalism, Bhagwati argues that multilateral institutions are losing their necessary supporter and enforcing power: 'As key defender of multilateralism through the post war years, its decision [of the USA] now to travel the regional route [in geographical and preferential senses simultaneously] tilts the balance of forces at the margin away from multilateralism to regionalism. This shift has taken place in the context of an anti multilateral ethos.' A harmful consequence for developing countries might be the effectiveness of the export-led strategy, which has triumphed through multilateral rules and preferential agreements and which are now being questioned by the European Union and, as well, by the United States. Furthermore, the shift to regionalism runs parallel with a new activism on the part of governments with respect to trade issues. Evidence of this can be seen in the strategic policies adopted by the Clinton administration, including Super 301 against Japan, or the 'social clause' aimed against exporters from less-developed countries (LDCs).[1] There is also the environmental concern, expressed by US consumer and environmental organisations at the Marrakesh meeting establishing the World Trade Organisation (WTO) in April 1994 recommending a three-year moratorium on global trade for food and agricultural products. These may be only the first steps of an escalating strategy of Northern countries to limit the export-led growth of LDCs.[2]

To free trade advocates, the new mood in trade regionalism suggests a return to protectionism and industrial policies. To others, state intervention is only an act to offset the practice of state support to trade and key industrial sectors in Europe and Japan.[3] In any case, the so-called return of the state in the management of trade policies is ambiguous. State action and vested interests have been and are perfectly alive in the field (Rugman and Gestrin, 1993, pp. 335–52).

The Core–Periphery Dynamic

To the extent that North–South regional schemes are likely to be implemented, a counter-intuitive dynamic may reemerge. Krugman (1993) calls this the 'core–periphery dynamic', a phenomenon already known to policy-makers of developing countries. Despite belief in this model, analysis has been inconclusive as to the 'dependencia theory'. Once introduced, policy initiatives alter the past. The story is telling with the success stories of the East–Asian Tigers where proactive policies were employed. According to Krugman (1993), now that economic geography is going to regain its own spontaneous dynamic, lost with obtrusive national barriers, a core–periphery model is likely to emerge in the deepening phase of European integration. In this situation of Europe in 1992, with the so-called four freedoms movements for labour, firm, services and capital, two distinct and related processes will take place:

1. The relocation of industries and services that are favoured with an attractive and richly endowed environment.
2. The specialisation of economies, which will favour regions with a 'head start' in production and attract industry away from those with less initial conditions. 'Foot-loose' industries, such as electronics, software companies, or accounting data processing services, will move towards a better-endowed environment (university network, science park, and so forth).

The emerging topology is one in which one or more cores are being surrounded by a hinterland (Krugman, 1991, pp. 84–90). The formation of cores and the hinterland is a self-organising process that occurred, for example, in the late nineteenth century in the United States. The struggle to occupy the core makes the present core–periphery model something completely different from the Dependence theory model (Krugman, 1993).

'Get the core' has a tremendous policy impact. The policy environment could be influenced so as to create favourable conditions for development through tax measures and programmes for infrastructural improvements. Sometimes the local administrative system plays a more effective role in achieving such objectives than national or federal governments. For instance, Krugman sees the establishment of the Silicon Valley as the product of personal initiative, namely, that of Fred Terman, Vice-President of Stanford University. Yet another example is that of Route 128, created through the endeavour of MIT's President Karl Compton, who encouraged the faculty to become entrepreneurs and to help mobilise private venture capital (Krugman, 1991, p. 64). North Carolina's Research Triangle, created through state support of a research park, is a direct emulation of Silicon Valley and Route 128.

THE CARIBBEAN ECONOMIC SPACE

Formation of the Caribbean Economic Space: An Overview

First, it was the 'triangular trade' (export of primary products and import of finished goods) of the colonial era, then multinational corporations and US hegemony and, more recently, International Monetary Fund (IMF) and World Bank structural adjustment programmes. These were the platforms that have defined Caribbean economic space over the past 40 years. From these analytical frameworks came the theories of dependence, neo-colonialism, economic marginalisation, and persistent calls with heavy moral and political overtures for protection, preferences, special consideration, aid, trade and investment support.

Caribbean economic dependence can no longer go unquestioned. Public policy imperatives designed for yesterday's world are today sterile in a world with no Third World, and what is disturbing is that such policies continue to inform long-term development plans.[4] The production of primary export commodities that have traditionally sustained many Caribbean economies, such as bananas, sugar and rum, are export earners that have managed to survive way beyond their natural lifetimes as a result of windfalls and preferences. New manufactures have also capitalised on preferential benefits. Special treatment has allowed Caribbean countries to enjoy a level of access to the international trading system that is incompatible with their levels of productivity and international competitiveness.

The situation that warrants concern for global trends is trade liberalisation through the reduction of tariff and non-tariff barriers. Competition, efficiency and productivity are the new watchwords. In this constantly changing environment, the Caribbean's underdeveloped productive capacity poses a severe hindrance to participation in liberalised trade. While Caribbean countries have realised that preferential treatment has not engendered a competitive production base, there is also the reasoning that preferential schemes can be a contributive factor in the short term in the attainment of desired levels of competition.

Globalisation of the world economy, however, threatens the very existence and foundation of such special arrangements between the Caribbean region and its traditional trading partners, namely, the United States, Canada and Europe. The formation of regional blocs, the new era of liberalised trade and reciprocity are indeed challenges for the Caribbean. A concerted policy response is imperative, both in the short and in the long term, in order to prepare the region for its 'new insertion' into the world economy.

CARIBCAN

A case for increased aid and greater access for Caribbean products to the Canadian market was proposed in 1985 by Edward Seaga, Prime Minister of Jamaica. Further interest was sparked by the US Caribbean Basin Initiative (CBI) programme of 1984, which provided duty-free access to the US for certain Caribbean products. Given the long-standing historical trade and cultural links between Canada and the Caribbean, the Canadian government responded with the introduction of CARIBCAN.

Canada previously extended preferential treatment to Commonwealth Caribbean goods through the Canadian General Preferential Tariff (GPT) (the arrangement ended on 30 June 1994), the generalised preferential programme for developing countries, GSP, and the British Preferential Tariff, BPT. The new bilateral agreement, CARIBCAN, which took effect in June 1986 through an amendment of the Customs Tariff Act, aimed at:

- enhancing bilateral commercial relations between Canada and CARICOM states;
- boosting CARICOM trade and export earnings potential;
- improving the trade and economic development prospects of the region;
- promoting new investment opportunities; and
- encouraging economic integration and cooperation in the region.

CARIBCAN is a non-reciprocal agreement that allows preferential duty-free access to the Canadian market for almost all imports from the

Caribbean (subject to rules of origin and shipping requirements). Products excluded from preferences under the programme continue to be eligible for special treatment under the GPT and BPT, where such benefits exist. Further, CARIBCAN incorporated measures designed to encourage Canadian investment and other forms of industrial cooperation within the region. Among these were provisions to assist training, to strengthen marketing skills, and to enhance promotional activity. There were also a number of business initiatives by the Canadian private sector arising as a direct result of the programme.

CARIBCAN was upgraded in 1990 with improved concessions in the areas of rum bottling, the inclusion of leather luggage, and certain vegetable fibre products. The effect was duty-free access to the Canadian market for about 98 per cent of all CARICOM goods. Complementary provisions in terms of investment, trade and industrial cooperation concentrated on the creation of linkages between the private sectors of Canada and the Caribbean. The private sector was depended upon to provide impetus to regional development.

No time limit was attached to the programme's provisions, but an extension of the waiver granted by the GATT in 1986 for a period of 12 years is to be renegotiated in 1998. The waiver exempted Canada from the requirement, contained under paragraph 1 of GATT, that the same duty-free treatment be extended to like products of any contracting party. Under CARIBCAN legislation, duty-free treatment may be suspended or withdrawn in whole or in part by the Canadian government from any beneficiary country. Beneficiaries of the programme are the Caribbean Anglophone countries in the region that maintain links with the Commonwealth. These number 18 to date.[5]

The Impact of CARIBCAN

Since the beginning of the programme, expectations were not very high, primarily because the value of dutiable products constituted a small share of Canadian imports as compared to the range of imports already accorded zero tariff access by such programmes as the MFN, BPT and GPT.

Henry Gill, consultant to the Latin American Economic System (SELA), made the observation that any evaluation of CARIBCAN's impact with respect to its goals had to contend with the difficulty involved in 'isolating the effects of this arrangement from others deriving essentially from the pre-CARIBCAN relationship' (Gill, 1992), noting that this was especially the case with the industrial cooperation activities. In examining the relationship of the three main areas of the agreement, namely trade, industrial cooperation and investment, Gill's findings of June 1992 were the following:

Trade

Generally speaking, CARIBCAN has shown little positive impact on Caribbean exports to Canada, and whatever positive impact was realised tended to concentrate on a few of the larger countries. Caribbean countries have expressed concern about various aspects of the trade provisions, notably the rules of origin, requirements for direct shipping and product exclusion. CARICOM Secretariat statistics noted that the Canadian share of CARICOM exports experienced considerable variance, ranging between 3.7 and 6.0 per cent during the period 1984 to 1990.

Caribbean exports to Canada did rise in value since the start of CARIBCAN in 1986 from EC$455.3 million to almost $498.3 million in 1990, but the increase was only 9.4 per cent and has lagged in relation to global exports, which rose 46.5 per cent over the same period. Major exporters have been Jamaica (66 per cent of total exports in 1990), Trinidad and Tobago, and Grenada. By contrast, Organisation of Eastern Caribbean States (OECS) countries experienced a marginal increase in exports between 1986 and 1988, with decreases in 1989 and 1990.

Figures compiled by Gill show imports valued at $11.2 million, representing 4.2 per cent of total trade and 2.7 times total CARIBCAN trade, did not meet the origin criteria requirement for direct shipping and other stipulations. An examination of the tariff-applied figures for 1987 shows that duty-free imports under CARIBCAN were valued at less than 1.6 per cent of duty-free imports and 1.5 per cent of overall imports. Other sources reflect a similar decline. Brewster and Thomas, examining Canadian trade with the Commonwealth Caribbean during the period 1982–89, show that Canada had a positive balance of trade with the Commonwealth Caribbean of C$91 million in 1988 but this fell to $48 million in 1989, in both years though there was a negative balance in Canadian trade with Belize, Guyana and Jamaica. Again, the point is made that:

> The volume of Caribbean goods entering Canada which are affected by the CARIBCAN program is minimal. It amounts to between 5 and 6 percent of Canadian imports from the Region and is made up

largely of agricultural, food and beverage items. The total amount in 1987 was about C$1.5 million which was approximately twice the 1986 level. The bulk of the trade originates in Jamaica, Trinidad Tobago and the Bahamas. (Momsen, 1992, pp. 501–13)

Momsen argues that, 'Despite the latest gestures aimed at increasing trade, it is probable that future links between Canada and the Commonwealth Caribbean will be largely at the personal level of migration, education, technical assistance, and tourism. Canada's success in its relations with the Commonwealth Caribbean is based on investment rather than merchandise trade' (Momsen, 1992, pp. 501–13).

However, Momsen's assertion of an investment effect at the personal level without a dynamic trade flow appears doubtful, particularly since trade relations historically have been a driving force in Canada–Caribbean relations. In this case the 'economic distance' between the two countries is likely to increase, as the Caribbean takes a smaller place in Canada's trade policy agenda.

Industrial Cooperation and Investment

Some success has been reported, particularly, with the establishment of National Development Foundations and Institutes in nearly all CARICOM countries. Funding was made available for over 376 business proposals emanating from the Caribbean. The bulk of activity has occurred under the Industrial Co-operation Programme, in the form of entrepreneurial and management training, standards development, investment promotion and institutional strengthening. Canadian investment in the Caribbean has centred mainly on the financial sector, communications and utilities. Another area of high investment that is of growing importance to the region is tourism.

CARIBCAN has become the focal point of a fair amount of activity that has led to strengthened commercial relations between Canada and the Caribbean over the years. Commencement of the CBI programme did spark some interest for greater commitment on the part of the Canadian government with respect to trade and investment prospects in the Caribbean. It is interesting to note, however, that some of the very arguments levelled at the CBI have also been pinned on CARIBCAN. The CBI and CARIBCAN arrangements, notwithstanding the overall increase in trade between the Caribbean and its North American partners, were felt to be not broad-based with benefits accruing moreover to particular countries.

Another criticism of CARIBCAN and the CBI is the reliance of these agreements on traditional imports. Thus, while there is virtue by way of non-reciprocal concessions to the Caribbean, little incentive is offered for the region to participate more fully in the North American market. Traditional products continue to be significant exports, although less favourable terms of trade for such items have witnessed some diversification in parts of the region with a surge in light manufacturing, particularly with regard to textiles and apparel. Overall, CARIBCAN and the CBI are felt to be largely ineffective.

In March 1996, a Summit of Heads of Government of CARICOM and Canada was held in St George's, Grenada. At this meeting the CARICOM heads indicated that they continued to place considerable importance on preferential access for Caribbean products to Canadian, European and US markets. Prime Minister Chrétien confirmed that Canada was seeking from the World Trade Organisation an extension of the waiver granted for its current preferential trade agreement, CARIBCAN. He also expressed the intention to explore the incorporation into CARIBCAN of those products currently excluded from the arrangement. In reviewing trade between Canada and CARICOM, the heads of Government agreed that renewed efforts should be made by Canada and the Caribbean states to cooperate on specific measures to improve the climate for trade and investment, particularly through foreign investment protection agreements.

BETWEEN ADJUSTMENT AND PROACTIVE POLICIES: A NEW APPROACH TO GROWTH

Export-led Growth and Proactive Polices

The economic success of the four tigers (Hong Kong, Taiwan, Singapore and Korea) has drawn attention to the strategy of 'export-led growth'. There are those in international economic institutions who recommend export policies as a model to emulate, a means to an end, to accomplish high rates of economic growth. Proponents argue that 'such a source of growth not only has real linkage effects and multiplier effects on the rest of the economy but also ensures that growth will not be constrained or halted by balance of payment difficulties, since it makes available any foreign exchange necessary to pay for additional imports required for expansion' (Pearce, 1992, p. 145).

Export promotion, however, is not that simple, and initial risks must be taken to derive success. In this regard, an efficient infrastructure is essential to achieving economies of scale. An efficient manufacturing capacity will allow for production and distribution at comparatively low costs. Capital, skilled personnel, technological capability and transport efficiency are also among the requirements needed. Export-led growth, however, is under serious scrutiny as a transferable model. Concerns are rising among industrialised and high-wage countries that should such a strategy be adopted by developing countries, it would certainly cause alarm. Hence protectionist moves are towards discouraging labour-intensive export production where such costs are considered to be relatively low. This may be inimical to the interest of poorer nations in their attempt to gain 'competitive advantage'. Further, removal of access to the export market for labour-intensive manufactures may lead to increasing unemployment in poorer countries.

It is sometimes argued that smaller countries are unable to benefit reciprocally by adhering to tariff reductions and export-led strategies. While this may be true, at the same time one cannot dismiss the increasing focus on 'national competitiveness', a theory that places less importance on the protection of labour-intensive industries and encourages, instead, boosting the industrial sector with a concentration on the export of knowledge-intensive services. Such arguments may perhaps be less significant if a coordinated set of policies within a regional grouping could be worked out. In the search for a new approach to deal with the question of 'export growth', Bernal (1993a) suggests the need for a strategic global repositioning in order to amplify and diversify the export range of Caribbean countries. This view appears to also have the support of strategic trade theorists (Krugman, 1993). Hence, proactive policy-making advocates that Caribbean countries assume an active posture in adjusting *ex ante*, instead of waiting to adjust *ex post*. Bernal suggests two platforms whereby Caribbean countries may create a 'fulfilling prophecy' in export and import policy:

1. Abandon traditional thinking and commence immediately with the formation of new development strategies; for example, skip the stage of exporting manufactured goods and move towards the export of services.
2. Focus on non-traditional exports, such as biotechnology, data processing, tourism, banking and insurance; and focus on new exports, including offshore medical services (Bernal, 1993b).

The list may be broadened to include joint-venture arrangements by Caribbean universities and North American and European science parks (France, Great Britain, Germany, Italy) for the establishment of biological stations with regard to basic science and biotechnology programmes.

Open Regionalism and Negotiating

The structural adjustment policy debate has focused substantially on the sequencing of measures and on a time period for the working of these policies. Hence the call for a transition stage to prepare for a level playing field, mitigation of social costs, restructuring of production and switching of national expenditure. These assertions are all valid in their own right, but, in totality, what is the new equilibrium after adjustment?

The evidence is clear, the Caribbean has had decades to adjust in the sugar and banana industries, but has adjusted only to a persistent low-level equilibrium. The argument that a transition period will allow the Caribbean to better prepare for the future is more likely to lead to post-ponement of a new strategy and recurrence of old situations. Forward-looking adjustment policies must focus on the targets of a new high-level equilibrium, and its sequencing and timing should be determined on that basis. Otherwise, the Caribbean would be engaged indefinitely in expectations outstripping performance, thus creating a 'reality gap' and the consequent 'politics of illusion'.

Many of the countries of the region have adopted stringent reform policy programmes for macroeconomic stability and growth. In so doing, less attention has been placed on the microeconomic conditions that are essential for macroperformance. For instance, instruments for export promotion such as duty-free access to imported inputs are some-times viewed as a surrogate to exchange rate policy. This is without appreciating that exchange rate policies change relative prices between the tradable and non-tradable sectors on an economy-wide basis, while instruments for export promotion only affect the costs of specific industries. Qualitatively, according to Rajapatirana (1993), exchange rate policy and export promotion measures are different and must be viewed as such. This illustrates the dichotomy between macro and micro-conditions and draws attention to the need to identify and alter the microeconomic conditions for economic and social adjustment.

The 'hub and spoke' argument, highlighted in the North American economic integration debate, suggests a US–centred 'hub' and other economies as the 'spoke'. Although not articulated in these words, the

Caribbean–Europe link is undergoing similar stress, and this has led to a disengagement period between the Caribbean and both Europe and North America. The question, therefore, is how would the Caribbean overcome these hurdles? In other words, what is the realistic capacity for the region to enter into the mainstream of income-generating activities in the world economy? What is the range of the economy? Many small countries of East Asia have dramatically extended their 'range' in production and trade and, in so doing, have secured an increasing share of world commerce. What conditions allow such targets to be realised? Is it a question of Caribbean transnationals, or strategic public policy interventions or issues of innovative management and production and competitiveness?

Bernal (1993b) has argued that CARICOM is a case of externally vulnerable economic integration, and that a grave issue affecting its vulnerability is the 'critical mass' requirement that is not satisfied in the present membership. Consequently, a priority today is to increase the critical mass and, hence, focus on the widening process. In order to facilitate this approach, Bernal has identified two immediate concerns, intraregional corporate integration and financial integration. The corporate and financial sectors are crucial to economic expansion, and these ought to be given priority on the open trading agenda.

Open regionalism captures the crossroads in which the Latin American and Caribbean nations have found themselves in promoting subregional integration. They do so in a period of uncertainty regarding the eventual outcome of the multilateral and minilateral trading systems.[6] Subregional integration is being promoted not as a protectionist grouping but as open systems to facilitate enhanced bargaining power in global accords. This concept transcends the 'insertion' theory argument, and responds more to Dharam Ghai's notion that the world is moving 'towards a single market for goods, services, technology, capital, and skills' (1992, p. 33). A world driven by the forces of technological advances and changes in world political power. Integration, therefore, is not simply a matter of economy and polity; equally dominant are technological superiority and hegemonic power.

National domestic economies are no longer the dominant players on the world stage. Rather, global and continental market forces shape the new economic order. Trade liberalisation calls for the removal of tariff barriers, reciprocal relations, and rejects the principle of special treatment. This is the web in which the Caribbean is entangled, and escape depends upon its ability to relinquish trade preferences and embrace free trade. Uncertainty grapples the region, as NAFTA, the European

Community, the successful completion of the Uruguay Round of GATT spell trade and investment diversion and the erosion of preferences.

Policy-making Apparatus

A new policy-making apparatus is urgent. Wholesale economic liberalisation is not an option for the Caribbean at this time, owing to the vulnerability of the smaller less diversified economies of the region. A period of transition is necessary, and 'asymmetric reciprocity' and 'parity' in trading arrangements are suggestions to prepare the Caribbean for a level playing field.

The NAFTA Parity Bill tabled in the US Congress in 1993 was introduced to enable Caribbean Basin countries time to undertake the necessary economic and structural reforms in the move towards full reciprocity. To offset the Caribbean fear of trade and investment diversion under NAFTA from the Caribbean to Mexico, the Bill proposed to upgrade the CBI whereby certain NAFTA benefits received by Mexico would accrue to CBI beneficiaries for a three-year period. This would have allowed some breathing space for adjustment, though minimal. However, in today's political circles the move is towards a more drastic adjustment by way of 'limited' NAFTA parity. The parity concession for CBI countries relates to apparel and is a far cry from the earlier NAFTA parity proposal in that it does not embrace 'similar treatment with respect to tariffs and quotas as Mexico for all U.S. imports from the Caribbean Basin not eligible for CBI treatment' (Suárez, 1996, p. 27).

Furthermore, application for limited NAFTA parity is not automatic. CBI countries will be required to meet certain reciprocal obligations similar to CBI criteria. The penalty for default is revocation of parity at the end of three years.

The other argument concerns the asymmetrical landscape of the Western hemisphere. Given the disparities in size, levels of development and economic structure of the region, what exists between North America, Latin America and the Caribbean is an asymmetrical interdependence relationship. The call, therefore, is for asymmetrical reciprocity to be able to advance the process of liberalisation of the Caribbean region. Changes in the tenure of trade relationships would be required to allow countries to 'advance bilaterally in accordance with their own conditions, but without increasing their trade barriers during the process' (Latin American Economic System, 1993a). It is interesting to note that such initiatives are already underway. Notably, there is the Venezuela–CARICOM non-reciprocal trade agreement of 1992, in which Venezuela grants duty-free access for CARICOM goods to the Venezuelan market. Venezuela's goal is towards eventual free trade by 1997 for a vast majority of CARICOM products (Latin American Economic System, 1993a).

Furthermore, there is the coming together of subregional groupings in the hemisphere with the aim of enhancing economic viability. Outward-looking as opposed to the earlier inward vision is now generally accepted and, no doubt, signals a desire to be a part of some larger unit rather than to be marginalised. NAFTA, the Southern Cone Common Market (MERCOSUR), the Andean nations, the Group of Three (Colombia, Mexico and Venezuela), the Central American Common Market (CACM) and CARICOM are said to 'have moved and are moving towards the formation of free trade markets, customs unions and common markets' (Latin American Economic System, 1993b).

The Association of Caribbean States (ACS) was born out of a report of the West Indian Commission[7] with the aim of furthering the goal of economic integration. The ACS has a market of approximately 204 million people, an estimated GDP of US$500 billion and annual trade of approximately $180 billion. The ACS's mandate is to focus on trade, tourism and transport. The 25-member ACS is comprised of the 13 member-countries of CARICOM, the Group of Three, Cuba, the Dominican Republic, Haiti, Costa Rica, El Salvador, Guatemala, Honduras, Nicaragua and Panama. The ACS Convention also made provision for associate membership. In May 1996, an agreement was reached between the ACS secretariat and the French republic in which the modalities for France's participation in the ACS as an associate member on behalf of Martinique, Guadeloupe and French Guiana were defined.

Financial resources are yet another critical factor in preparation for the free trade challenge. Caribbean economies have traditionally been dependent on external financing to supplement domestic savings and insufficient foreign exchange earnings with which to meet external needs. Now that the geopolitical landscape has changed with the fall of the Iron Curtain, making Caribbean countries less strategically important, the future appears bleak. There is also the view that Caribbean countries have attained a certain level of development and, therefore, their needs are less urgent than those of poorer nations. If these arguments are accepted, external aid to the region may not be readily forthcoming, and in fact the World Bank has taken note of decreased aid to the region. A 1994 report published by the Bank, for example, indicates a reduction in external financing from bilateral and multilateral agencies to the region. It is believed that this decline will continue. 'Net lending from multilateral sources amounted to only $72 million in 1992 compared with $546 million in 1982. Net bilateral lending actually turned negative in 1992 amounting to –$32 million compared with $603 million in 1982 (World Bank, 1994, p. xiv).

Although the United States has always been a major source of financing to the Caribbean, recently aid has been reduced. This picture is grim: US$217 million in 1992 to an approximate $180 million in 1993 (US Agency for International Development, 1992, pp. 29, 38). Yet another instance of United States budgetary constraints is the decision by the US State Department to close some of its embassies in the Caribbean. Grenada, Antigua and a regional office of the Agency for International Development (AID) in Barbados were on the list. The *New York Times* (1994) reported that such a move is 'part of an effort to shift resources to Eastern Europe and the Former Soviet Union'.

It has been argued that since official external funding has declined, the Caribbean should take advantage of direct foreign investment (DFI) opportunities, which are on the rise and which are important sources of foreign capital to many countries. Support for the argument drew on the following statistics. 'In 1993 approximately $60 billion worth of DFI flowed into developing countries of which $13 billion went to Latin America and the Caribbean (Suárez, 1996, p. 132). Furthermore, the World Bank reports that DFI to the region has increased significantly:

> Whereas, in the mid-1980s DFI to the Caribbean countries amounted to US$ 100–200 million per year, with much of it destined for the Trinidadian petroleum and petrochemical sectors, the Caribbean countries have attracted US$500–600 million in each of the last three years. The FDI level reached $656 million in 1992. Trinidad and Tobago is no longer the single main recipient. The Dominican Republic, Jamaica and St. Lucia have increasingly been able to attract foreign investment. (Suárez, 1996)

CONCLUSION

The Caribbean must reassess its position in light of new market realities, and notions of sovereignty and regionalism may require revision.

What is perhaps also needed is a genuine move towards what theorists call 'linked loyalties' and 'pooled sovereignties': a pooling of the region's bargaining power to achieve greater effective sovereignty. Robert Keohane (1993) makes a distinction between 'formal sovereignty' and 'operational sovereignty': 'During the coming decades, the operational sovereignty of formally sovereign and politically autonomous governments is likely to continue to be eroded by their own decisions, shaped by interdependence, to seek effectiveness at the expense of legal freedom of action'.

The need is timely and compelling, as international negotiations – whether on matters of trade, conflict resolutions or diplomatic initiatives – are being conducted through regional groupings and megablocs. There is no voice for small nations, no tolerance for their small size and no conduit for their concerns to be considered at major summits. The Caribbean must choose not to be a victim of circumstances. The task ahead is to undo the models that have imprisoned the region, a restructuring that undoubtedly would greatly impact on the lives of the people and on the ability to maintain levels of income, production, employment and welfare.

The benefits accruing to Europe, the United States and Canada through economic and social links with the Caribbean have historically been significant and should not be underestimated. This is not a moment of closure for the Caribbean. Reciprocity, parity and preferences are vital concerns. The argument has often been made and the facts of the case attested. Will the Caribbean speak with a new voice in the integration strategy? Will Europe and North America provide necessary cooperation to allow the Caribbean to find its niche in a world of equals? This is a test of political generosity, statesmanship and leadership foresight – a matter of political economy!

Notes

1. The topic is drawing even greater attention. *The Financial Times*, on Monday 18 April 1997, comments on a speech by Lawrence Summers, the US Treasury Undersecretary to the Inter-American Development Bank. Summers advised Latin American governments 'to do what they can to strengthen trade unions', and *The Financial Times* critics note that 'the risk is that the emphasis on social issues will raise conflicts which play into the hands of those wishing to block further necessary reforms...' More ominously, the new American emphasis on social ideals has parallels with

its stance on labour and environmental standards in trade negotiations. Developing countries may ask what lies beyond these arguments. Is the United States really worried about work conditions in Peru, or is it looking to hobble competition from poorer countries? Some of these concerns can be alleviated by the multilateral approach. But Washington must take care not to impose its ideas on Latin America. Otherwise, its new drive for social justice in Latin America will be seen as a covert way of pursuing the perceived commercial interests of the United States.

2. The strategic trade theory has been forged at MIT by P. Krugman and is now identified with Laura D'Andrea Tyson, Chief of the Economic Committee at the White House.

3. Dornbusch and Thurow at MIT have spoken of the death of GATT.

4. For an elaboration of this view, see Winston Dookeran (1994), 'Caribbean Integration: An Agenda for Open Regionalism', *The Commonwealth Journal of International Relations*, July.

5. Included are the 13 English-speaking CARICOM countries, plus Anguilla, Bermuda, British Virgin Islands, Cayman Islands and the Turks and Caicos Islands.

6. The term 'open regionalism' was separately coined by researchers at ECLAC, Santiago and Stanford University. Open regionalism implies that a strategic path for small-size economies will be to secure commitments from both multilateral and regional trading arrangements. See Dookeran (1994), 'Caribbean Integration: An Agenda for Open Regionalism', *The Commonwealth Journal of International Relations*, July.

7. The proposal for an Association of Caribbean States was made by the West Indian Commission, *Time for Action*, 1992.

References

Bernal, R.L. (1993a) 'CARICOM: Externally Vulnerable Regional Economic Integration', paper presented to the workshop on Economic Integration, Institute of International Studies, University of Notre Dame, Indiana, April.

Bernal, R.L. (1993b) 'The Compatibility of Caribbean Membership in LOME, NAFTA and GATT', paper presented at the Sixth Europe/Caribbean Conference, Santo Domingo, Dominican Republic, November.

Bhagwati, Jagdish (1991) 'Regionalism vs. Multilateralism: an overview', presented at World Bank and CEPR Conference on New Dimensions in Regional Integration, 2–3 April 1991.

De Melo, P. (1993) *Dimensions of the New Regionalism* (Cambridge: World Bank Publication, Cambridge University Press).

Dornbusch, R. (1992) 'The Case for Trade Liberalization in Developing Countries', *Journal of Economic Perspectives*, vol. 6, no. 1 (Winter), pp. 69–85.

Dookeran, W. (1994) 'Caribbean Integration: An Agenda for Open Regionalism', *The Commonwealth Journal of International Relations*, July.

Dunne, N. (1994) 'US Concern on Food Safety Rules', *The Financial Times*, 14 April.

Ghai, D. (1992) 'Structural Adjustment, Global Integration and Social Democracy', discussion paper of the United Nations Research Institute for Social Development, October.

Gill, H.S. (1992) 'Canada and the Commonwealth Caribbean: Evaluation of the CARIBCAN Experience since 1986', *Latin American Economic System (SELA)*, June.

Goldstein, J. (1993) *Ideas, Interests and American Trade Policy* (Ithaca, NY: Cornell University Press).

Graham E.H. and P.R. Krugman (1991) *Foreign Direct Investment in the United States*, 2nd edn (Washington, DC: Institute for International Economics).

Haar, J. and E.J. Dosman (eds) (1993) *A Dynamic Partnership: Canada's Changing Role in the Americas* (Coral Gables, FL: North–South Center).

Keohane, R.O. (1993) 'Sovereignty, Interdependence, International Institutions', in L.B. Miller and M.J. Smith (eds), *Ideas and Ideals: Essays on Politics in Honor of Stanley Hoffman* (Boulder, CO: Westview Press).

Krugman, P. (1991) *Geography and Trade*, Gaston Eyskens Lecture Series. Cambridge, MA: MIT Press.

Krugman, P. (1993) 'Toward a Counter Revolution in Development Theory', *World Bank Observer*.

Krugman, P. (1994) *The Age of Diminished Expectations: US Economic Policy in the 1990s*, revised edition (Cambridge, MA: MIT Press).

Latin American Economic System (SELA) (1993a) *Evolution of Regional Integration (1992–1993)* (Caracas: Latin American Economic System).

Latin American Economic System (SELA) (1993b) *Intensification of Regional Integration and Establishment of a Hemisphere Free Trade Area*, July.

Momsen, J.H. (1992) 'Canada–Caribbean Relations: Wherein the Special Relationship?', *Political Geography*, vol. 11, no. 5 (September), pp. 501–13.

New York Times, May 1994.

Nogues, J.J. and R. Quintanilla (1993) 'Latin America's Integration and the Multilateral System', in P. DeMelo (ed.), *Dimensions of the New Regionalism* (Cambridge: World Bank Publication, Cambridge University Press).

Oye, K. (1992) *Economic Discrimination and Political Exchange: World Political Economy in the 1930s and 1980s* (Princeton, NJ: Princeton University Press).

Pearce. D.W. (ed.) (1992) *The MIT Dictionary of Modern Economics* (Cambridge, MA: MIT Press).

Rajapatirana, S. (1993) 'Policy Recommendations for Export Promotion', paper presented to the annual meeting of the Chilean Economic Society, Santiago, May.

Riggs, A.R. and T. Velk (1993) *Beyond NAFTA: An Economic, Political and Sociological Perspective* (Vancouver: The Fraser Institute).

Rugman, A.H. and M.V. Gestrin (1993) 'US Trade Laws as Barriers to Globalization', *World Economics*, November.

Suárez, E.M. (1996) 'The Caribbean in Economic Transition', in W.C. Dookeran (ed.), *Choices and Change: Reflections of the Caribbean* (Washington, DC: Inter-american Development Bank (IDB)).

US Agency for International Development (1992) *Latin American and the Caribbean Selected Economic and Social Data* (Washington, DC: US Agency for International Development), April.

West Indian Commission (1992) *Time for Action* (Black Rock, Barbados: West Indian Commission).

World Bank (1994) *Caribbean Region: Coping with Changes in the External Environment* (Washington, DC: World Bank).

Conclusion

Jerry Haar and Anthony T. Bryan

TOWARDS A NEW PARADIGM OF CANADIAN–CARIBBEAN RELATIONS

The 1990s mark a turning point in Canadian–Caribbean relations. The presence and convergence – as well as divergence – of global, regional and national forces have led Canada and the Commonwealth Caribbean to rethink, reassess and, in a number of areas, recast their special relationship.

At the heart of this shift is a paradox: at the very time in which the Americas has become of far greater priority in Canadian foreign policy, the importance of the Commonwealth Caribbean has diminished. And at the core of this paradox is an irony: the traditional and fundamental values of Canadian foreign policy (especially partnership and middle power cooperation), which have been manifest most vividly, extensively and successfully in the Caribbean, are perceived as critically important assets by Canada's hemispheric neighbours. Coupled with the paradox and the irony is an indisputable reality: the major issues affecting the Commonwealth Caribbean, and the rest of the region, such as trade, immigration, the environment, security and narcotics trafficking, directly impact upon all Canadians as well.

New global realities, and economic ones at home, have forced Canada to shape and adopt a new paradigm in its relations with the world. Its 1994 Foreign Policy Review serves as a significant departure from its post-World War II modus operandi. It seeks to meld, rather than discard, fundamental beliefs and values in which Canadian foreign policy is rooted, with meaningful responses to the dynamic and monumental global changes in trade and commerce, technology, communications and culture. Essentially, Canadian foreign policy has not been narrowed but *broadened* and *reordered*: additional issues and a recasting and reweighing of existing ones more accurately describe the evolution of Canadian foreign policy in the last decade of the twentieth century. Strengthening civil society, promoting democratic governance, and supporting economic and social development remain pillars of Canadian foreign policy *vis-à-vis* the Commonwealth Caribbean. However, the agenda has been expanded to include neoliberal economic reform, including privatisation, deregulation and a diminishing role for the state; trade, investment and financial services liberalisation, modernisation and widened market access; sustainable development; enhanced peacekeeping and anti-drug trafficking assistance.

The Review is also fully cognisant of the domestic milieu in which the nation has spent the last decade: economic recession, ethnic and cultural tensions, the Québec separatist movement and rumblings from other provinces for greater independence and a lesser federal role, budgetary cutbacks, corporate downsizing, high levels of unemployment, and periodic trade skirmishes with the United States.

Consequently, Canada's relationship with the Caribbean is one in transition, being influenced, shaped and formed by domestic and international events and trends. Unquestionably, the one issue that is the most important to both Canada and the Caribbean – in their relationship with other nations as well as with one another – is trade (and, by extension, investment and finance as well). A trading nation historically, Canada is two and one-half times more trade-dependent, as a percentage of GDP, than the US – the nation that accounts for more than three-fourths of Canada's trade. Beginning with NAFTA, Canada has been able to expand and deepen its trade and commercial relationship with the nations of the Western hemisphere. Whether through a free trade agreement with Chile, the next candidate for NAFTA accession, or Cuba, the US's nemesis in the hemisphere, Canada is genuinely determined to play an active and equal role in the Americas – within and beyond trade. During the last decade, the rate of export growth to the region and the percentage of manufactured versus agricultural exports have grown more dramatically than to any other region of the world.

Ironically, and unfortunately for the Commonwealth Caribbean, two-way trade has declined, even with the incentive of CARIBCAN. Granted that CARIBCAN has contributed to an increase in the size and composition of non-traditional exports from the Caribbean, on the whole the programme has been only modestly successful. At the same time, the wider and intrinsic benefits derived from multilateral relationships signal future benefits for the Commonwealth Caribbean, including quite possibly accession to NAFTA.

It remains to be seen whether, due to political interest or *noblesse oblige*, Canada will assume a proactive role by expanding CARIBCAN product coverage, extend the agreement for another ten years, and target development assistance to the most competitive, high valued-added sectors and industries in the Commonwealth Caribbean. Canada is deeply concerned about trade and investment diversion from the CARICOM countries and will work assiduously with these nations and within international bodies to help ameliorate the region's declining competitiveness. The harsh reality for the Caribbean is that Canada's visibility and profile, and more importantly its economic and political interests in the hemisphere, lie in Mexico, the Southern Cone, and MERCOSUR and Chile; moreover, the Canadian government's foreign affairs budget – regardless of goodwill and intentions – has forced Canada to make hard choices in targeting a declining amount of resources and commitments to an increasing agenda. This bodes ill for the scores of Canadian NGOs that have been major beneficiaries of governmental largesse. (The salutary effect for the Canadian taxpayer, however, is that the scope, efficiency, effectiveness and accountability of Canadian international development programmes will be scrutinised like never before.)

Not surprisingly, deteriorating economic conditions in the Commonwealth Caribbean have precipitated a continuing trend of immigration to Canada from the region, in spite of an economic sluggishness and a high rate of unemployment. Economic conditions being relative, Canada's economy is undisputedly much healthier than that of the islands of the Caribbean. However, Canadians' perception of the Caribbean and receptivity to immigration have changed in recent years, due to the different class status of many immigrant cohorts in comparison with the waves of professionals who comprised earlier immigration. Criminal activity, particularly among Jamaican gangs, has sullied the image of West Indians. On the other hand, the West Indian diaspora has been an important consumer group – especially for non-traditional imports from the region – and a source of working class labour, particularly in the services sector.

In the area of sustainable development, Canada has been in the forefront on global efforts to elevate thought, policy and action to sustain all facets of development in the present, without compromising the ability of future generations to meet their own needs. Canada has actively participated in global environmental fora and organisations. At the United Nations Conference on Environment and Development, held in Rio de Janeiro in 1992, and in the World Business Council for Sustainable Development, Canadian involvement has sought to optimise public and private solutions to the problems of sustainable development. At the federal level, Canada has embodied a holistic approach to sustainable development in its foreign affairs and development assistance policies.

Canada and the Caribbean share ecological links through the Gulf Stream, migration of birds and mammals, and other environmental connections. The transfer, application, and diffusion of Canadian environmental technology and technical assistance to the Commonwealth Caribbean have been able to promote sustainable development, ecologically and economically – controlling pollution, utilising renewable resources and preserving biodiversity.

Canada's involvement in the Caribbean in security affairs has been that of a reluctant partner. As a surrogate protector for Great Britain following independence in the Caribbean, Canada's role has evolved as a counterweight to US dominance in the region, a provider of peacekeeping forces and military and police training, as well as technical assistance. Since joining the OAS in 1989, Canada's presence in the security arena has expanded significantly, concurrent with other multilateral initiatives such as UN peacekeeping activities in Central America and police training in Haiti. Canada's concern that drug trafficking poses a serious threat to democracy and stability in the Caribbean (as well as rising crime and health and social problems within Canada) has led to an increase in support for security and antidrug training in the Caribbean. A more targeted approach utilising scarcer dollars will complement US assistance in the area and enable Caribbean nations to spread their dependency in this sensitive area upon both their northern neighbours.

Canada's relations with the nations of the Western hemisphere will expand and intensify well into the next century:

> The recognition of the Americas as a priority region for Canada will require an appropriate shift of resources and attention to strengthen our understanding and management of a complex set of relationships. Moreover, it will only be effective within a coherent, consistent and effective overall foreign policy towards the region. (West Indian Commission, 1994)

How and where the Commonwealth Caribbean fits into Canada's relatively new policy of active, multifaceted engagement with its hemispheric neighbours, and their own evolving relationship with their northern neighbour, will depend upon the understanding and desire of both to forge new traditions to respond to new global realities.

Countries of the Commonwealth Caribbean have always perceived themselves as having a long-standing and special relationship with Canada. Canada shares common legal and legislative institutions with many

Commonwealth Caribbean countries. Historically, there has been a steady movement of people between the two regions, and commercial linkages have existed for over two hundred years. As the contributors to this volume have described in detail, aside from bilateral relations, the Caribbean and Canada have a number of common interests and both are confronted with rapid changes in the global economy, which demand that they consider how best to position themselves.

In the Caribbean, Canada still enjoys a favourable image because of what it is not. It is not a superpower that regards the Caribbean as its backyard or its *mare nostrum*; nor does it carry the burden of being a former colonial power (Levitt, 1988, pp. 225, 247). But there is an awareness in the Caribbean that Canada's interest in the Americas is gradually extending beyond its traditional ties to the Commonwealth Caribbean. In the area of trade, as NAFTA and the FTAA evolve, it will lead to greater interaction between Canada and the Latin American countries. Such ties will create a range of competing interests with those of CARICOM countries and will eventually erode the privileged trade position of CARICOM countries in the Canadian market. Consequently, because of a plethora of competing regional and hemispheric economic interests, CARICOM will be relegated to the back burner of Canadian concerns. From the business perspective, Latin America and other Caribbean countries, such as Cuba, are becoming more promising areas for Canadian private sector investment and expansion. Some Canadian critics already argue that the Commonwealth Caribbean receives too large a proportion of Canadian aid, given the region's size and level of development. While Canada still defines CARICOM as an area of special interest as far as economic and technical assistance are concerned, as less Canadian aid money becomes available, it will be directed to less economically fortunate areas in other parts of the globe.

While the 'special relationship' may be in jeopardy, the CARICOM region still has some advantages on which to build a creative and sustained relationship. CARICOM governments must seek to continue the encouragement of Canadian investments in the (historic) sectors of finance, communications and other utilities, and tourism. They should also seek to reinforce Canadian interest in traditional areas, such as assistance in higher education, infrastructural development (particularly regional transportation), law enforcement and security (including now the fight against drug trafficking), and the conservation of the marine environment (West Indian Commission, 1992, pp. 436–41). There should also be an overall CARICOM strategy that includes the strengthening of strategic alliances with the Caribbean diaspora in Canada; the promotion of joint ventures with Canadian business interests, in which there is a perceived competitive advantage; the development of business links directly with Canadian provinces (such as New Brunswick, Nova Scotia and Prince Edward Island), where there are developing niche industries and where there is interest in developing investment relationships with other countries; and active public relations and lobbying efforts to promote the Caribbean at all levels in Canada.

In sum, while the Commonwealth Caribbean is the oldest and strongest of Canada s bilateral relationships in the Caribbean, it may in the future no longer be the most important one. But there still remains the recognition by the governments, businesses and the public in both regions that the Commonwealth Caribbean is the meeting ground between traditional Canadian ties to Europe and the new magnet of the Americas. However, in this interesting paradigm shift comprising the European Union, NAFTA, an emerging SAFTA (South American Free Trade Area) and the FTAA, Canada itself is also simply just one of several options and poles of interest for the Commonwealth Caribbean.

References

Canadian Foundation for the Americas (1994) *Toward a New World Strategy: Canadian Policy in the Americas into the Twenty-First Century* (Ottawa: FOCAL).
Levitt, K. (1988) 'Canada and the Caribbean: An Assessment', J. Heine and L. Manigat (eds), in *The Caribbean and World Politics* (New York and London: Holmes & Meier).
West Indian Commission (1992) *Time for Action: The Report of the West Indian Commission* (Black Rock, Barbados: West Indian Commission).

Index

Note: page numbers in **bold** type refer to tables.

ACCC (Association of Canadian
    Community Colleges)   12
acid deposition problem   95
ACS (Association of Caribbean
    States)   18, 101, 225
African-Americans in posse
    operations   31
Agency for International
    Development   226
Agenda 21   *see* Rio Earth Summit
Agricultural Development
    Corporation   200
agricultural problems, regional
    approach to   100
agricultural technology,
    Canadian   5, 24
agricultural workers
    from Caribbean in Québec
        and Ontario   12
    from Mexico in Canada   12
agriculture   94
    Canadian   **108**
    Caribbean   12, 199–200
Ahmad, J.   38
aid, Canadian   5
    to Caribbean   8–9, 135
    to Cuba   9
    to Haiti   9
Airports Maintenance Project,
    CARICOM   157
Alaska   109
Alcan   25
Ali, D.A.   81
Allen, T.F.H.   85
Alleyne, F.E.   81
All-Island Cane Farmers
    Association   200
alumina   5, 24, 175
aluminium ores   119

American Revolution   24,
    57, 154
American War of
    Independence   131
Americas, the
    Canada's involvement with   19
    as focus for Canadian interests   73
    trade liberalization in   19
Andean Commission of Jurists
    (Peru)   68
angostura bitters   132
Anguilla   162, **163, 176**
animals   24
Antigua and Barbuda   162, **163,
    176, 178, 179, 180, 181**
Antilles, French   x
apparel   8
    effect of NAFTA on trade in   6
apples   132
aquaculture   94
Argentina   15, 19, 61
arms trafficking   55
    and drugs   30
Army Commanders Conference
    (Argentina, 1995)   68
arrowroot   132
Aruba   72
Asia and Canada   73
Association of Canadian Community
    Colleges   *see* ACCC
Association of Caribbean States
    see ACS
athletes, Canadian, with Caribbean
    connections   13
Atlantic Canada Opportunities
    Agency   116
Augustine, Jean, MP (Canada)   13
Australia   96
Axworthy, Lloyd (Canada)   18, 23

Bahamas   26, **114**, 162, **163**
    and consolidation centre   117
    market size of   **120**
    trade with   **174, 176**
Bailey, S.   46
balance of payments assistance for
    CARICOM   135, 160
bananas   132
banking   4, 5, 155
Bank of Jamaica   202
Bank of Montreal   24
Bank of Nova Scotia (BNS)
    24, 193
Baranyi, S.   159
Barbados   x, 12, 23, 26, 62,
    114, 124, 162, **163**
    and consolidation centre   117
    market size of   **120**
    trade with   172, **174**, 175, **176**,
        178, 179, 801, 802
Barbados Advocate News   160,
    161–2
Barbados Summit of
    Canada–CARICOM
    (1990)   169–72, **170**
Barclays Bank   24
Barnet, R.J.   81
Basdeo, S.   4–6, 9, 12, 24,
    133, 134, 154
Baum, J.B.   193
Baumgartner, F.   49
bauxite   5, 24, 175
beef   132
beer   175
Belgium   96
Belize   162, **163**, 218
    cadet training for   14, 62
    Defence Force   71
    recognition of   71
    security of   71
    trade with Canada   26,
        **174, 176, 178, 179,
        180, 181**
Bermuda   24, 162, **163**
    trade with   172, **174, 176**
Bernal, R.M.   193, 221, 223
Berry, G.R.   43
Bertasi, S.   108
Bhagwati, J.   213

biodiversity, loss of   87
Bird, Prime Minister V.C. (Antigua
    and Barbuda)   148
Bishop, Maurice   159
Black, D.R.   203
Blaikie, P.   82
Boardman, R.   102
Bogota, RCMP in   16
Bolivia   19
Bonney, J.   111
BPT (British Preferential
    Tariff)   173, **174**
'brain drain' from Caribbean
    to Canada   43
Braveboy-Wagner, J.A.   38,
    39, 40
Brazil   19
    as major player in the
        Americas   74
Brennan, J.   111
Brewster, H.R.   192
Britain   *see* United Kingdom
British colonial trade system   191
British Empire   61
British Preferential Tariff
    see BPT
Brown, J.H.   94
Brown, Rosemary (Canada)   13
Brundtland Commission
    see UNCED
Brunterm (Saint John)   124
Bryan, A.T.   33
budgetary cuts in Canada   xi
Burns, R.   110
Bush, President George   63
butter   132

cabotage restrictions   109–11
cadet training for Jamaica
    14, 62
Caldwell, L.K.   87, 88
Callender, V.   193
Cambior   25
Campbell, K.   134
Canada
    Americas in trade and foreign
        policy of   231
    Asian dimension of foreign
        policy of   63

Caribbean community in 10, 12–13, 158
diplomatic missions of 23
Dominion status of 61
duty-free access to markets of, by CARIBCAN 138
economic assistance to CARICOM countries 190–207, **192, 197, 203**; *see also* ODA
economy of 142
export performance 26, 140
fiscal problems of 72
future role of 232–3
immigration policy of 12–13, 140, 143, 150
importance to US security of 56–7
as major player in the Americas 74
military contribution to British security 61
parliamentary structure of 45–6
paternalism and exploitation by 11
railways in 112
relations with CARICOM since 1980s 131–51
review of policy towards CARICOM 134–5
security context of 56–8, 135
seen as less threatening than US 39
as 'substitute Great Britain' to Caribbean 42
as target for US conquest 57
trade of 108–9, **108, 112**, 113–16, **114, 116**, 146–7
trade policy and Caribbean 7, 156–9
see also immigration; investment; Senate Foreign Affairs Committee; separatism in Québec; trade
Canada–British West Indies Economic Conference (1911) 132
Canada–Caribbean Business Cooperation Office *see* CCBCO

Canada–Caribbean relations
ecological links and 234
new paradigm of 231–6
Canada–Caribbean Seasonal Workers Programme 158
Canada–Caribbean trade agenda 210–28
Canada–CARICOM Conference (1979) 134
(1996) 185
Canada–CARICOM Protocol on Rum 168
Canada–CARICOM Trade and Economic Cooperation Agreement (1979) 134, 138, 145, 156, 165
Canada–Commonwealth Caribbean Prime Ministers' Conference 132, 155
Canada–Commonwealth Caribbean relationship 25
Canada Fund for Local Initiatives (Canada Fund) 12, 158, 194, 202, 204, 205
Canada and Latin American Security 33
Canada–US Free Trade Agreement *see* CUSFTA
Canada–West Indies Trade Agreement (1925) 132, 134, 192
Canada–West Indies Reciprocity Treaty (1912) 132, 155, 192
Canada and the World (Defense White Paper) 73
Canadian Agricultural Trust Fund 198
Canadian–Caribbean Latin American Association 182
Canadian Commercial Livestock Fund 199
Canadian Confederation 41–2
Canadian Executive Services Organisation *see* CESO
Canadian Exports Association *see* CEA
Canadian Forces *see* CF
Canadian Hunger Foundation 204

Canadian Imperial Bank of
    Commerce   24, 193
Canadian International Development
    Agency   *see* CIDA
*Canadian Journal of Political
    Science*   33
Canadian National Railways   *see* CN
Canadian Pacific Railways   *see* CP
Canadian Technical Cooperation
    Fund   *see* CTCF
Canadian Training Awards
    Programme   *see* CTAP
Canadian University Service
    Overseas   *see* CUSO
CANEXPORT (Canadian export
    promotion)   200, 207
Caribbean
    communities in Canada   9–10,
        43
    'critical mass' and   223
    definitions of   69–70
    independence celebrations,
        Canadian presence at   14
    policy-making apparatus
        for   224–6
    as reduced priority for
        Canada   73
    security context of   58–60
    social change in   11
Caribbean Action Plan   *see*
    Programme on the Environment
    of the Caribbean
Caribbean Association of Industry
    and Commerce   x, 182
Caribbean Basin Initiative   *see* CBI
Caribbean, Commonwealth
    (English-speaking)   37, 131
    in Canadian foreign policy   3
    parliamentary structures
        of   45–6
Caribbean Community and
    Commonwealth   *see*
    CARICOM
Caribbean Conference of
    Churches   10
Caribbean Development
    Assistance studies   9
Caribbean Development Bank
    see CDB

*Caribbean Development Bank
    News*   199
Caribbean, Eastern
    cadet training for   14
    Canadian assistance to   204–5
    economic growth in   9
    Economic Reform Project   205
Caribbean economic space   215–20
    CARIBCAN and   216–18
    overview of   215–16
Caribbean, English-speaking   *see*
    Caribbean, Commonwealth
Caribbean Environmental
    Programme   *see* CEP
Caribbean Epidemiology
    Centre   205–6
Caribbean Examinations
    Council   *see* CXC
Caribbean infrastructure   158
Caribbean Investment Opportunities
    Conference (1991)   171–2,
        182
Caribbean Maritime Training
    Assistance Programme
    see CMTAP
Caribbean Regional Institutional
    Strengthening Project
    see CRISP
Caribbean Trust Fund   89
CARIBCAN   x, xi, 4–6, 25–6,
        36, 37–8, 106, 138–49
    assessment of problems and
        prospects of   153–88
    description of   162–6, **163**
    early years of   166–9
    historical background to   154–6
    origins of   159–62
    review of (1988)   140–2
    trade, investment and industrial
        cooperation under   172–83,
        **174, 176, 177, 178, 179,
        180, 181**
CARICOM (Caribbean Community
    and Common Market)   x, 4–6,
        7, 20, 107, 123, 146, 162–87, 235
    Canadian assistance to   205–6
    exports to Canada from   147, 156
    as externally vulnerable
        integration   223

Grenada Summit (1996) of 220
Jamaica Summit (1982) of 136
relations with Canada since
1980s 131–51
Carnival holiday in Toronto 43
cars, from Canada to Cuba 27
Cartegena Convention *see*
Convention for the Protection
and Development of the Marine
Environment
Carter, President Jimmy (US) 66
Castro, Fidel 26, 63
Castro, R. 81
Cathcart, P.G. 111
Cavanagh, J. 81, 102
Cayman Islands 72, 162, **163, 176**
CBI (Caribbean Basin Initiative)
x, 4, 26, 137–40, 145, 159,
164, 183, 187, 219
CCBCO (Canada–Caribbean
Business Cooperation
Office) 5, 171, 182, 186
CDB (Caribbean Development
Bank) 158, 198–9, 207
CEA (Canadian Exporters
Association) 171
Cedras, General Raoul (Haiti) 66
cement 132
CEMPOL (Control and Evaluation
of Marine Pollution) 88
Central America 19, 38, 65, 194
Central Vermont Railway 112
CEP (Programme on the
Environment of the
Caribbean) 88
see also CEPNET, CEPPOL,
ETA, IPID, SPAW
CEPNET (Information Systems for
Management of Coastal and
Marine Resources) 88
CESO (Canadian Executive Services
Organisation) 204
CF (Canadian Forces) 62
use for anti-drug purposes 67
see also RCMP
Chambers, Prime Minister (Trinidad
and Tobago) 137
cheese 132
chemicals 98, 118

Chile 19, 232, 233
Chinese in drug operations 31
Chodos, R. 155
Chrétien, Prime Minister Jean
(Canada) 8, 148, 149–50, 220
CIDA (Canadian International
Development Agency) xi, 9,
12, 19, 24, 37, 81, 106, 136, 158,
164, 171, 191, 193–207
bilateral programmes of 89–90
decentralizing 135
Industrial Cooperation
Programme of 90
Partnership Programme of 90
cigars from Cuba 27
Clairmonte, F. 102
Clark, Joe 133
climate change, global 87
Clinton, President Bill 212, 213
clothing 5, 193
Clouthier, M. **114, 116**
CMTAP (Caribbean Maritime
Assistance Programme) 62,
157
CN (Canadian National
Railways) 112, **112**
CN North America railway
system 112
Coast Guard
and drug-trafficking 67–8
Canadian, training by 29, 136, 153
cobalt from Cuba 27
cocoa beans 132
cocoa butter 132
coconuts 132
cod, Canadian 24
coffee 84, 132
Cold War 55, 133–4
end of 4, 14, 23, 63
Reagan stance on 39–40
Colombia 19, 69–70
Canadian assistance for anti-drug
operations in 68
insurgency in 29
in NAFTA 74
Colombians in posse operations 31
colonial history 25, 58–9
Commission on Hemispheric
Security (OAS) 32

Commonwealth 16, 55, 74
  Canadian membership of 58
  Caribbean *see* Caribbean,
    Commonwealth
Commonwealth Caribbean–Canada
    Trade and Economic
    Committee 132
Commonwealth Caribbean and
    Canada heads of government
  meeting (1990) of 143–4
  meeting (1996) of 149–50
Commonwealth Heads of
    Government Meeting
  at Edinburgh (1997) 8
  at Melbourne (1981) 136
  at Nassau (1985) 138
Commonwealth Parliamentary
    Association 43, 47
communications 98
communism, collapse of 145
community development,
    Caribbean 12
Compton, Prime Minister John
    (St Lucia) 137
computer science 98, 135
Connor, D. 124
consolidation centre,
    Canadian–Caribbean, proposed
    (Saint John) 116–23
  complementary centre in
    Kingston, Jamaica 121
  concept and definition of
    117–18
  potential traffic through 120–1
  requirements of 122–3
  shippers' views on 121–2
  transportation system analysis
    for 121
Constitution Act 1982 (Canada) 45
consumer goods, Canadian 5, 24
container movement 113
Control and Evaluation of Marine
    Pollution *see* CEPPOL
Convention for the Protection and
    Development of the Marine
    Environment of the Wider
    Caribbean Region 88
'core–periphery' model
    (Krugman) 211, 214–15

corruption and drugs trade 16, 30
Costa Rica 19, 70
CP (Canadian Pacific
    Railways) 112, **112**
CP Rail System 113
crime and drugs 30
CRISP (Caribbean Regional
    Institutional Strengthening
    Project) 205
Cropover holiday in Toronto 43
Crosbie, J. 187
CTAP (Canadian Training Awards
    Programme) 157
CTCF (Canadian Technical
    Cooperation Fund) 199
Cuba x, 3, 19, 56, 63, 169
  balsero crisis (1994) 69
  Canadian relations with 16–19,
    23, 232
  as Canadian tourist
    destination 17
  Canadian trade with 26–8,
    118, 17, 113, **114**
  characteristics of 70
  and consolidation centre 117
  economy of 17
  'exporting revolution' 60
  and immigration 15, 69
  isolation of 20
  longevity of Castro government
    in 14–15
  market size of **120**
  and Mexico 16
  peaceful change in 29
  problems of shipping from 125
  racial composition of 59
  security problem of 68–9
  US embargo against 17, 59, 70
  see also Cuban Democracy Act;
    Helms–Burton Bill
Cuban Democracy Act 125
Cubukgil, A. 110
Cuff, R.D. 58
CUSFTA (Canada–US Free Trade
    Agreement) 4, 107, 166,
    167, 171, 184–5
CUSO (Canadian University
    Service Overseas) 11
customs duty 165

Customs Service and
   drug-trafficking 67
Customs Tariff Act (1986)
   (Canada) 162
Customs Tariff and Excise Act 165
CXC (Caribbean Examinations
   Council) 157

Daly, H.E. 83, 99
d'Arge, R.C. 99
Davidson, A. 84
DDT, effects of 85–6
Deans, E. 121
debt, official 143–4, 153, 169,
   170, **170**, 193, 206
decolonization, postwar 60
Defense Department, National
   (Canada) 72
Delaware and Hudson Railway 113
De Melo, P. 211, 213
Dence, M. 84
Denmark in Caribbean 59
De Palma, A. 28
Department of State (US) 81
'dependence theory' model
   (Krugman) 214
development *see* growth and
   development
development assistance *see* ODA
Dewitt, D. 75
diamonds, Caribbean 24
diversity, cultural and political 100
Dominican Republic 23, 70,
   114, 124, 162, **163**
   and consolidation centre 117
   market size of **120**
   trade with **176**, **178**, **179**, **180**, **181**
Dominicans in posse operations 31
Donley, C. 38
Dosman, E.J. 16, 41, 48, 75, 159, 185
Drucker, P.F. 82
drugs trade 14, 29, 30, 55, 56,
   70–1, 72, 150, 159, 169
   Canadian assistance for Caribbean
      in 16, 30–1, 143, 171
   and free trade 15
   as security threat 15–16, 67
   see also Colombia; Jamaica
Dube, S.C. 81

Duluth, Winnipeg and Pacific
   Railway 112
Dupont Corporation 111
Dziedzic, M. 30

East Asian 'Tiger' economies 214,
   220
Eastern Canada
   analysis of trade with
      Caribbean 118
   definition of 117
Eastern Caribbean *see* Caribbean,
   Eastern
EC (European Community) 107,
   211, 224
Eccles, W.J. 57
ECLAC (Economic Commission
   for Latin America and
   the Caribbean) 88
ecological footprint (Wackernagel
   and Rees) 95–7
Economic Commission for Latin
   America and the Caribbean
   see ECLAC
economic development assistance
   see development assistance
economic growth
   as challenge for eastern
      Caribbean 9
   and development 82–3
   and environment 86
   and poverty 99
   and wealth 83, 99
economic recovery programme
   (Guyana) 203
economy, global 99
   generators of transformation
      of 107
Ecuador 19
education, Caribbean 12
Education, Training and
   Awareness *see* ETA
Edwards, P.J. 93
EEC (European Economic
   Community) 139, 157
Eldridge, A. 45
electrical equipment from
   Canada to Cuba 27
El Salvador 19

emigration from West Indies 134
  see also immigration
ENACT (Environmental Action
    Programme, Jamaica) 20, 201
energy 195–6
English language 159
Enterprise for the Americas
    Initiative 212
environment xii, 20, 82,
    153, 169, 195–6, 231
Environmental Action
    Programme *see* ENACT
environmental costs and economic
    benefits 82, 86
environmental degradation,
    cumulative effects of 92,
    95–8
Environmental Foundation of
    Jamaica 201
environmental planning,
    anticipatory 94
Environmental Training Network
    (UNEP) 91
ETA (Education, Training and
    Awareness) 88
EU (European Union) 86,
    212, 236
  opposition to Helms–Burton
    Act 18
European Community *see* EC
European Economic
    Community *see* EEC
European Free Trade Area 107
European integration 212
European Union *see* EU
exchange rate policy 222
Excise Act (Canada) 168
exports
  from Canada to Caribbean
    4, 26, 140
  growth led by 220–2
  to India 4
  see also Canada; trade
Express, The 172
External Affairs, Ministry of
    (Canada) 37, 116, 165

'family ties' in special
    relationship 42–4

farm workers *see* agricultural
    workers
FAO (Food and Agriculture
    Organization) 90
FCL *see* full container loads
FEMA (Foreign Extraterritorial
    Measures Act 1984)
    (Canada) 18, 28
Fertilizer Line of Credit
    project 204
Finan, J.S. 72
Finance, Department of 194
Finlayson, J.A. 108, 110
fisheries 94
fish products
  from Canada 118, 132
  Caribbean 5, 24, 154
Flemming, S. 72
flour 118, 132
Food and Agriculture
    Organization *see* FAO
food
  security 195–6
  supply, finite 83
food products
  Canadian 5, 24, 27, **108**, 118
  Caribbean 24
  Puerto Rican 119
footwear 5, 132, 103
Ford 81
Foreign Affairs and International
    Trade, Department of
    (Canada) 73, 194
foreign assistance *see* development
    assistance
Foreign Extraterritorial Measures
    Act *see* FEMA
Foreign Policy Review (1994)
    (Canada) 231–2
forest destruction 84, 93
forestries 94
France 89
Francophonie, La 15,
    36, 55, 58, 74
free market *see* free trade
Freestone, D. 89
free trade 95, 145, 184, 213, 223
  in the Americas 19
  and drug trade 15

as generator of global
change 107
and environmental
protection 98–9
Free Trade in the Americas, Senate
of Canada Report on 6–7
Free Trade Area of the
Americas *see* FTAA
Freudman, A. 27
fruit
Canadian 12
Caribbean 24, 175
FTA (Free Trade Agreement)
109, 113
FTAA (Free Trade Area of the
Americas) (proposed) 7–8,
147, 148, 187, 235, 236
FTL *see* full truck load
fuel oil 175
Fuentes, E.R. 100
full container loads (FCLs) 117, 122
full truck loads (FTLs) 117
future, lack of interest in 84

Gaia Hypothesis 85
García-Amador, F.V. 75
García Muñiz, H. 34
Garments, US 807 Special Access
Programme for 167
Garrié Faget, R. 60
GATT (General Agreement on
Tariffs and Trade) 107, 108,
138, 156, 164
General Agreement on Tariffs and
Trade *see* GATT
General Preferential Tariff,
Canadian *see* GPT
genetic engineering 98
Geoghegan, T. 81
Germany 96
Gestrin, M.V. 214
Ghai, Dharam 223
Gill, H. 154, 156, 182,
183, 217–18
Giller, P.S. 92
Gilpin, M. 92
Global Environment Facility 87, 90
globalization, economic 106,
107–9, 210

'global village' (McLuan) 107
gold
from Caribbean 24
from Guyana 25
investment in 25
Gold Star Resources 25
GPT (General Preferential
Tariff) 173, 193, 216
Graham, G. 160
Granatstein, J. 58
Grand Caribe 27
Grand Trunk Western railway 112
grapefruit 132
Great Britain *see* United
Kingdom
Great Lakes 110
Grenada 162, **163**
religious expeditions to 131
revolutionary government
in 133
trade with **176, 178, 179,
180, 181**
US invasion of 159
Grenadines 46
Griffith, I.L. 25, 28, 29, 33, 62,
71, 74
Griffith, M. 81
Group of Seven (G7) 158
Group of Three (Colombia, Mexico,
Venezuela) 225
growth and development, distinction
between 82–3
see also economic growth
Guatemala 19, 61, 70
peace process 29
return to democracy in, 71
Gulf Stream 93
Gunst, L. 33
Gupta, A. 98
Guy, J.J. 38–9, 41–2, 155
Guyana 23, 162, **163**, 218
bauxite from 25
cadet training for 14, 62
Canadian assistance to 203
dispute with Venezuela 71
gold from 25
religious expeditions to
British 131
security of 71

Guyana (*contd.*)
    trade with Canada by 26, **174**,
        175, **176, 177, 178,**
        179, 180, 181
Guyana Support Group 158
Guyana Volunteer Consultancy
    Programme 204
Guyanese in posse operations 31

Haar, J. 16, 48, 75
Haila, Y. 86, 98
Haiti 14, 15, 19, 23, 29–30,
        144, 159, 169
    Canadian assistance to 202, **203**
    Canadian security and 66
    characteristics of 70
    coup d'état (1991) 30, 66
    environmental degradation in 84
    and immigration 15
    US intervention in 59, 63
Halifax 115, 124
Hamilton, posse drug
    operations in 31
Hamm, K. 46
Hammond, S. 47
Hancock, A. 45
Hanski, I. 92
Harbron, J. 40
Harmel, R. 46
Harrison, P. 81
Hatch Report (1980) 195
Hawaii 109
Hay-Pauncefote Treaty (1901) 59
Head, I. 84, 93, 97
health
    Caribbean 12
    problems, regional approach
        to 100
hegemonic stability, theory of 213
Helms–Burton Act 3, 17, 125,
        148, 150
    opposition to 18, 20, 28
Helms–Burton and International
    Business 28
Hewitt, V. 46
Hirsch, H. 45
historical perspective on political
    commonalities 37–42
Hoffman, S. 23

homeostatic mechanisms 85
Honduras 19, 70
Hong Kong 157
Hosten-Craig, J. 6
'hub and spoke' argument 222–3
Hudson River 98
human resource development 153
Hurricane Gilbert (1988) 84
Hyett, C. 24, 25

IDB (Inter-American Development
    Bank) 7, 90, 158
IDRC (International Development
    Research Centre) 81, 90
IMF (International Monetary
    Fund) 135, 160, 170, 203
immigration, 153
    from Africa to Caribbean as
        slave labour 59
    from Caribbean into Canada
        xii, 12–13, 43, 231, 233
    from Europe to Caribbean 59
    and visitors' visa 13
impact assessment 95
income inequalities in the
    Americas 19
India 4
industrial cooperation 153,
        182, 219–20
Information Systems for
    Management of Coastal and
    Marine Resources *see*
    CEPNET
information technology as generator
    of global change 107, 109
Institutional Strengthening Project,
    Canadian 169
insurance 4, 5, 155
Integrated Planning for Industrial
    Development *see* IPID
Inter-American Development
    Bank *see* IDB
interdependence of economies 107
International Assistance
    Envelope 196
international community,
    interdependence of 22–34
International Development Research
    Centre *see* IDRC

International Journal 33, 48
International Monetary Fund
  see IMF
investment, Canadian
  in Caribbean xii, 5, 141, 153,
    167, 171, 182, 219
  in Cuba 27, 163
IPID (Integrated Planning for
  Industrial Development) 88
Ircha, M.C. 115, 121
Irving Corporation (New
  Brunswick) 124
Isaacs, Chief Justice Julius
  (Canada) 13
island biogeography 92–3

Jackson, L.A. 190, 200
Jamaica x, 6, 23, 70, 124,
  162, **163**, 218
  agriculture in 199–200
  bauxite from 25
  cadet training for 14, 62
  and consolidation centre 117
  crime and drug problems 71
  criminal gangs (posses) from
    13, 30, 68, 233
  marijuana from 30
  market size of **120**
  ODA to 199–202
  RCMP in 68
  trade with Canada by 26, 113,
    114, 172, **174**, 175, **176**,
    177, **178**, **179**, **180**, **181**
Jamaica Agricultural Society 200
Jamaican Gleaner 162
Jamaica Promotions
  see JAMPRO
Jamieson, A. 72
JAMPRO (Jamaica
  Promotions) 200
Japan 157
Jefferson, O. 192
Joint Trade and Economic
  Committee *see* JTEC
joint ventures, Atlantic
  Canadian–Caribbean 124
'Jones Act' 109–11
*Journal of Commonwealth and
  Comparative Politics* 33

JTEC (Joint Trade and Economic
  Committee) 5, 6, 7,
    166, 168–9, 183
  establishment of 134, 160–1
  meeting (1981) of 137
  meeting (1989) of 142
  meeting in Georgetown (1995)
    of 185
  meeting in Ottawa (1996) of 8
  meeting in Guyana (1997)
    of 185–6

Kakoschke, Q.C. 111
Kegley, C.W. 23
Kempe, R.H. 38
Kent Lines 124
Keohane, R.O. 22, 227
Kingston Container Terminals 121
Kirk, J.M. 16, 26, 76
Kitchener, posse drug operations
  in 31
Klepak, H.P. 11, 13, 14, 16, 29,
    33, 58, 62, 64, 68, 70, 75
  knowledge in wealth creation as
    generator of change 107
Korea 157
Korean War 62
Kornberg, A. 45
Kornblith, M. 49
Kronberg, B.I. 100
Krugman, P. 211, 214–15, 221

Lafeber, W. 59
Lake Erie 98
Lanctot, G. 57
Lane, P.A. 84, 94, 95, 102
lard 132
Latin America
  Canadian relationship with 3, 56
  Caribbean as trading base
    to 123–4
  security in 15
  similarities of Caribbean to 11
Latin America and Africa, Secretary
  of State for (Canada) 17
Latin American Economic
  System *see* SELA
Laurier, Prime Minister Wilfred
  (Canada) 155

LCL   *see* less than container load
LDC (least developed country)
    states 213
    of Eastern Caribbean 135
least developed country   *see* LDC
leather 5, 193
Leeward and Windward
    Islands x, 173
    Canadian ties with 37
    trade with 172, 173, **174**
Lemaitre, E. 59
Lemco, J. 46
Le Moyne d'Iberville 61
less than container load
    (LCL) 122
less than truck load (LTL) 117
Levins, R. 86, 94
Levitt, K. 25, 37, 39, 40, 193
Liberal Party (Canada) 133
limes 132
Loewenberg, G. 45
Lomé Convention 139, 145,
    159, 183
London (Canada), posse drug
    operations in 31
Lovelock, J.E. 85
LTL   *see* less than truck load
lubricating oil 5, 193
luggage 193
lumber, Canadian 24, 27, 132, 154

Maastricht 72
MacAulay, A.M. 64
MacDonald/Cartier
    government 24
MacDonald, Marci 75
mace 132
machinery, Canadian 5, 24
machine tools 175
MacKenna, P. 75, 203
'macroecology' (Brown) 94
Mahler, G. 46, 48
Malaysia 157
Malthus, T. 83
Manifest Destiny (US) 59
Manley, President Michael
    (Jamaica) 148, 170
Manning, Prime Minister Patrick
    (Trinidad and Tobago) 148

manufactured goods
    Canadian 27, **108**
    Puerto Rican 119
Margulis, L. 85
marijuana, Jamaican 31
Mariñez, P.A. 76
May, R.M. 93
McCallion, K. 185, 186
McGrudy, W.A. 111
McGuigan, M. 134–6, 138, 157,
    160–1
McIntyre, A. 193
McKibben, B. 98, 101
McLuan, Marshall 107
McQuire, F. 124
medicine 98
Merchant's Bank of Halifax
    see Royal Bank of Canada
MERCOSUR (Southern
    Cone Common Market)
    225, 233
Merle, M. 63
Metals Enterprise 27
methanol 5, 146, 171, 193
Mexico xii, 3, 15, 19, 69, 184–5
    access to markets of 111
    Canadian trade to 113, 233
    cheap labour in 39
    and Cuba 16
    investment in 111
    as major player in the
        Americas 74
    methanol from 146
    in NAFTA 29, 56, 145–6
    opposition to Helms–Burton
        Act 18
Mexico City
    Canadian military attaché in 65
    RCMP in 16
Mezey, M. 49
MFA (Multi-Fibre Agreement) 6
MFN (most favoured nation)
    status 173, **174**
Miami Herald 28
militarization 82
milk 132
mining 25, 94
    see also bauxite
missionaries 155

molasses, West Indian   5,
   24, 154, 175
Momsen, J.H.   219
monetary regulation, Canadian
   model of, in Caribbean   38
money laundering   150
   see also drug trafficking
Montreal   113, 115
   as port of choice for container
      centre   122
   posse drug operations in   31
Montreal Gazette   167
Montserrat   162, **163, 176,
   178, 179, 180, 181**
Mooney, H.A.   100
Morris, N.   27
Morrison, D.R.   195, 196
Morton, D.   57
most favoured nation status
   see MFN
Mulroney, Prime Minister Brian
   (Canada)   40–1, 133,
   137–8, 142–4, 169–71
Multi-Fibre Agreement   *see* MFA
multinational companies   *see*
   transnational corporations
Musolf, L.   45
Myers, A.A.   92
Myers, S.L.   28

NAFTA (North American Free
   Trade Agreement)   xii, 3–4,
   6–9, 14, 18, 20, 28, 29, 36, 56,
   63, 86, 106, 107, 109, 113,
   145–6, 184–5, 211–13,
   223–5, 232, 235,236
   and Canadian security   65
   Parity Bill   224
   and regional security   15
   as threat to CARICOM   6,
      12, 39, 42
National Defense University
   (US)   65
National Development
   Institutes   182
National Forum on Foreign Policy
   (Canada)   23
National Resources Conservation
   Authority   *see* NCRA

nation-state, obsolescence of   82
NATO (North Atlantic Treaty
   Organization)   14, 58,
   62, 64, 73
Nelson, D.   49
neoliberal reforms in Caribbean   xi
Netherlands   96
New Brunswick
   and Caribbean   106–26, 236
   consolidation centre and   117
   Department of Commerce and
      Technology   116
   missionaries from   155
   recent initiatives in
      Caribbean   123–5
   trade with Caribbean   115, **116**
   trade missions to Latin
      America   113
Newfoundland and proposed
   consolidation centre   117
New France
   and French West Indies   61
   population of   57
newsprint   118
New York Carib News   25
New York, Port of   113
New York Times   226
NGOs (non-governmental
   organizations)   10, 158
   Canadian support for
      Caribbean   12
Nicaragua, 70, 159
   ODA to   19
   US intervention in   60
nickel
   Caribbean   24
   from Cuba   27
Nigerians in posse operations   31
Nogues, J.J.   212
non-governmental organizations
   see NGOs
non-tariff barriers   139, 141, 183
NORAD (North American Air
   Defense)   58, 67–8
Norgaard, R.B.   86
North American Air Defense
   see NORAD
North American Free Trade
   Agreement   *see* NAFTA

North Atlantic Treaty
Organization *see* NATO
Northern model of
sustainability 98–9, 101
Nova Scotia
and Caribbean 106–26, 236
consolidation centre and 117
missionaries from 155
recent initiatives in
Caribbean 123–5
trade with Caribbean 115, **116**
trade missions to Latin
America 113
NRCA (National Resources
Conservation Authority) 201
nutmeg 132
Nye, J.S. 22, 23, 63

Oakley, R. 30
OAS (Organization of American
States) x, 14, 36, 55, 90, 197
Canadian membership of 20,
63, 64, 144, 158–9, 185
Charter 65
Commission on Hemispheric
Security 32
Cuban membership of 17
meetings on security 32
OECD (Organization for
Economic Cooperation and
Development) 18
and regional security 15
Unit for Promotion of
Democracy 65
ODA (Official Development
Assistance), Canadian 19,
143, 161, 169–70
by Canada to Caribbean xi, xii,
7, 37, 39, 153, 190–207,
192, **197**, **203**, 235
by Canada to Cuba 17
historical overview of 191–3,
192
institutional mechanisms
for 193–6
OECS (Organisation of Eastern
Caribbean States) 137,
204, 218
official debt *see* debt, official

Official Development
Assistance *see* ODA
Ogdensburg 66
Ogelsby, J.C.M. 75
oil crisis 133
Olsen, D. 45
Omai Gold Mines Ltd 25
Ontario 115
consolidation centre and 117
ONUCA (UN observer group in
Central America) 64
ONUSAL (UN observer mission
in El Salvador) 64
ores 5
Organization of American
States *see* OAS
Organisation of Eastern Caribbean
States *see* OECS
Organization for Economic
Co-operation and
Development *see* OECD
Ornstein, J. 63
Oshawa, posse drug operations
in 31
Oueuille, P. 59
Owen, L.A. 83
ozone depletion 87

Pacific Rim states 157
PAHO (Pan American Health
Organisation) 90, 205
Panama 19, 63, 70
Panama Canal 29, 59–60
Panamanians in posse operations 31
Pan American Health
Organisation *see* PAHO
Pan American Union 60
Pantin, D. 81
paper 118
Paraguay 19
Parliamentarian, The 49
passenger pigeon 98
Patterson, Prime Minister P.J.
(Jamaica) 148
Patterson, S. 45
peacekeeping operations, Canadian
involvement in 14
Pearce, D.W. 84, 99, 220
Pearl Harbor 66

Peru 19
petroleum, Caribbean 5, 24
Philip Morris 81
Pickering, K.T. 83
pineapples 132
pine production in Jamaica 84
PIOJ (Planning Institute of
Jamaica) 201
Pitre, F. 110
Plan d'Urgence de Reconstruction
Economique *see* PURE
Planning Institute of Jamaica
see PIOJ
police training, Canadian xii,
29, 153
political commonalities and
convergences 36–49
political structures and institutions as
Canada–Caribbean ties 43–4
Ponting, C. 84, 93
population, world 83
pork 132
posses *see* Jamaica, criminal
gangs from
potatoes 118
poverty 195–6
in the Americas 19
and growth 99
in Haiti 202
power without paternalism 22–34
Pratt, C. 194
Preston, R.A. 41, 57
Prince Edward Island 124, 236
consolidation centre and 117
Programme on the Environment
of the Caribbean
see CEP
Progressive Conservatives
(Canada) 133
Puerto Rico 59, 109, **114,
124,** 141–2, **167**
and consolidation centre 117
market size of **120**
trade with Eastern Canada
118–19
pulp, Canadian 27
PURE (Plan d'Urgence de
Reconstruction Economique)
(Haiti) 202

Québec 145
consolidation centre and 117
exports from 115
fall of (1759) 57
separation of 148
Quintanilla, R. 212

racism 13
Rajapatirana, S. 222
raw materials, Canadian **108**
RCMP (Royal Canadian Mounted
Police) 15, 62
in Haiti 66
post in Kingston (Jamaica) 16, 68
Reagan, President Ronald (US)
4, 137
anti-Cuba stance of 39–40
Redclift, M. 80
Rees, W. 83, 96
Regional Industrial Expansion,
Canadian Department of 164
regional integration at CARICOM
level 7, 210–28
and North–South pact 210–15
rationale for 10
slow pace of 10
Regional Seas Programme
(UNEP) 91
regional self-sufficiency 100
regions and nations 85–91
regulatory frameworks,
environmental 95
religious expeditions to
Caribbean 131
resource commodities 5
Rio Earth Summit (1992) 90–1
Rio Pact 65
Ritter, A. 76
Robbins, L. 49
Roberts, N. 92
Robertson, H. 154
Rochlin, J. 62, 64, 75
Rodgríguez Beruff, J. 34
Rogozinski, J. 80
Roseau Basin Water Development
Project (St Lucia) 205
Royal Bank of Canada 24, 193
Royal Canadian Mounted
Police *see* RCMP

Rugman, A.H. 214
rules of origin restrictions 140,
    146, 164, 171, 184
rum
    Caribbean 5, 24, 132,
        141, 154, 171
    from Cuba 27
rural development, Caribbean 12

SAFTA (South American Free
    Trade Area) 236
Saint-Amand, A. 17
St Christopher/Nevis 162, **163**
St Clair-Daniel, W. 49
Saint John, port of 113, 115
    see also consolidation centre
Saint John Port Days 113
St Kitts and Nevis **176, 178,
    179, 180, 181**
St Lucia 162, **163, 176, 178,
    179, 180, 181**
St Vincent 46, 162, **163, 176,
    178, 179, 180, 181**
Santo Domingo 59
Sauvé, P. 111
Schoultz, L. 68, 75
Schumacher, E.F. 99
science and technology in
    environmental control 98
seafood, Cuban 27
Seaga, Prime Minister Edward
    (Jamaica) 137, 160–1, 200
Second World War 14, 60, 61
security xii, 14–16
    Canadian and Caribbean 55–76,
        153, 231, 234
    Canadian contribution to
        Caribbean 37, 40
    Caribbean perspectives
        on 69–72
    and democracy 28
    and governance 28–32
    influence of Haiti on 56
    policy thinking, Canadian 29
SELA (Latin American Economic
    System) 154, 156, 217, 224
self-sufficiency, regional 100
Senate Foreign Affairs Committee
    (Canada) 6, 8

separatism in Quebec 3
Serbin, A. 59
Sherritt Inc. of Alberta 27
shipping 4
Simberloff, D. 92
Simmons, D.A. 206
Sinclair, J. 28
Singapore 157
Slack, B. 118
small and medium-sized
    enterprises *see* SMEs
SMEs (small and medium-sized
    enterprises) 149–50
Smillie, I. 11, 13
Smith, Adam 95, 99
SNAP (Soil Nutrients for Agricultural
    Productivity) 201
Soberman, R. 110
Soil Nutrients for Agricultural
    Productivity *see* SNAP
Sokolsky, J. 63
Somalia 63
Soo Line railway 113
South Africa 144
South America 19, 194
South American Free Trade
    Area *see* SAFTA
Southern Cone Common
    Market *see* MERCOSUR
South Korea 96
sovereignty, national, and
    drugs 30
SPAW (Specially Protected Areas
    and Wildlife) 88, 89
Specially Protected Areas and
    Wildlife *see* SPAW
special relationship,
    Canada–Caribbean 41–2
spices, West Indian 5, 24,
    132, 175
Stabroek News 185, 187
Stanley, G. 57
Starr, T.B. 85
Statistics Canada 118
steel, Caribbean 5, 24, 175
Stewart, Christine 28
stone 118
structural adjustment 145,
    195–6, 222

Stuart, I.A. 38
Suárez, E.M. 224, 226
Suárez Salazar, L. 68
sugar
  from Cuba 27
  West Indian 5, 24, 59,
    131–2, 175
Summit of the Americas (1994)
  19, 212
Surinam 149
sustainable development in
  Caribbean 79–102, 233
  as academic ruse 81–4
  application of Northern model
    to 95–9
  definition of 79–80
  economists' views of 82–3
  examples of 100–1
  as holistic and hierarchical
    concept 86
  at national level, sufficiency
    of 91–5
  as regional priority 84, 86–7,
    87–91, 99–101
  relevance to Caribbean–Canadian
    relationship 80–1
  and survival 83
  WCED rationale for 91–2
Swardson, A. 28

Taiwan 157
tariff preferences conceded to
  Mexico 6
technical and consulting services,
  Canadian 5, 24
technical and scientific cooperation,
  Canada–Caribbean xii,
    135, 153
telecommunications equipment,
  Canadian 5, 24
Tennyson, B.D. xi, 155
terrorism 55, 82
test of common sense (TOCS)
  79–102
textiles, Caribbean 5, 8, 24,
  39, 171, 175, 193
Third World crisis 55
Thomas, C. 37, 38, 81, 192
Thomas, P. 47

tobacco
  in Canada 12
  Caribbean 175
TOCS *see* test of common sense
Toronto 113
  posse drug operations in 31
tourism, 94, 171
  Canadian, to Caribbean x,
    5, 37–8
  Canadian, to Cuba 27
  and security 14
Townsend, K.N. 99
trade
  Canada–Caribbean 4, 23–8,
    37, 38, 40–1, 61, 106,
    113–16, **114**, **116**, 139–40,
    146–7, 153–4, 155,
    156–9, 231
  Canada–CARIBCAN 72–83,
    176, 177, 178, 179, 180, 181
  Canada–Cuba 17
  Canada–US 111–12, **112**
  Caribbean 119–20, **120**
  Eastern Canada–Caribbean 118
  history of preferential 192–3
  seaborne 106
  world, increase in 107–8
Trade and Economic
  Cooperation Agreement
  see Canada–CARICOM
trade liberalization
  see free trade
transnational corporations,
  increasing role of 81–2,
    94, 99, 210
transportation 98
  in development of world
    economy 109
  in FTA and NAFTA 109–13,
    112
  intermodal 117
  sea 171
Transportation, US Department
  of 112
Transport Canada 109
Trinidad Guardian 166,
  167, 170
Trinidad, religious expeditions
  to 131

Trinidad and Tobago 7, 24, 26, 49, 70–1, **114**, 124, 162, **163**
  CCBCO office in 186
  and consolidation centre 117
  market size of **120**
  trade with 172, **174**, 175, **176**, **177**, **178**, **179**, **180**, **181**
Trinidadians in posse operations 31
Trudeau, Prime Minister Pierre (Canada) 14, 20, 62, 136, 137
  speech at St Lucia 40
  visit to Havana (1976) 16–17, 26
Turks and Caicos Islands, 62, 72, 162, **163**, **176**
  Canadian ties with 37

UNCED (United Nations Commission on Environment and Development) (Brundtland Commission) 90
UNDP (United Nations Development Programme) 90, 158
UNEP (United Nations Environmental Programme) 87–8, 89, 90, 91
UNHCR (United Nations Higher Commission for Relief) 90
UNICEF (United Nations International Children's Fund) 90
United Kingdom 4, 89, 96
  immigration policy 140
  trade with Caribbean by 191–2, **192**
United Nations 16, 55, 87
  Canada's contribution to 15, 58, 62
  expansion of security role of 14–15, 64
United Nations Commission on Environment and Development *see* UNCED
United Nations Conference on Environment and Development 233
United Nations Development Programme *see* UNDP

United Nations Environmental Programme *see* UNEP
United Nations First Development Decade 194
United Nations Food and Agriculture Organization *see* FAO
United Nations Higher Commission for Relief *see* UNHCR
United Nations International Children's Fund *see* UNICEF
United States 4, 69, 89
  attitude of CARICOM to 190
  Canadian dependence on 14
  Cuban embargo by 17
  immigration policy 140
  military interventions in Central America and Caribbean 59, 63, 159
  National Drug Intelligence Center 31
  trade with Caribbean by 191–2, **192**
  see also Helms–Burton Act
University of New Brunswick Transportation Group 116
University of the West Indies 8, 143, 157, 169, 205
Uruguay 19
Uruguay Round of GATT 108, 224

Vail, B. 111
value-added criteria 166
vegetable fibre products 5
vegetables 118
Venezuela 19, 61, 70, 72, 89, 124
  in NAFTA 74
Venezuela–CARICOM trade agreement 225
Venture Capital Fund, need for, in CARICOM 183
Virgin Islands
  British 162, **163**
  US 141, 167
Voluntary Restraint Agreements *see* VRAs
VRAs (Voluntary Restraint Agreements) 141, 171

Wackernagel, M. 83, 96
Warsaw Pact assistance, end of 70
water pollution, international 87
WCED (World Commission on
    Environment and
    Development) 79–80,
    83, 91–2
wealth and growth 83
wealth and poverty 99
Webb, N.R. 93
Weinberg, G.M. 98
Wells, J. 27
Western Hemisphere Free Trade
    Area 74
Western Hemispheric
    Commonwealth Countries,
    Summit Meeting of (1983) 137
West Indian Commission 10, 157
Westminster model of
    government 43–8
    Caribbean variations on 46
    concept of 'Westminster family'
        in 44–5
    legislative committee in 47
    and party discipline 46
    structures of 45–8
wheat 118

white females as drug runners 31
White, G. 45
Williams, Prime Minister E.
    (Trinidad and Tobago) 133,
    136
Wilson, M. 146, 184
Wilton Properties Ltd 27
Windsor (Canada), posse drug
    operations in 31
women, status of 19, 195–6
World Bank 7, 87, 90, 158,
    170, 203, 225–6
World Commission on Environment
    and Development see WCED
World Food Programme 90
World Trade Centre 124
World Trade Organization
    see WTO
WTO (World Trade
    Organization) 8, 18, 28,
    107, 108, 148, 211, 213, 220

Yee, P. 109, 110

Zedillo, President (Mexico) visit
    to Ottawa (1996) 66
Zwier, R. 47

DATE DUE

~~APR 0 9 2003~~			
~~MAY 2 1 2003~~			
~~APR 3 0 2008~~			
			Printed in USA

HIGHSMITH #45230